Higher Education Assessment and Techniques

Higher Education Assessment and Techniques

Dr. Parul Agarwal
&
Prof. Surinder Pal Singh

RANDOM PUBLICATIONS
NEW DELHI (INDIA)

Higher Education Assessment and Techniques

ISBN 978-93-5111-498-7

Published in 2015 in India by

RANDOM PUBLICATIONS

4376-A/4B, Gali Murari Lal, Ansari Road
New Delhi-110 002
Phone : +9111-43580356, 011-23289044, 011-43142548
e-mail: sales@randompublications.com,
info@randompublications.com, randomexports@gmail.com

Reprint 2021

Type Setting by : Friends Media, Delhi-110089
Digitally Printed at : Replika Press Pvt. Ltd.

Preface

Fundamental to education is the need to evaluate student learning and the effectiveness of teaching methods and the programs offered. Assessment allows faculty to determine what, and how well, students are learning. Assessment also allows faculty to fine tune teaching methods. Finally, assessment allows department or division heads to evaluate the effectiveness of entire programs.

Regardless of the assessment strategies used, all assessment must focus on improving students' learning, with a secondary focus of improving teaching methods. Since assessment requires students' active participation in the process, it is to the teacher's advantage to get the students to buy into the assessment strategy. By continually showing your interest in students and your investment in their learning, students will be more motivated to participate in assessment methods. As students become more used to ongoing assessment, they will begin to see that ongoing assessment reinforces their learning and adds to their self-assessment skills.

Assessment strategies—whether of the individual, the course, or the entire program—give faculty an impressive tool to measure learning. Assessment strategies must be related to the course material and relevant to students' lives. Provide assessment strategies that relate to students' work, such as product analysis or portfolios. Have students use simulated activities for computer courses, keep a log of performance ratings or references, or role play job interviews, mock trials, or historical moments.

Higher Education: Assessment and Techniques provides guidance for assessing and promoting institutional effectiveness. The book contains a wide range of issues, from measures of effectiveness to communicating with the public. It will be an essential resource for university leaders for achieving institutional effectiveness.

Author

Contents

Preface v

1. Higher Education: Status and Trends **1**

Contributions of Higher Education 3

Role of Higher Education Institutions 6

Role of Research and Innovation 8

Higher Education in a Knowledge-driven Economy 10

Higher Education: Global Concerns 17

Globalisation and Issues in Higher Education 22

Global Higher Education Market 28

Importance of Quality Assurance in Higher Education 29

2. Assessment and Evaluation: Basic Concepts **34**

Meaning of Assessment 34

Purposes of Assessment 35

Assessment in Open and Distance Education 37

Reliable and Valid Assessment 39

Methods of Assessment 40

Computer Based Assessment 43

Meaning of Evaluation 48

Difference between Assessment and Evaluation 50

Purposes of Evaluation 50

Evaluation in Distance Education 52

3. Program Evaluation Methods **57**

Concept of Programme Evaluation 60

Programme Evaluation in Distance Education 61

Types and Purposes of Program Evaluations 64

Designing and Conducting a Program Evaluation 65
Performance Measurement 76
Programme Evaluation at IGNOU 78

4. Quality Assurance Instruments **83**

Concepts of Quality and Quality Assurance Instruments 83
Dimensions and Terms 88
Dynamics of Quality Assurance 89
Two Decades of Quality Assurance History 90
Changes in Concepts of Quality in Use 94
Multiple Functions of Evaluation and Quality Assessment 96
Uses of Question Bank 107

5. Quality Assessment **115**

Practising Quality Assessment: Problems and Difficulties 122
Quality Assessment Systems: A problem of ownership 132
Quality Management 134
Quality Assessment as an Information Tool 136
Quality Assessment as a Compliance Tool 138
Quality Assessment as a Substitute for Trust 142
Quality Assessment as a Supranational Policy Tool 144

6. Assessment of Assignments **148**

Types of Assignments 148
Assignment Response 150
Types of Tutor Comments 152

7. Development of Accreditation Systems **158**

Concepts and Definitions 160
Emergence of Evaluation Schemes in Europe 161
Causes for the Establishment of Evaluation Schemes 163
Initial Disinterest in Accreditation 164
First Steps Towards Accreditation System 166
Recent Growing Interest in Accreditation 167
Actual Development of Accreditation Schemes 169
The future of Accreditation Systems 171

Accreditation in the Netherlands 173
Some Important Changes 181

8. Peer Evaluation 185

Grant Peer Review 186
Fairness of the Peer Review Process 187
Predictive Validity of the Peer Review Process 188
Meta Evaluation of Peer Review-based Study Programme Evaluation 190
Evaluation of Study Programmes 192

9. Improving evaluation Methods 196

New Educational and Economic Contexts 197
Access to the Labour Market 199
Improving the Evaluation Processes 201
Insufficiencies of the National Evaluation System 202
Quality Charts 205
Offensive Strategy of Evaluation 207
Stability Amidst a Storm of Evaluation 208
Increasing Evaluation Costs with Dubious Results 218

10. Assessment and Grading in Open and Distance learning 223

Assessment Systems 225
Design of Assessment Tasks 227
Role of Publishers 228
Summative Assessment 228
Drivers and Barriers for E-assessment in Open Learning 229
Specific issues for Distance Teaching Universities 230
Future Capabilities 231
Grading in Distance Education 232

11. Assessment Versus Accountability 242

The Focus 243
The Argument 243
The Role of the State 245
Comparative Methodology 247

Assessment Principles 248
Collegiate Learning Assessment 250
Notes for Reconciliation 252
A Strategy for State-Based Comparisons 254

12. Management of Educational Assessment 256

Social Context of Assessment 256
Management and Quality Assurance 261
Staff Assessment Instruments 266
Stakeholders' Reaction to Instruments 270

Bibliography 278

Index 282

1

Higher Education: Status and Trends

While it may not yet be possible to think of higher education as a global system, there is considerable convergence among the world's universities and higher education systems. The medieval European historical origin of most of the world's universities provides a common antecedent. The basic institutional model and structure of studies are similar worldwide.

Academic institutions have frequently been international in orientation—with common curricular elements and, in the medieval period, a common language of instruction—Latin. At the end of the 20th century, English has assumed a role as the primary international language of science and scholarship, including the Internet. Now, with more than one million students studying outside their borders, with countless scholars working internationally, and with new technologies such as the Internet fostering instantaneous communications, the international roots and the contemporary realities of the university are central.

Higher education systems have also been moving from elite to mass to universal access, as Martin Trow pointed out in the 1960s. In North America, much of Europe, and a number of East Asian countries, academic systems approach universal access, with close to half the relevant age group attending some kind of post-secondary institution and with access increasingly available for non-traditional students.

In some countries, however, access remains limited. In China and India, for example, despite dramatic expansion, under 5 percent of the age group attends post-secondary institutions. In some countries with relatively low per capita income, such as the Philippines, access is high, while in some wealthier nations, it remains a key point of challenge. Throughout Africa, access is limited to a tiny sector of the population. Access is an increasingly important issue everywhere, as populations demand it and as developing economies require skilled personnel. Demands for access come into conflict with another of the flashpoints of controversy of the present era—funding.

Higher education is an expensive undertaking, and there is much debate concerning how to fund expanding academic systems. Current approaches to higher education funding emphasise the need for "users" to pay for the cost of instruction, as policymakers increasingly view higher education as something that benefits the individual, rather than as a "public good" where the benefits accrue to society. This new thinking, combined with constrictions on public expenditures in many countries, have meant severe financial problems for academe. These difficulties come at a time when higher education systems are trying to provide expanded access.

Higher education's problems have been exacerbated in many of the poorer parts of the world by the idea, popular in the past several decades and stressed by the World Bank and other agencies, that basic education was most cost-effective—as a result, higher education was ignored by major lending and donor agencies. Now, higher education is back on the agenda of governments and multilateral agencies just as academe faces some of its most serious challenges.

Academic systems and institutions have tried to deal with these financial constraints in several ways. Loan programmes, the privatisation of some public institutions, and higher tuition are among the alternatives to direct government expenditure. In many parts of the world, including most of the major industrialised nations, conditions of study have deteriorated in response to financial constraints.

Enrolments have risen, but resources, including faculty, have not kept up with needs. Academic infrastructures, including libraries and laboratories, have been starved of funds. Less is spent on basic research. Conditions of study have deteriorated in many of the world's best-developed academic systems, including Germany and France. Students have taken to the streets in large numbers to protest declining budgets and poor conditions for the first time since the 1960s. There has also been a dramatic decline in academic conditions in sub-Saharan Africa and in some other developing areas.

While these trends vary to some extent from country to country, there is considerable convergence. Academic leaders worldwide worry about the same set of topics. Specific conditions vary from one country to another, and there are certainly major differences between the Netherlands and Mali. Yet, solutions from one country may be relevant, at least in terms of suggesting alternatives, elsewhere. For example, there is much interest in Australian ideas concerning a "graduate tax"—a repayment scheme based on postgraduate income. The United States, as the world's largest and in many respects leading academic system, experienced the challenges of universal access first, and American patterns of academic organisation are of considerable interest elsewhere.

We live in a period of rapid change in higher education, a period when we can learn much from the experience of others. In short, higher education has gone global but with a variety of accents. These global concerns or issues are actually not discrete topic areas. They are better understood as issue clusters.

Contributions of Higher Education

In the last three centuries, the evolution of society has been amazing and has proceeded by many steps: from the agriculture society, to industrialisation, the post-industrial society, the information society, and, last, the knowledge society. The interacting context for people has changed dramatically. From the village, to the region, to the nation, to the continent, to the whole world, that characterises the knowledge society and the globalisation phenomena.

In the agriculture society, the larger part of the population lived and worked in the countryside or in small villages. Most of them could not read or write, they were taught by their relatives how to cope with the problems connected to cultivation and breeding, and learned on the job. Few people went to school and only very few reached a higher education level.

During the 17th and 18th centuries the development of science and technology produced the industrial revolution, with less and less people involved in the hard work of agriculture and more and more people leaving the countryside to live in big cities and to work in manufacturer industries. The industrial work asked for workers able to read and write and therefore primary education became soon compulsory in all the industrialised countries.

The French revolution produced the new concepts of national state and citizenship. The organisation of the society changed and new professions aroused to tackle the new needs of the population. Higher education institutions, and in particular universities, provided the professional skills and training, and educated the leaders for the new society. Universities became also the institutional places for producing knowledge through research activities.

In Europe up to the mid 20th century only a few percent of young people attended the university courses to reach a professional degree. After the Second World War the fast and widespread development of scientific knowledge and the impressive technological innovations produced a new displacement of people from the countryside to the cities and the new manufacturer industries asked for more and more educated workers. Therefore in Europe the compulsory period of studies of 5 years changed and shifted first to 8 years, then to 10-12 years. In the 60's and 70's the number of students attending the university courses was growing, reaching in some countries like USA the 50% of the age rank and in Europe about 20-30%.

Development of information and communication technology (ICT) and the great progress in transports – as high speed trains, cheap cars, larger and faster airplanes – improved a lot the mobility of people, goods, news, and ideas, giving rise to what we call today 'globalisation'. Information society in fact has been characterised by the spread of information that can bring to each person, every day, news about the whole world.

These developments affected deeply the geopolitical situation of the world and extended the complexity of the society. Today we talk of Asia, Europe, North America, etc. more than of single nations. Events like Olympic Games, world championships as well as regional wars like those in Kosovo or in Iraq are followed on television by billions of people all around the world. In the developed countries only a few percent of people are still involved in agriculture and only between 10-20% in industry. More and more are in fact engaged in the so-called 'third sector' in which are included all the services like national health services, teaching, research, transports, information and communication, sport and leisure activities, etc.

The incoming knowledge society puts on the table new problems and asks for new solutions. Land and natural resources have become less important; on the other hand human resources are crucial and strategic for the future of each country, thus making the investment in education and research the most fruitful. Through the media (television, newspapers, internet, etc) people share every day what happens in every part of the world and often the dramatic events prevail in this information. Therefore those who still live in undeveloped countries in poor conditions, becoming aware of their low level of living, ask for a better living environment and expect to reach the living standard of more evolved countries in a short time. At the same time people belonging to definite cultures and religions get in touch with people of different cultures and religions and the problem of how to manage a multicultural society arises.

The degree of development of one country is measured as the percent of growth in Gross National Product (GNP) and also as life expectation for the new generations. In fact the economical parameters are often the only ones taken into account. On the other hand the world resources limits do not allow the six billion people living today in our world to consume the average resources per person that is used in USA. Other problems as air pollution, drinking water availability, waste management, etc. can be faced and solved only at global level through global collaboration.

These are the reasons why the information society is becoming the knowledge society and the 'knowledge society' should evolve in the 'wisdom society' in order to face properly the new world situation. This asks for a deep change of mind and behaviour primarily in developed countries. To preserve the level of quality of life reached by developed countries it is necessary that other people improve faster their living conditions to reduce the gap between rich and poor countries. We can maintain our better conditions, but because of the limited resources in the world, we should at the same time reduce energy consumption, pollution, waste production, etc. In other words to measure the degree of comprehensive development for a country we have to introduce other non economic parameters such as the degree of education, the efficiency of the public health systems and of the public transports system, the impact on environment, etc.

Knowledge is an aware utilisation of information; wisdom means to behave following a shared knowledge in order to enhance the well being of everybody in the awareness that personal actions have a social consequence, and that today each part of the world is connected to the others. The knowledge is not only the scientific one which refers specifically to the natural world. It concerns also the artistic and humanistic world, and last but not least the spiritual and metaphysical world. In particular the spiritual and humanistic dimensions of the human being play a major role in giving meaning to the human life and contribute a lot to improve the quality of life.

If we want to contribute to realise a 'wisdom society' in which there is a wise use of knowledge it is necessary to develop in each person, in a well balanced way, the different dimensions of his/her being, i.e. the knowledge and economic dimensions together with the creative and spiritual dimensions. Each person should be aware of his/her responsibility to fully exploit his/her own potentialities and at the same time to act as a member of a society. In other words, everyone has to recover the consciousness of the social impact of his/her actions. If these are the real frames and the most likely perspectives of our society, it is very important to educate and train people for living and acting properly in this new, dynamic, and more and more complex society in the global context.

Role of Higher Education Institutions

Universities, colleges, higher education institutions, research centers have therefore to play a crucial role. As for information and knowledge society twelve years of school have been considered necessary, to shift from the knowledge to the wisdom society it is very important to extend as much as possible the higher education, both providing university courses and/or post baccalaureate courses to the largest possible number of young people and providing the opportunity to resume education many times during the life.

The wisdom society is a continuous learning society: every person has to act at the same time as learner and teacher in every context, therefore everybody must be taught how to learn and how to communicate; this should be not only the task of primary and secondary schools, but in particular the goal of higher education. In a knowledge society as well as in a wisdom society knowledge is expected to disseminate quickly and easily. This may create a tension between the needed knowledge certification and the needed knowledge diffusion. Many examples can be given: the knowledge on nuclear energy production and safety, the knowledge on the risks in the diffusion of GMO (Genetically Modified Organisms), or on the propagation of electromagnetic fields. More and well educated people are necessary although this can not be sufficient. Therefore we have to extend higher education almost to everybody. Higher education should be supported mainly by public funds, because of the general needs that it has to fulfil and also to guarantee more independence to education and research. On the other hand we judge positively the payment of some fees by the students as thus they become more aware of the value of acquiring new knowledge and professional skills and therefore they feel compelled to a stronger engagement in their studies. Of course the principle that the students should contribute to the costs of their studies is a strong conflicting issue which needs to be reconciled with the possibility of access for everybody. Different solutions are possible with good results, provided they are coherent with the particular context.

The Bologna process is going on in Europe with different trends but to the same goal. A problem is still there: how to implement the teaching and learning for the cleverest people in order to exploit completely their potentiality? This is their own interest but also the interest of the whole society. In other words, how can we fulfil both the needs of mass education and the necessity to prepare good leaders? This can be done differentiating the institutions in mass and elite institutions or organising in the universities different support and opportunities for the best students, but both solutions can also be applied together.

Other problems have to be solved by higher education institutions. For example, what kind of competences should be developed by higher education, considering the fact that society is in fast evolution and that we have to provide young people with competences that must not become obsolete too fast? Higher education should be focused in developing primarily the 'core competences', i.e. the skills necessary to live in a complex, very interacting, and continuously changing society. Some of these 'core competences' are the capability of learning, listening, interacting, communicating, being active and proactive, solving problems, understanding other cultures and religions, etc. This implies for example to be able to manage the information and communication technologies, to speak and understand other languages, to be aware of one's own cultural identity.

Curricula and the teaching methods need to be changed and shaped for the new objectives. A greater flexibility in curricula is necessary, as well as more personalised interactions between students and teachers. A multidisciplinary approach to the problems should also be encouraged. Moreover 'education' must not remain a theoretical learning but the transfer of knowledge must be integrated with practical experience. Stages in working contexts are unavoidable means to educate young students to act, to be proactive and to learn how to evaluate themselves.

The new young generations come from families where the parents have been more engaged in realising themselves than in educating their children; they live in a continent where the traditional values have become weaker and people are opportunist and consumers. When they enter the University they seek the meaning of their life: they dream to meet the right person to create a real family, they hope to find a good job after graduation, and they also would like to contribute to change the society they know in a better one.

Universities have to take into account all these expectations and hopes, and provide their young students suitable opportunities and new means in order to facilitate their search of the meaning of life. Young students have to learn how to distinguish what is more important from what is trivial for their life. Universities should also present to the students models of behaviour, how to build up their own personality, and how to strengthen their own independence.

Role of Research and Innovation

A word which synthesises well the need of new approaches, new solutions, and new educational targets is 'innovation'. It is necessary to innovate in every field: technology, social sciences, politics, organisation, etc.: to innovate we have to develop in all these fields research activities, and we have to train more and more people to have an active role in research, in research transfer, and in exploitation of research results.

Intensive research universities are the main agents for basic research; they have the capability to be dynamic and effective engines for the development of knowledge society and economy, and a magnet for international talents. Europe must invest more money in basic research which is the source of creation of new knowledge and of most innovation in society. A clear and acceptable balance should be reached between the pursuit of knowledge for its own sake and the demand for basic research aimed at a tangible return to the economy and society at large.

The knowledge society not only needs excellence and top rate research but also depends on a larger number of highly educated people who, while not engaged in active research, have sufficient knowledge to make good use of the latest research results. To learn 'core competences' and to be trained in employability skills more and more students should have the opportunity to make stages in research groups and in other working environments, not only at doctoral level but also at graduate and undergraduate level.

As higher education and research are becoming more and more strategic activities for a new kind of development for our knowledge society the governments should proportionally increase their investments in research and higher education institutions. Universities seem to be the most suitable institutions for developing integrated activities of higher education, research, and innovation, and therefore they should be the main destinations of new public and private funds devoted to development. On the other hand, to optimise the exploitation of public and private funds given to universities it is necessary to enlarge the universities autonomy, to introduce both internal and external evaluation procedures, and to improve the social responsibility awareness of teachers, researchers and students.

The governments have the responsibility for the allocations of public funds and therefore they have to incentive and support the transfer of research results from laboratories to society. This can be done in different ways: certainly the more effective is through the mobility of people involved from labs to industry and society and vice versa. Again this can be enhanced if bureaucratic obstacles are removed: the mobility of researchers should not have negative consequences on their careers and in particular on social benefits as health care and future amounts of pensions. This asks for a new legislation at European level that overcomes the single state present rules.

Due to the limitation of public funds for research, also in case they would be increased as everybody asks for, the problem of setting the priorities is ever present. The public funds for research should be divided in three categories: the first should be devoted to fertilise the free research, and allocated according to the quality of researchers. The second should be devoted to basic research and allocated to the large fields evaluated more important for society growth. The third should be devoted to applied and finalised research, taking into account the actual needs of society.

In a democratic country the division of research funds between these categories must be responsibility of the government and the parliament. Then the allocation of each part should be decided by the scientific and academic community for the first two categories; for the third, the academic and scientific community can decide jointly with people coming from industry and other productive realities.

The 'wisdom society' should be characterised by a greater institutions autonomy, more personal responsibility, and fewer rules: the governments must facilitate and fund more research in humanities and social sciences to educate people to manage properly at personal and global level science achievements and technological development, in order to foster the personal and social growth. To improve personal responsibility based on shared strong values it is better to trust the role of faiths and religions as traditional regulators of good personal behaviour than to try to control the growing complexity of the society and the personal actions only by augmenting the number of laws and rules approved by parliaments or governments.

Higher Education in a Knowledge-driven Economy

In the era of knowledge-driven economy and learning societies, both formal and informal education is playing an increasingly vital role in promoting economic solidarity, social cohesion, individual growth, sustainable development, and a culture of peace and world citizenship. Whereas our views about the way we live, learn, work, and 'think about work' have changed, the acquisition of knowledge and skills provided by a traditional formal educational setup do not correspond. Therefore, a new paradigm must evolve that is developmental, human-centered, environmentally sound, and all-inclusive, so as to prepare learners to be contributors to knowledge and not just mere recipients of knowledge. It has opened up new challenges and opportunities for higher education institutions – whether public, private, or hybrid. Just a few years ago, we could not have imagined a university without classrooms, or a library without books. Nor could we imagine a university existing 10,000 miles away from its students. Nor could we imagine technocrats rather than faculty and academic staff managing sensitive information and knowledge 'online'. Yet all of this is true today. The University of Phoenix, for example, one of the most dynamic amongst the distance learning universities, has an enrolment of over 200,000 students across the world.

Science and technology parks have lately emerged in the education sector, based upon public-private partnerships for research activities. We find such science parks in Taipei, Japan, and Singapore. In Taipei, for instance, there is a science-based industrial park at Hsinchu. It has been built near the major universities with both government and private support, and it has attracted the attention of many hi-tech firms in China and other parts of the world.

Additionally, some university-owned firms, partly funded by the private sector, are producing certain products for the educational market. A number of universities are entering into contracts with private publishers. Similarly, a large number of private enterprises are entering into agreements with various universities to meet their technological and other requirements or to help them with the distribution of their knowledge-based products. There are abundant examples of private booksellers, food services, and providers of other services, academic and non-academic alike.

Given the increasingly corporate culture in higher education, it is not surprising that 'education' has been included as a 'service' or a 'commodity' under the General Agreement on Trade and Tariffs (GATT) and World Trade Organisation (WTO). Though UNESCO has been striving hard towards protecting and strengthening higher education as a common good at the global level by promoting pluralism and diversity, on the one hand, and equitable access, capacity building, and sharing of knowledge, on the other, the GATS and WTO are striving equally hard towards reducing the barriers to 'trade' in higher education. No wonder, then, that we find the academic institutions and business enterprises of the North actively selling educational programmes to middle-income and emerging economies in the South.

The former have made collaborative arrangements with overseas institutions or offshore campuses via distance or online education. They are able to use new technologies and international collaboration effectively and rapidly for the education of approximately 84 million students attending about 2000 universities and colleges worldwide. These institutions operate in a largely unregulated environment, although organisations like GATE (The Global Alliance for Transnational Education) have recently come to the forefront with the aim of fostering and maintaining quality in cross-border higher education enterprises.

The concept of private higher education is not new. In Asia, private institutions have always been a central part of higher education. Private higher education has been playing a major role in Japan, South Korea, Taiwan, Taipei, Indonesia, and the Philippines. In these countries, up to 80 percent of students attend private institutions. Private higher education is reported to be rapidly growing in China, Vietnam, Cambodia, and other central Asian republics as well. Generally, private post-secondary institutions are found to be at the lower end in terms of prestige, though there are some high quality private universities, such as Waseda and Keio in Japan, De La Salle and the Ateneo de Manila in the Philippines, Yonsei in South Korea, and Santa Dharma in Indonesia. These universities are among the oldest in their respective countries and share a reputation of training the elite class.

Another category of new private institutions comprises those specialising in fields such as management, technology, or education, with the sole aim of offering high quality academic degrees having market acceptability. The Asian Institute of Technology in the Philippines and the National Institute of Information Technology in India fall in this category. Besides private universities and colleges serving the mass higher education market on a massive scale, there are some non-selective institutions run by individuals or families. There are also some institutions sponsored by private, non-profit religious groups or ethnic organisations.

Many Asian countries already have considerable experience in managing private higher education institutions on a large scale, whereas other countries have picked this up during the last 25 to 30 years. Whereas we find a long tradition of private higher education in Asia, we find dramatic changes in terms of the public-private mix in Eastern Europe in the last few years. There are 91 private business schools in Poland, 29 in the Czech Republic, 21 in Armenia, 18 in Romania, and 4 in Bulgaria. In the Cote d'Ivoire, professional training is exclusively in the private domain, and in Gambia 44% of skill-based education and training is privately provided. About 75% of tertiary education in India is supposed to be under private management. Whereas most of the private colleges are affiliated with the open schools or public universities, we also find examples of new private universities being set up under the Private Universities Acts passed by some of the newly emergent states in India such as Chattisgarh or Uttaranchal.

China has more than 1200 private higher education institutions today, though not all of them enjoy official government authorisation. By the end of 2002, only 4 private colleges had been authorised to award the bachelor's degree and 129 were authorised to grant degrees below the level of the bachelor's. The private sector accounts for 10% of the total enrollment in post-secondary education in China. Whereas the public-private educational institutions in Shanghai and Beijing enjoy reasonably good reputations, the schools in Shenyang are not doing so well. These Minban Gongzhu (owned and supported by the government through property and infrastructure) are seen as breeding corruption, sacrificing quality for the sake of profit, and putting unnecessary pressures on students and their families.

The notion of private ownership is different in China from that prevailing in the western world. Minban or Sili (private institutions) remain only partly owned by the government and administered by independent parties. On 28 December 2002, China promulgated its first national legislation on private education. The law aimed at facilitating private growth and initiated a longer process to accredit, merge, dismantle, or change institutions at higher level. China's initial recognition of private education under the 1982 constitution was quite vague and timely action was required to provide legitimacy to the private institutions engaged in higher education.

These institutions are now playing an important role in filling the gap between demand and supply, on the one hand, and stemming the brain drain by providing job opportunities to many local Chinese, on the other. Unlike China, private higher education in post-communist Russia is only a decade old and public involvement in the creation of private higher education institutions has been substantial. Russian private higher education institutions are generally referred to as 'non-state' institutions to demarcate them from both the government and private institutions. Though these institutions are not funded by the central government, they rely considerably on support and resources from other state-run organisations and agencies. Often their connection to government bodies is much closer than is openly declared.

There are more than 500 private institutions that account for roughly 10 percent of enrollment in higher education, mostly under market-related programmes such as economics, law, psychology, sociology, social work, business administration, and other such fields that do not require much investment, equipment, or research facilities. Similarly, in Vietnam, about 12% of the students attend "nonpublic institutions". There the first non-public institution, known as the Thang Long University, was established in 1989 on an experimental basis. By 2002-3, Vietnam had 23 non-public post-secondary institutions. Out of these, 16 were people-founded universities, 2 were people-founded colleges, 1 was a semi-public university, and 4 were semi-public colleges. People founded institutions are owned and managed by the NGOs or private associations, whereas the semi-public institutions are owned and operated by the public authorities with some private support. In future, private individuals may also own and operate nonpublic higher educational institutions along with some foreign-owned institutions.

In Malaysia there has been rapid growth of private higher education. There are 691 private colleges and universities and 4 foreign university campuses. Malaysia is one of a few countries that had long ago allowed private higher education, without granting it full status. Recently the government has put restrictions on funding study abroad programmes. Instead it is striving hard to attract foreign students from neighboring countries by making Malaysia an educational hub. In fact, between 1997 and 2000, foreign enrollment grew by 60% in Malaysia. Malaysia relies on the private sector both to meet the excessive demand for higher education and technical skills, and to generate revenues from abroad.

The private sector is making inroads into higher education in the Middle East, as well. For instance, in Afghanistan, along with political and economic changes, we find equivalent changes in the education sector. The Afghan government is actively planning for the first private university, the American University of Afghanistan. This university is to be American style, with English as the medium of instruction and mainly American professors as faculty.

In Saudi Arabia, the government has given permission to private organisations to set up 2 new universities and 36 colleges as part of its privatisation policy. The colleges are to be spread over the 9 cities and are to be in addition to 6 already existing private colleges with licenses from the Ministry of Higher Education.

In Latin America, the oldest universities are private institutions set up by the Catholic Church. But now the trend is in favour of for-profit private universities. For instance, the University of the Americas, owned by Sylvan Learning System, is making big profits despite deriving criticism from Chile's academia for lower quality and higher fees. This private university, however, prides itself on offering access and international ties. Surprisingly, the private sector in Chile is allowed to function *de facto*, even if it is not granted *de jure* status. But in Argentina, private higher education institutions have been allowed full license for a provisional period of time. The private sector has now captured a fifth of university enrollments and a fourth of total higher education enrollments there.

There is a long tradition of private career colleges in Canada. Today even the public universities are working very hard to pursue private links. Their focus is on internationalisation as a proactive response to the worldwide circulation of ideas, technology, capital, and people. There is a wide range of private post-secondary institutions working in Canada, offering programmes in areas such as aviation, business, computer training, hospitality, tourism, and English as second language, among others. While these institutions are required to register with the provincial government, they are not accredited directly by the government. Rather, the institutions may be encouraged to apply for accreditation by the Private Post-secondary Education Commissions in their respective provinces. Canada is the first country to have passed the Private Postsecondary Education Act in 1996 in order to protect the interests of students and their families as consumers.

In the United States, some of the private institutions are able to focus on 'quality education' and 'narrow purpose'. The rationale behind private post-secondary education seems to be high quality, high costs, and high prestige, on the one hand, and cultural distinctiveness and additional services, on the other. No wonder the private for-profit post-secondary institutions are doing well, whereas traditional public universities and colleges are often struggling financially.

In the case of private post-secondary education, the market and short-term considerations have an edge over academics and long-term goals. Private equity funds are investing hugely in the US for profit higher education market in the wake of increasing job market and political acceptance of these institutions. Traditional colleges and universities are also investing in private for-profit education themselves.

Whereas private higher education is growing worldwide in response to a number of factors and with a variety of goals—meeting the demand for advanced levels of knowledge and technological skills that exceeds the supply; providing more choices or differentiated products to meet the specific demands of the students as consumers and clients; more feasibly implementing variable fee structures on the basis of ability to pay; adopting practices from business management to increase accountability and economic efficiency; shouldering some governmental burdens; rectifying inegalitarian, over-, or mis-use of public provision of higher education; making the government focus on its prime duty towards literacy and basic education; saving public subsidies for public goods; generating revenues and making innovations through experimentation—there can be significant variations at the socio-cultural and national levels.

Most of the Western European countries are still dominated by public universities, while private higher education is becoming more successful in Eastern Europe. In the United Kingdom and many other countries, the distinction between public and private colleges is getting blurrier by the day. One of the reasons is the competition from the new private post-secondary institutions that are more affordable and market-oriented. Another is the change in public policies regarding private initiative in post-secondary education. We also find some new institutions financed by a mixture of public and private resources. Governments are no longer indifferent or hostile to the private sector in most countries.

But there is no dearth of examples of the post-secondary private institutions unable to survive in the wake of harsh competition and demand for quality education. For instance, many institutions were forced to close down in Japan. Poor economic performance, falling birth rates, and a decade-old recession were reported to be the prime factors responsible for their closure. Some of the private higher education institutions could not survive as, in Japan, faculty salaries were accounting for 60-70% of operating costs.

In Mexico, where the number of private universities rose from 67 in 1975 to 1368 in 2003, the government has had to close 88 private universities over the past two years for failing to comply with basic educational standards. In the same vein, the Ugandan government has had to clamp down on private tertiary institutions operating illegally. The National Council for Higher education in Uganda published a list of 13 private degree-awarding authorities that it licensed and warned against enrolling in non-authorised institutions. Uganda is representative of most African countries, where we find a sharp rise in private higher education. Most of it has occurred as "unregulated surprise" and "unanticipated development". In most of these cases, the governments are engaged in more clearly defining roles in private higher education, regulating these institutions, and guarding the interests of the students as clients against low quality suppliers in open markets.

Kenya, on the other hand, provides another example where the number of students seeking private higher education is declining. In Kenya, private higher education has a longer history than in most other states in Africa, but their share in student enrollment is declining as a result of the adoption of the Module II programme by the public universities. Here the private universities are also facing challenges from entrepreneurial foreign universities from South Africa, the UK, and Australia.

In most African countries, the assessment and accreditation bodies have been set up by national or provincial governments to regulate quality, curricula, fee structures, faculty competence, accessibility, etc. A large number of private higher education institutions end up filling the gap between supply and demand or performing traditional socio-economic functions. Most of them remain public as far as their missions are concerned. Private institutions worldwide are generally criticised for their privateness, their lack of quality or accessibility, or their contribution to the commercialisation or commodification of higher education.

It is not generally recognised, however, that it is always the 'private' that dominates both the public and the private. Neither privatisation nor nationalisation could have occurred without the prior consensus or nexus between business and politics. Moreover, the private sector can cater to diversified needs on a smaller or more select basis more easily than can the public sector. In fact, the private sector can also be given credit for the expansion of higher education in most countries in the last three decades. It can provide quality education to the elite, vocational education to the needy, and low quality education to those who neither merit nor can afford a better education. It can also provide education to those who are already employed, through distance or online education on an "anytime, anywhere" basis.

Higher Education : Global Concerns

In the last decade, higher education has emerged as a key sector in the social and economic transition taking place in countries around the world. The concerns of the public and of politicians have focused on higher education in a number of ways. The world society suffered a critical loss of intellectual resources due to national disintegration, political purges, brain drain, and market restructuring. Higher education has provided an important recruitment base for the newly emerging political arena. Faculty and students have become part of a new breed of public personalities, which allows representatives of the sector to gain more influence and thus retain or even enhance their political privileges.

Higher education is increasingly seen as a leading force to help transitional societies catch up with wealthy nations. In many countries, higher education as a sector has experienced deprivation and crisis, given the problems of feasibility and sustainability. In countries that have gone through civil conflicts and violent confrontations, the resulting physical destruction has made costly rehabilitation programmes necessary that are hardly feasible. In countries that have experienced economic and financial deterioration, the inadequately maintained infrastructure and devalued salaries have left higher education in turmoil, as sustaining quality or even basic services does not seem possible.

Higher education has profoundly changed in the past two decades, and those involved in the academic enterprise have yet to grapple with the implications of these changes. Academic institutions and systems have faced pressures of increasing numbers of students and demographic changes, demands for accountability, reconsideration of the social and economic role of higher education, implications of the end of the Cold War, and the impact of new technologies, among others. While academic systems function in a national environment, the challenges play themselves out on a global scale.

We identify several themes that seem to be central to current developments in higher education worldwide. These themes deserve elaboration and analysis. They affect countries and regions differently, although we believe that all are relevant internationally, and that a discussion of implications can lead to understanding that will be useful for both comparative and national analysis.

— Education and work are activities that should feed one another. The links and transition points from initial education to the work force are weakly articulated. This is true in the developed world as well as in the developing world. Educators and business leaders rarely discuss, let alone agree upon, a set of skills and orientations that are prerequisites for successful employment. The formal structures by which education systems prepare students for tomorrow are similarly weakly developed. Models developed in Germany, through the linking of post-secondary education and apprenticeship arrangements, or community college system are currently being explored in several areas. Professional education often links well to employment in many countries, but education in the arts and sciences is less well articulated. It is not clear how close an articulation is possible, but the issues are worthy of further consideration.

— While the initial transition from school to work may be poorly articulated, the demand for education throughout the life cycle is becoming apparent. Fed by rapid changes in technology and the creation of employment categories that did not exist 10 years ago, workers and employers must continually attend to the educational dimension. As the nature of work has evolved, so have the needs of those in the workforce to continually upgrade their capacities. This has led to the development of a variety of educational forms beyond the bachelor's degree. In Germany, recent changes in the degree structure have led to the modularisation of graduate degrees. In the United States, certificate programmes and short-term courses of study are being rapidly developed. By one recent estimate corporations in the United States alone will spend $15 billion over current expenditures by 2005 just to maintain current employee training levels. Others estimate that worldwide expenditures on training amount to many billions of dollars annually to ensure that their workforce has the skills necessary to compete in an ever-competitive and high-velocity business environment. In many countries, especially in the developing world, graduate education is coming into its own as the need for advanced skills and for continuing education becomes increasingly clear.

— It has become a point of banality to remark on the changes that technological developments have wrought. Indeed, many of the dislocations in school-to-work transition and the press for lifelong education are partially the result of these developments. More directly, however, technology has made possible a revolution in distance education that has important implications for the accreditation of educational institutions and assurance of quality in such circumstances. Technology is also beginning to have an impact on teaching and learning in traditional universities. It is also a truism that this technology is expensive, subject to rapid obsolescence, and requires high initial investment simply to get into the game. For many developing countries, cost is at present prohibitive, and it is precisely these areas where technology can provide the greatest short-term improvement. Technology is also central to the communication, storage, and retrieval of knowledge. The traditional library is being revolutionised by web-based information systems, as are the management systems of many universities.

— As the market for individuals with transnational competencies has grown, so have opportunities for individuals with marketable skills in other countries. Currently, the transfer of talent has been from developing countries such as India and China to the developed world. In the United States, the stay rates for advanced students in the engineering disciplines and the sciences can be higher than 75 percent for students from particular countries. From the perspective of national education authorities, these students may represent a considerable hemorrhaging of talent that has been developed by the students' countries of origin. If nations are to develop, a means must be found by which talent can flourish in the soils that originally nurtured it. Related issues of internationalising the curriculum and providing a global consciousness to students, including instruction in foreign language, and ensuring that the academic profession is linked internationally are central to any discussion of the internationalisation of higher education.

— Although seldom discussed, one of the areas of greatest expansion worldwide has been graduate education—the post-baccalaureate training for the professions as well as for science, technology, and teaching. Graduate education offers great opportunities for international links and cooperation. Countries can take advantage of graduate training capacities elsewhere, and the new technologies can provide key links. Highly specialised and advanced-level teaching and research deserve careful analysis.

— The privatisation of higher education is a worldwide phenomenon of considerable importance. In Latin America and some parts of Asia, the fastest-growing parts of the academic system are private institutions. In Central and Eastern Europe, private initiative is also of considerable importance. Public universities are in some places being "privatised" in the sense that they are increasingly responsible for raising their own funds. They are asked to relate more directly to society. Students are increasingly seen as "customers." The expansion of the private sector brings up issues of quality control and accreditation since in many parts of the world there are few controls as yet on private-sector expansion. Access is also a central issue. As some developing areas, such as sub-Saharan Africa, will soon be experiencing the growth of private institutions, understanding in a comparative context the problems and possibilities of private higher education is an urgent need.

— The academic profession is in crisis almost everywhere. There is a rapid growth of part-time faculty members in many countries, and traditional tenure systems are under attack. The professoriate is being asked to do more with less, and student-teacher ratios, academic salaries, and morale have all deteriorated. The professoriate is being asked to adjust to new circumstances but is given few resources to assist in the transition. Without a committed academic profession, the university cannot be an effective institution.

— Access and equity remain central factors, but in the current policy context are sometimes ignored. While academic systems worldwide have expanded dramatically, there are problems of access and equity in many parts of the world. Gender, ethnicity, and social class remain serious issues. In many developing countries, higher education remains mainly an urban phenomenon, and one that is reserved largely for wealthier segments of society. Although women have made significant advances, access for women remains a serious problem in many parts of the world.

— Accountability is a contemporary watchword in higher education. Demands by funding sources, mainly government, to measure academic productivity, control funding allocations, etc. is increasingly a central part of the debate on higher education. Governance systems are being strained, sometimes to the breaking point. To meet the demands for accountability, universities are becoming "managerialised," with professional administrators gaining increasing control. The traditional power of the professoriate is being weakened.

— Expansion brings with it increased differentiation and the emergence of academic systems. New kinds of academic institutions emerge, and existing universities serve larger and more diverse groups. In order to make sense of this differentiation, academic systems are organised to provide coordination and the appropriate management of resources.

These are some of the key topics that affect contemporary post-secondary education worldwide. While this is by no means a complete list, it provides the basis for discussion and cooperation. International and comparative analysis can help to yield insights on how to deal with these topics in individual countries.

Institutions of higher education have historically played an important role in serving the globe. Today, like many other elements of our society, higher education is under stress, with rising tuitions, growing barriers for low income and minority students, and increasing privatisation of public institutions. Conservative anti-tax/anti-government ideology has taken its toll as states struggle to fund their public universities and community colleges. At the same time, the open academic environment and academic freedom have become increasingly vulnerable to commercial pressures, attacks on science, government security measures and occasional right-wing political monitoring of individual faculty members. Institutions of higher education remain remarkable in their diversity, intellectual strength and commitment to openness. These are opportunities that should be accessible to all citizebs, not a privileged elite. The democratising of access to universities will only strengthen and improve education. Harnessing the intellectual energy of universities for enlightened public ends will strengthen the nations.

Globalisation and Issues in Higher Education

Globalisation is a newly emerging phenomenon. It has been defined as a set of processes by which the world is rapidly being integrated into one economic space via increased international trade, the internationalisation of production and financial markets; the internationalisation of a commodity culture promoted by an increasingly networked global telecommunication system. It transcends socio-economic and political barriers that the countries of the world are prone to build around themselves. It is not only a process integrating just economy, but culture, technology and governance. It is giving rise to new markets, foreign exchange and capital markets linked globally, new tools, internet links, cellular phones, media network, new actors; the World Trade Organisation with authority over national governments, the multi-national cooperation with more economic power than many states, new rules, multi-national agreements and intellectual property, multi-lateral agreements on trade.

Globalisation is expected to have a positive influence on the volume, quality and spread of knowledge through increased interaction among the various states. 'In a globalised world, as technology becomes its main motor, knowledge assumes a powerful role in production, making its possession essential for nations, if they are successfully to pursue economic growth and competitiveness. Education, being the most potent instrument of creation, assimilation and transmission of knowledge, assumes a central role in the process.

In a market oriented competitive world, unleashed by the forces of globalisation, education has to assume a somewhat different role. It cannot afford to be conventional, rigid and impervious to change. It has to keep abreast of the latest developments in various fields and be capable of creating, absorbing and transacting neo-technology and information systems that are sweeping across the countries of the world. There has also to be a paradigm shift in the contents of education with substantial emphasis on the productivity aspect of the curriculum. It would also call for adequate emphasis on research and development. It is, however, necessary to guard against being swept off our feet by the new 'cult of technology', and consequently, 'the diminution of respect for spiritual and cultural values'. An unfettered and ruthless pursuit of economic goals, without regard to considerations of moral and social values is bound to be disastrous for the people, particularly in developing countries.

In spite of the cataclysmic changes brought about in most countries, it would be wrong to consider globalisation as a panacea for all economic and social ills. The accelerated process of liberalisation and globalisation in the world has increased the opportunities for growth and development, but it has also added new complexities and risks in the management of global interdependence". Some of the complexities identified at the international level are:

— Globalisation is forging greater interdependence, yet the World seems more fragmented – between the rich and the poor, between the powerful and the powerless.

— Economically, politically and technologically, the world has never seemed more free – or more unjust.

— If the present global progress continues at such a snails' pace, it will take more than 130 years to rid the World of hunger.

— Globalisation is a "tricky term for some, it connotes free flow of ideas, capital, people and goods around the world. For others, it implies the hegemony of the capitalist system, the domination of rich nations and corporations and the loss of national identity.

It would thus appear that globalisation is not an unmixed blessing. It may promote "growth through increased technology and knowledge transfers in developing countries but it could also be sometime a source of instability.

The changes to which higher education all over the globe increasingly is exposed, are complex and varied, even contradictory, and the comprehensive concept of globalisation are far from clear and well defined. Nevertheless, the concept of globalisation indicates that the various changes are somehow interrelated and creating new forms of interdependencies between actors, institutions and states.

Education, as a service industry, is part of globalisation process under the umbrella of General Agreement on Trade in Services (GATS). There is, however, distinct possibility that this might force countries with quite different academic needs and resources to conform to structures inevitably designed to service the interest of the most powerful academic systems and corporate educational providers breeding inequality and dependence. Globalisation can lead to unregulated and poor quality higher education, with the world wide marketing of fraudulent degrees or other so-called higher education credentials. While these are obvious problems, globalisation can also have advantages, particularly for India, which has a large educational system and infrastructure and diverse human capabilities.

Given the array of theoretical and epistemological perspective presented in the general social science literature on 'globalisation', it is difficult to assess not only the nature and dimensions of globalisation, but also what it might mean to the field of education. Very few educational researchers or theorists have attempted to make connections between the economic, political and cultural dimensions of globalisation and the policies and practices of education.

It appears as though the phenomenon of globalisation will mean many different things for education. Most certainly, in the near future, "it will mean a more competitive and deregulated educational system modelled after free market but with more pressure on it to assure that the next generation of workers are prepared for some amorphous 'job market of 21st century'. It will also mean… "that educational system will increasingly provide the sites of struggle over the meaning and power of national identity and a national culture. And finally, schools will no doubt also be the sites of various counter-hegemonic movements and pedagogies".

Globalisation, though a recent phenomenon, is a reality, which cannot be wished away. It is, however, difficult to measure its long-term effect on the course of socio-economic development in various countries. In fact, because of the large disparities in the economic position of the countries inhabiting the globe, it would be imprudent to arrive at any standardised formula of assessing the effects. Each country is an entity in itself and requires to be studied differently. It is however necessary to stress that a thoughtless and unimaginative entry into the globalised market would not be in the best interests of the countries, particularly those, which are striving to grapple with the problems of slow economic and social development.

The impact of the various trends and challenges related to globalisation on higher education institutions and policies is profound, but also diverse, depending on the specific location in the global arena. There is a danger of generalisation and oversimplification when dealing with globalisation; diversity has to be recognised but also to a certain extent promoted. Nevertheless, an attempt can be made to define some general tendencies in higher education that in one way or another relate to globalisation:

Globalisation and Knowledge Society

Globalisation and the transition to a knowledge society seem to create new and tremendously important demands and exigencies towards universities as knowledge-centres. Scientific research and development of technologies are crucial activities in a knowledge and information driven society and will become even more important in the future. Not only in the core countries of the developed world, but increasingly also in other parts of the globe will research and development activities become the motor of economic growth and social development. Because there is a move away from the traditional scientific research paradigm and towards more 'Mode 2' oriented research, and because of the fact that also outside the fields of natural sciences research becomes strategically important for corporations and governments, the role and importance of science and technology will continue to grow. Since long, scientific research is intrinsically internationally oriented, but the internationalisation of research has accelerated strongly during the last years.

International communication (publishing, conferences, electronic networking) within the scientific community and quality norms for scientific personnel benchmarked to international standards have to be developed by universities that aspire the quality label of research universities. As a side effect of the globalisation of research and development, the academic profession itself becomes more mobile and an highly competitive international market of researchers is emerging, with organised migration of researchers and brain drain as one of the consequences. The new role of universities as 'knowledge centres' stretches out to other functions than science and research however. Universities are called upon to take up responsibilities in society and culture at large, to act as mediators in conflicts, to deepen democracy, to dynamise cultures, to function as centres for critical debate and ethical conscience. The high demands placed upon universities worldwide create tensions in institutions, and at the same time stimulate other organisations to engage also in those kinds of activities, sometimes with the idea in mind that traditional universities will not be able to meet those new demands.

Increasing Demand for Higher Education

Many observers expect an increase in the demand for higher education worldwide. In the developed world the knowledge society will ask for even more highly qualified knowledge workers. Economic development, modernisation and demographic pressure will fuel the demand for higher education also in other parts of the world, only limited by the inability of the poor to finance the cost of higher learning. Local institutions nor governments will have enough resources to deal with this massification of demand in many countries, leaving an unmet demand in the upper and middle classes of many countries in the ex-Soviet Union and the southern hemisphere to international and virtual providers.

The demand for higher education will not only grow quantitatively but will also become more diverse. Despite some decline in their value as credentials on the labour market in the developed world, traditional qualifications (degrees and diplomas) will remain the most important product of higher education institutions, but they will be supplemented by specialised programmes, vocational and competency-oriented training and modular courses adapted to a new lifelong learning demand, even if higher education institutions are not the main providers in these fields in many countries. In other parts of the world however, credentialism still is on the rise, sometimes leading to a kind of 'paper chase', fuelled by the (sometimes overrated) expectation that degrees and diplomas are the gateway to economic prosperity and social security by promising a job in the public sector.

New communication technologies and the Internet provide new opportunities for a more flexible delivery of higher education, thereby creating a new demand in some countries and meeting demand in others where traditional institutions are incapable to do so. All together, these developments underpin the assertion that higher education will become one of the booming markets in the years to come. This expansion and massification will not be matched by a proportional rise in public expenditure, leading to an increase in private and commercial provision and creating huge problems of access and equity.

Regulatory Issues

Internationalisation and globalisation lead to an erosion of the national regulatory and policy frameworks in which universities are embedded. Most modern higher education institutions are product of national developments and policies and are fully integrated in national educational systems. In an increasingly international environment—marked by a globalised and liberalised marketplace, globalising professions, mobility of skilled labour, an international arena of scientific research and academic personnel, and international competition between universities and between universities and other institutions and companies –, the national character of policy frameworks creates more and more tensions. Institutions already acknowledge this and are developing partnerships, consortia and networks to strengthen their position in the global arena.

Mobility programmes, such as ERASMUS/SOCRATES or UMAP, and schemes such as the European credit transfer system have tried to stimulate internationalisation in higher education with full respect to the various national policy frameworks. Globalisation challenges this more or less voluntaristic policy and asks for more thorough international harmonisation of policy frameworks, higher education structures, degree systems and even curricula.

The process started with the Bologna-Declaration in Europe is a clear example of this, but in the context of free-trade agreements, like for example NAFTA or MERCOSUR, similar tendencies of international harmonisation of higher education systems exist also in other parts of the world. In the longer run this eventually will lead to the generalisation of the bachelor/ master-degree structure, the hegemony of English as the lingua franca in higher education and scientific research, the development of compatible credit transfer and accumulation systems to recognise, transport and validate teaching and learning experiences, the international recognition of degrees and diplomas, a negotiated consensus on core knowledge and competencies and their place in curricula, especially in specific professional fields, etc.

Like in other social fields, globalisation will create resistance and counter tendencies in the field of higher education, asking for the recognition of the importance of the national language, the specific degree architecture, the cultural embeddedness of curricula, etc. Such tendencies are not always to be seen as retrograde or counter- productive to globalisation. Globalisation in higher education does not necessarily imply international standardisation and uniformity, but asks for policies balancing the global and the local.

To a large extent resistance to globalisation in higher education is also motivated by a rejection of the marketisation perceived to be inherent in globalisation and a defence of a 'public good' approach to higher education. However, many make the error to identify a 'public good' perspective towards higher education with an exclusively national policy framework. An international regulatory framework is needed to transcend the eroded national policy contexts and to some extent to steer the global integration of the higher education systems. Without such a framework the globalisation of higher education will be unrestrained and wild, generating a lot of resistance and protest.

Global Higher Education Market

One of the most visible manifestations of globalisation is the emerging 'borderless' higher education market. The huge increase in the worldwide demand in higher education, the budgetary and capacity problems of many nations to meet this demand, and the opportunities created by new communication technologies and the Internet, shape an environment in which new, mostly for-profit providers successfully can expand the supply of educational services. Universities from North America, Europe and Australia take initiatives to reach out their educational provision to this international higher education market, by active recruitment of international, fee-paying students to the home institution, by establishing branch campuses or franchising and twinning agreements with local institutions, or via distance education and e-learning and other transnational activities. The international demand for higher education has also invited new providers from outside the higher education sector to enter the scene.

The 'business of borderless education' comprises various forms and developments, among which also combinations are possible, such as new for-profit private universities, corporate 'universities', media companies delivering educational programmes, professional associations becoming directly active in higher education, and companies with high training needs establishing their own training facilities. Many of these new providers extensively use the Internet as delivery channel; in some cases they develop into real 'cyber-universities' with a very limited physical presence. Drifting away from the old academic culture of traditional universities – and sometimes even openly questioning it –, and blurring the distinctions between academic, research-driven education and vocational training, they defy the age-old identity of universities.

In some niches, such as business administration studies, their substantial growth poses a direct threat to the market position of existing traditional universities, although in many other sectors of mass delivery of initial higher education degrees their capacity to compete with the publicly funded institutions is very limited.

However, in some countries, mainly in Eastern Europe, the former Soviet Union and the developing world, their presence even on this level is substantial, due to insufficient domestic public supply and the growth of demand in middle classes willing to pay for higher education. Although there are also less reputable initiatives and real 'diploma mills', the reaction of national governments and traditional universities in some countries to these new providers is sometimes exaggerated. To some extent their development even enriches the higher education sector, awakes innovation also in the old institutions and challenges productively the academic tradition. Still, important issues of access and equity on the one hand and quality on the other are raised by the global rise of private, for-profit higher education.

Importance of Quality Assurance in Higher Education

In the previous decade quality assurance and accreditation systems in higher education have been developed in many countries. By far the most of them are national schemes, oriented to the domestic higher education systems. As a consequence, transnational activities of universities and especially distance education and e-learning activities in many cases are not covered by these national quality assurance and accreditation schemes. Since there is a great variety in and limited international communication on standards and benchmarking, the readability and transparency of these quality assurance and accreditation systems to other countries, foreign institutions and international students is low, and therefore the relevance of these national schemes in the context of globalisation of higher education is limited as well. In a number of countries accreditation schemes have been developed as an instrument to regulate and control the higher education market. There is no generally accepted definition of accreditation in higher education, and in many cases the term is used also to indicate procedures of recognition of institutions, ex ante authorisation or licensing of programmes of new providers, approval of nationally controlled curricula, etc. Here, we use a rather pragmatic definition of accreditation, namely the formal and public statement by an external body, resulting from a quality assurance procedure, that agreed standards of quality are met by an institution or programme.

An accredited status can have specific consequences, for example regarding the degree-awarding capacity, the recognition of those degrees, funding, credit-transfer, access to postgraduate programmes in third institutions, etc. The situation with regard to accreditation internationally is very diverse, with the differences mainly concentrating on the issue of the role of the state in accreditation. In some countries, such as the US, voluntary accreditation of institutions has a long tradition. The American example has led to the development of accreditation in many other countries, but mostly driven by the national authorities willing to control the domestic higher education market. In Europe accreditation is a much debated issue in the context of the Bologna process and opinions are divided, with countries moving to various kinds of accreditation schemes and others opposing it, some institutions seeing it as a necessary instrument to guarantee quality and to differentiate the market and others seeing it as an intolerable attack on their autonomy.

It is clear that, a Dutch-Flemish experiment excepted, there is a strict national focus in the European debate on accreditation and a resistance against any form of transnational accreditation system. And those who think about international accreditation, sometimes see it as a strategy to differentiate a specific group of countries or institutions from those outside, and thus to create new divisions. This is often also the case with networks of universities developing mutual inter-institutional accreditation procedures. This short overview illustrates that inter- or transnational accreditation virtually is non-existing and that sometimes accreditation even is used to protect the domestic higher education market and to counteract the development of private and transnational higher education.

The establishment of transnational professional accreditation compensates the absence of truly inter- or transnational public accreditation systems to some extent. Already clearly developed in the fields of engineering (ABET) and management studies (EQUIS), but in development in other professions, these schemes of international professional accreditation fill in the gap left by the national authorities and the higher education community.

Another development is the import of foreign accreditors, as is the case of American accreditors or the British Open University validation scheme asked to accredit programmes or institutions in other countries. The establishment of organisations specifically devoted to the accreditation of transnational accreditation is another interesting case, although up to now the most important endeavour in this field, GATE, has not be very successful due to its links with a particular for-profit provider.

These developments have in common that they originated outside the higher education community and policy fields, demonstrating the inability of the global higher education world itself to develop its own systems of transnational self-regulation. They also indicate that international accreditation is becoming a reality, although external to the international higher education community itself, and that institutions in the future will be facing a situation of 'multiple accreditation' coming from various origins.

There is a growing agreement on the viewpoint that globalisation in higher education urgently asks for a transnational approach to quality assurance and accreditation, but there are huge differences of vision on how to achieve this and which steps have to be taken. A minimal strategy is to improve communication and exchange among national quality assurance agencies, in the hope that this will lead to a kind of harmonisation and international benchmarking of trustworthy standards and methodologies and the gradual mutual recognition of agencies and schemes. This minimal strategy, defended for example by ENQA, legitimating the quality assurance and accreditation competencies of the national states, risks to take too much time and to remain too voluntaristic in the light of the profound and accelerating impact of globalisation.

A second strategy is to develop a kind of soft validation and approval procedure for existing quality assurance and accreditation systems. International associations such as IAUP think of the possibility to establish a clearinghouse of trustworthy quality assurance and accreditation systems in the world, based on a mutually accepted definition of concepts and basic standards and criteria.

Following on this, a third strategy could be the development of real meta-accreditation on an international scale. There are no real significant examples of this for the moment and it is difficult to imagine where such an initiative would derive the authority and legitimacy from to take up a well-defined and trustworthy position in the field. However, the fact that some international professional accreditation schemes succeed in establishing their authority suggests that in principle it would be possible also for the international higher education community to do the same. International organisations such as UNESCO could provide the moral authority and legitimacy to start some experiments in this area.

A fourth strategy, the development of a real international accreditation agency, seems to be very unrealistic for the moment, given the unwillingness of national states to transfer that kind of crucial competence to an international agency, but also because many fear that this will lead to a very bureaucratic, costly apparatus escaping any kind of control from governments and higher education institutions.

There is no doubt that this issue asks for urgent consideration and action on an international level. The impact of globalisation is such that without a trustworthy international quality scheme of whatever kind that could balance the development of the global higher education market, we will have to face severe problems in the future of which especially the countries in the less developed parts of the world and their students will be the victims. It is difficult to underestimate the risks associated with various kinds of rogue providers and diploma mills.

Growing insecurity about the quality status of foreign degrees will lead to even more severe checks at the level of national governments and a more protectionist attitude among institutions, creating more problems regarding recognition of qualifications and mobility of professional labour that those already existing today, and further inhibiting that development of transnational higher education. It is in the self-interest of the global higher education community to develop transnational quality assurance and accreditation systems that can counterbalance the globalisation of higher education.

References

Allan, J.. *Learning Outcomes in Higher Education*, Studies in Higher Education, 21, 1, 93-108.

Breton, G. and Lambert, M. (eds) (2003) *Universities and Globalization: Private Linkages, Public Trust*, UNESCO Publishing/Université Laval/Economica, Paris/ Quebec.

Gibbs, P. (2001) Higher education as a market: a problem or a solution? *Studies in Higher Education* 26(1), 85–94

Orsingher, C. (ed.) (2006) *Assessing Quality in European Higher Education Institutions*, Physica-Verlag, Heidelberg.

Pascarella, E. and P. Terenzini. (2005*). How College Affects Students: A Third Decade of Research.* Jossey-Bass.

Patton, M. Q. (2011). *Developmental evaluation: Applying complexity concepts to enhance innovation and use.* Guilford Press

2

Assessment and Evaluation: Basic Concepts

Assessment is an essential component of the teaching learning process. Teachers in schools, professors/lecturers in universities/colleges and trainers in training institutes are inevitably involved in assessing learners and/or trainees. Every teacher/lecturer/trainer should, therefore, have a clear knowledge of designing and carrying out assessment in their respective fields.

Meaning of Assessment

The term 'assess' originates from the Latin word 'assidere', which means 'to sit by' (in judgement). According to The Oxford English Dictionary the word 'assess' means (i) estimate the value of (a property) for taxation etc., (ii) fix the amount of (a tax etc.) and impose it on a person and community, (iii) fine or tax (a person, community etc.) in or at a specific amount, (iv) estimate the size or quality of (something).

The first three meanings are related to fines or taxes. The last meaning has some relation with the teaching and learning process.

Since the middle of the twentieth century educationists have been using the word 'assess' in the field of education and psychology. The latest use of its meaning is: to judge the extent of students' learning.

Here, we would like to introduce and explore some key terms and issues in assessment. We have looked at the issues from the open and distance learning perspective.

Explaining Assessment

There are many definitions and explanations of assessment in education. Let us look at the definitions of Rowntree and Erwin.

Assessment in education can be thought of as occurring whenever one person, in some kind of interaction, direct or indirect, with another, is conscious of obtaining and interpreting information about the knowledge and understanding, or abilities and attitudes of that other person. To some extent or other it is an attempt to know that person.

Assessment is a systematic basis for making inferences about the learning and development of students... the process of defining, selecting, designing, collecting, analysing, interpreting and using information to increase students' learning and development.

The above definitions emphasise a couple of significant common themes. They are:

- Assessment is a human activity which involves interaction aimed at seeking to understand what learners have achieved. Rowntree implies that assessment may occur in formal or informal ways, and it may be descriptive than judgemental in nature.
- The role of assessment is to increase students' learning and development, rather than simply to grade or rank student performance. Naturally, one cannot grade student performance without first assessing it, but it is implied that grading is a secondary activity to the primary goal of helping learners to diagnose problems and improve the quality of their subsequent learning.

From the above definitions, we could reconceptualise assessment as the engine that drives and shapes learning, rather than simply an end of term examination that grades and reports performance.

Purposes of Assessment

Assessment has different purposes. The main purposes related to the teaching learning process are:

i) Selecting the students: Assessment helps in selecting the students for a course (general, professional, technical and so on).

ii) Certification: Assessment helps in certifying that a student has achieved a particular level of performance.

iii) Stimulating learning: Assessment can stimulate learning in different ways, e.g. motivating the students, providing information/feedback, suggesting practice, and so on.

iv) Improving teaching: Assessment information helps to review the effectiveness of teaching arrangements.

Rowntree and Freeman and Lewis have identified a number of purposes of assessment such as selection; certification/accreditation; maintenance of standards; description; improving learning; and improving teaching. From the above statement, it can be stated that the purpose of assessment varies as per the need of the target group and the context higher/open and distance learning/training. But, one can realize that there are two distinct interpretations of 'assessment'. They are:

(i) Assessment is interpreted in terms of the routine tasks that students undertake in order to receive feedback on their learning and a mark or grade signifying their achievement.

(ii) Assessment as applied to processes at the institutional level, for example, programme evaluation or course evaluation.

As a teacher/trainer in open and distance education system, we come across different meaning of assessment and assessment strategy and use of appropriate assessment vehicles in a variety of teaching contexts i.e. in terms of individual learning, independent learning, group learning and self assessment. But the most consistent message we receive from the teachers/trainers is the need for evidence to judge the extent of student's learning and the extent of the competencies developed by the trainees. For example, "Student learning research has repeatedly demonstrated the impact of assessment on learner's approaches to learning....... Ask them to explain the physics and chemistry of muscle contraction, but test them on the names of the muscles, and they will 'learn' the names but not be able to explain how contraction happens.

Evidence of the extent of students' learning comes from their behaviour. Students' behaviour may be specific to a course or more general one. It may include various types of activities like written, verbal or practical work. The students may 'produce' a report, an assignment response, a story and so on; and they will follow some 'process' for doing these. So, two things are involved: a product and a process. Both of these constitute the 'evidence' on which the judgement may be based. In short, assessment may be defined as the judgement of a sample of relevant student behaviour.

There has been a change in the assessment scenario. We observe that there is a change from testing conceptual or disciplinary knowledge to testing the application of that knowledge in different contexts, together with a wider appreciation of or sensitivity to the boundaries and changing nature of knowledge.

Now a days the tests are developed in more flexible and contingent ways so that not only the disciplinary knowledge is tested but the general skills and abilities of students are also tested within the disciplinary contexts.

Lifelong learning skills have become an important and explicit feature of the open and distance education curriculum and the need for evidence to judge the 'knowledge, understanding, transferable or generic skills and attributes in learners (for example oral and written communication, teamwork, self management, creativity, inquiry and problem solving etc.) emphasises more demands on assessment.

The need to demonstrate understanding and application of knowledge, together with generic skills, has moved assessment practice towards new vehicles. It is clear that while a handwritten, three or four hours essay type examination may be able to legitimately test something, it cannot measure all, especially the generic skills that students have developed. This has led to integrated assessment. In such assessment, complex simulations, case studies, role plays or multi faceted projects are used to assess a range of knowledge, skills and attitudes in the single assessment (Nightingale, 1996, p.03). In situations where self assessment is important, reflective journals or reflective moments in portfolios have become popular. So, testing what learners can actually learn and can do, and how they have developed the skills and attitudes and need to continue their learning, marks a significant shift in approach to assessment. At the same time, sometimes assessment faces a few risking challenges such as cheating, plagiarism and a variety of assessment problems. So, while designing assessment tools considerable care has to be taken and ensure that the purpose of assessment has been achieved.

Assessment in Open and Distance Education

In face to face teaching, you get to know your learners through lectures, tutorials and individual consultations. The students in face to face settings have a range of opportunities to demonstrate their learning which are not confined to formal assessment tasks. Their interest, motivation, questioning and interactions are all on display throughout a learning encounter. As open and distance learners rarely enjoy these varied opportunities to communicate their learning, they are much more dependent on formal assessment tasks. They have also less opportunity in which to diagnose their own errors or mistakes before they go for a formal assessment task. For example, it may not be until midway through a course, when a student's first assignment is returned, that a simple error is discovered, to the detriment of the student's final grade.

While face to face learners can often rectify these problems long before they submit an assessment task, open and distance learners do not have the same kind of opportunities to check their understanding of an assessment task, or to compare approaches or methods with other students. So, distance learners are more dependent upon effective, early communication of assessment requirements, together with well designed and cohesive assessment tasks, useful and timely support, and a transparent marking scheme that explains how judgements are to be made. They are also more dependent on rapid turn around of assignments, so that the feedback can contribute to subsequent efforts and help maximise the valuable formative functions of assignments. Assessment activities do not have the same level of flexibility as they do in face to face settings. They must be thoroughly planned, communicated and managed.

Who Needs Assessment?

There are a number of stakeholders in the assessment process and it involves the students, teachers, trainers, institutions and the community at large. Nightingale et al categorise these needs into four groups. They are:

1. Students' needs
    - to know how they are progressing with their studies/courses
    - to know whether they are achieving the required standard
    - to gain certification of a level of achievement
2. Teachers' needs
    - to know whether students are attaining the intended learning outcomes
    - to know whether course materials and distance teaching activities are effective
    - to be able to certify that students have achieved standards or met requirements.

3. Institutions' needs
    - to provide evidence of achievement of institutional aims
    - to know whether programmes are effective in their stated aims
    - to certify that learners can practise in specific vocational areas
    - to make judgement about admission to courses/programmes
4. Community needs
    - to know whether institutions and teachers are effective and deserve continued funding
    - to know whether students are adequately prepared for their careers
    - to know whether education is being geared to meet the broad, long term needs of the society.

Reliable and Valid Assessment

Reliability and validity are terms used for educational assessment. In this context validity refers to what we really measure and what we are supposed to measure as per the detailed objectives. For validity to be high:

- The assessment must analyse student's performance on each objective.
- The assessment should provide the appropriate situation possible for measuring the specific abilities being measured.

For example, if the objective is to test learner's practical skills, we should not set a question for oral development measuring skills. Reliability is about the consistency or precision with which the assessment item measured the desired objective.

Whenever we make an assessment, it may or may not be reliable. We should try our level best to make it reliable.

Reliability or consistency operates at two levels:

- individual assessor; and
- more than one assessor.

As a reliable assessor, you should make the same decision on a particular assignment response whenever you grade/mark it. It means whenever you go through an identical response/solution of problem, every time you give the same grade/mark. Then you will be called consistent or reliable.

The key component in determining reliability of an assessment is consistency in marking. There is always the opportunity for human error, particularly when more than one assessor is assigned to a group of students assignment responses. If all the assessors make the same judgment — then reliability is achieved.

It is not possible to attain complete reliability due to various factors. We may try to make assessment more reliable with the help of a few guidelines as mentioned below:

To achieve more reliability in assessment

1. cover all objectives (learning outcomes);
2. create and use clear assessment criteria;
3. ensure that the assessors understand the criteria;
4. monitor assessors' marking; and
5. use moderator where necessary.

The most important way is to create, communicate and use clear criteria against which student performance is measured/assessed. The good criteria are those which are explicit, understood and agreed by all assessors and also by the students.

Methods of Assessment

There are various methods of assessment. The main methods are the following:

Objective Questions

Here, the word 'objective' refers to the method of marking the questions. This marking is a simple mechanical process. This can be done by an individual or by a computer. There are various types of objective type questions like, true false, fill in the blanks, multiple choice, matching, and so on.

Short Answer Questions

Short answer questions may be of different types like one sentence answer, completing a table/diagram, preparing a list, writing a paragraph, and so on. (For example, write the features of self learning material within 300 words).

Long Answer Questions

Long answer questions also may be of various types like essay, reports, dissertations, etc. (For example, prepare a self learning unit of 1200 words of a theme of your choice).

Performance Methods

These methods do not require a separate assessment device. We may assess the presentation itself. Examples of performance methods include making a presentation, acting, dancing, singing and playing a musical instrument.

Presentations

Presentation is a popular method of assessing. When presentation is used to assess presentation skills, the method has high validity, if it is assessed by a group. To assess presentations, suitable assessment criteria may be developed. These may include: appearance of presenter, introduction of self, introduction of presentation, content of presentation, logic and order of presentation, eye contact, audibility, handling questions, use of visual aids, and so on.

Formative Assessment

This method of assessment helps to form and develop student learning. It provides support and feedback to learners to improve their ongoing learning. This comprises of all those activities designed to motivate, to enhance understanding and to provide learners with an indication of their progress. These are in the form of self assessment questions and tests given in the SIMs that help the learners monitor their own progress feedback from the assignments or from peers or mentors or counsellors and interaction with the teachers and tutors.

Summative Assessment

It provides a total feedback or a report on what the distance learners have already achieved, whether this be a grade or a written assessment. The purpose of summative assessment is to record or report an estimate of students' achievement. These will often take the form of end of course examinations, course work assignments that contribute to a final grade or mark, supervised practical demonstrations, the project reports, etc. Depending on the setting and goals, it might entail awarding marks, grades, written reports or achievement or recognition of acquired competencies.

In most open and distance learning contexts, assessment usually involves both formative and summative component. Assessments are often designed in such a way that one assignment builds upon the next, with formative feedback from the first contributing to the next, and so on. This is referred to as continuous assessment. Marks are awarded for each assignment, which taken together, form a final grade. Continuous assessment plays a key role in open and distance education.

In open and distance education context, the role of continuous assessment is to:

- provide some structure to distance learning;
- break down the assessment load into manageable chunks;
- encourage, motivate and develop confidence in the distance learners;
- work as a source of ongoing dialogue or two way communication between teacher and learners or institution and learners; and
- provide insight for learners into their progress, including their understanding and mastery of the subject.

An end of course examination or term end examination which has a summative function might also be included in a final grade.

Criterion Referenced Assessment

This method uses clearly stated criteria and performance standards against which each student's achievements are judged. If the criteria and standards are met, the student achieves the corresponding grade, irrespective of how others in the group have performed or how many others have achieved the same grade. Although criteria may be achieved in norm referenced assessment to assist in marker's judgements, criterion referenced assessment provides a clearer focus to assessment, for both learners and evaluators, and a clear description of what learners have achieved and the standard of achievement.

Norm Referenced Assessment

This method uses the achievement of group of students to set the standards for specific grades awarded to learners. Initially, learners are ranked using a scale (0-100) in order of achievement among the members of the group. A predetermined formula is used to nominate which percentages of students achieve the top grade, the lowest grade, and the range of grades in between. This method of assessment provides a description of where a student's achievement lies in relation to others in the group, rather than the particular qualities or competencies that students individually achieve. This method promotes competition between students for limited grades, rather than a detailed description of students' progress or abilities.

To sum up, criteria referenced and norm referenced assessment refer only to the method of interpreting the learners' performance on test and other evaluation instruments.

As educators and trainers, on the one hand, we are working with learners to review and support learning, and on other hand, we are making judgement regarding their merits and their achievements. In the context of open and distance learning, we have embraced self assessment, continuous assessment and terminal evaluation. In distance education, teacher assessment is no longer pre eminent and there is no immediate feedback and reinforcement. The learner has to assess her/himself and for the purpose the distance teaching materials provide questions and answers which enable the learners to evaluate their progress frequently and provide immediate feedback. This is carried out through self assessment questions. The functions of self assessment are to help the student to check that the content is understood; to reinforce memory or understanding and stimulate the student to go forward in his or her thinking.

The continuous assessment in open and distance education is through tutor marked assignments (TMAs) and computer marked assignments. Assignments carry, weightage of 25% to 30% to pass an examination. Terminal evaluation carries 70% to 75% weightage in the final results. In case of IGNOU the terminal evaluation or term end examinations of various courses and programmes are held in the months of June and December every year. Distance learners are free to appear at any of these examinations either for specific courses or for the whole programme provided that the minimum period of study prescribed for the relevant course/programme is completed.

Computer Based Assessment

Computer technology is an important device for assessing students' learning in different subjects as it opens up opportunities for developing innovative assessment tools in distance education. The nature of computers as information processing tools, the role of computer technology in user friendly interactive learning environments, and the possibility of designing instructional tools to meet individual needs of distance learners, make computers potentially powerful tools for assessment. Computer based assessment applications are used in different subjects, such as computer based and Computerized Adaptive Testing, Figural Response Item Testing, Computer Simulations and Anchored Assessment etc. Computer based tools are found to have a positive impact on student's attitudes in learning.

Guidelines for Computer Based Testing

In testing and assessment applications, computer has changed the ways in which tests and assessments are developed and administered. Computer based tests are defined as tests or assessments that are administered by computer in either stand alone or networked configuration or by other technology devices linked to the Internet or the World Wide Web (www). In the face of the rapid growth of computer based testing, the Association of Test Publishers sponsored the development of formal, written guidelines to ensure high measurement quality of computer and internet based tests and to provide direction for the principles and procedures used for developing and administering those tests. Guidelines for Computer Based Testing are intended to supplement, extend, and elaborate on the recently published Standards for Educational and Psychological Testing (Joint Standards) as they apply to computer based and internet based testing and assessment.

All computer based tests must be used in accordance with fundamental measurement standards for test fairness, including fairness in testing and test use, in the right and responsibilities of test takers, in testing individuals with diverse linguistic backgrounds of distance learners and in testing individuals with disabilities. So, the purpose of statement of 'standards' is to provide criteria for the evaluation of tests, testing practices, and the effects of test use.

The Standards applied to computer based testing are:

1) The rationale and supporting evidence for computerized adaptive tests should be documented. The documentation should include procedures used in selecting subsets of items for administration, in determining the starting point and termination conditions for the test, in scoring the test and for controlling item exposure.

2) Instructions to test takers should clearly indicate how to make responses. Instructions should also be given in the use of any equipment likely to be unfamiliar to test takers. Opportunities to practice responding should be given when equipment is involved, unless use of the equipment is being assessed.

3) If a test is designed so that more than one method can be used for administration or recording responses — such as marking responses in a test booklet, on a separate answer sheet, or on a computer keyboard

— then the manual should clearly document the extent to which scores arising from these methods are interchangeable.

The following six steps are presented to illustrate the essence of the guidelines and the standards:

Step I

Planning and Design A wide variety of computer based tests can be designed and developed to meet different purposes. The test specification for computer based tests should include: the test purpose, the content domain definitions, the content structure for the test items, required response formats for the test items, sample test to be developed and administered, scoring and reporting formats and procedures, and test administration procedures. The test specification should be thoroughly documented.

Step II

Test Development The test delivery environment should be evaluated before item authoring begins. It is important to make sure that items being created can be properly displayed in the test delivery environment and that test taker input and results can be collected, aggregated, and reported. For example, graphics constraints need to be identified so that item writers do not create items that have too many colors or require a screen resolution that is too high for the current test delivery environment.

Step III

Test Administration The test sponsor should provide test takers with clear and concise information regarding procedures to register for an examination, obtain an authorization for testing document, and scheduling a test appointment.

Step IV

Scoring and Score Reporting The accuracy of computer scoring algorithms should be established prior to implementation of the computer based test.

Step V

Psychometric Analysis Determine appropriate reliability indices if different test takers are given different items or exercises or pictures.

Step VI

Stakeholder Communications Developers of computer based tests should provide sufficient information concerning the test purpose, and test content specifications to test users, prior to when the test is available for widespread administration. This test information /instructions should be kept accurate and as up to date as possible.

The above six guidelines show that the guidelines provide supplemental and elaborative information on the standards for individuals and organizations seeking to develop computer based or internet based tests and assessments. The guidelines can be appropriately used by a wide variety of audiences. They are:

- Test development organizations — for specifying procedures for designing, developing, field testing, and validating computer based tests.
- Test publishers and administrators and test delivery organizations — for establishing common institutional guidelines for communication of test items, examination scores, and item response information to and from computer based testing locations.
- Test delivery organizations — for providing information about how to achieve high quality delivery of computer based tests.
- Test takers — for providing information about the types of test items, tests, and test score interpretations and test orientations they might encounter when they take a computer based test.
- Research and evaluation specialists — for providing information on current and expected future uses of computer based tests.
- Teachers at educational institutions that administer or use computer based tests — for providing information about interpreting test scores about examinations and using the test scores appropriately, improved psychometric methods, and expanded or up dated question bank or item bank etc., as well as about helping students to prepare appropriately for computer based tests.

Designing Computer Based Testing

All computer based tests should be designed by using the fundamental standards identified in the six technical areas. These areas are:

1) Test construction, evaluation, and documentation;
2) Reliability and errors or measurement;

3) Test development and revision;
4) Scales, norms, and score comparability;
5) Test administration, scoring, and reporting; and
6) Supporting documentation for tests.

The Advantages of Computer Based Testing

There are a number of reasons why computer based testing is more helpful for a distance teaching institution. First, computer based testing can be more responsive to the needs of both the test provider or the institution and the distance learners. For example, where "on demand" testing of examinees is needed, the use of computer based testing is more useful.

Computer based assessment works on a completely different model than paper and pencil administration and offers benefits the latter can not match.

Smaller numbers of candidates can be tested throughout the year rather than larger numbers several times a year. Candidates can register just two days before the test, as opposed to weeks in advance for paper and pencil testing. Centers can offer different tests at the same time, because exams are delivered on Personal Computers (PCs) using a Local Area Network (LAN).

The computer selects test questions from a pool, so candidates taking the same exam will not be answering identical questions, which would, enhance test security. Computers eliminate the need for test booklets and answer sheets, that increase the security levels. Self paced tutorials show candidates how to use a mouse and other testing tools, ensuring that even those without computer experience are comfortable. Candidates can use either paper and pencil or word processing for essay questions, depending on their own preference. Computer based assessment allows for a diverse range of question types, which is a better test of a candidate's competency. Technology based assessment improves the link between instruction and assessment, providing a profile of candidates' strengths and weaknesses, and matches questions and the order in which they are presented to the ability of each test taker.

Computer based tests are scored immediately or shortly after administration. The paper and pencil test results usually take four to six weeks to process. Scores are sent electronically to universities or licensing and certifying agencies. So, fast scoring helps for publishing results quickly.

Disadvantages of Computer Based Testing

The disadvantages of computer based testing are all related to the resources required. These resources are a sufficient numbers of computers, a room to install them, appropriate software, and adequate technological expertise.

To sum up, in computer based testing the computer continuously re evaluates the ability of the distance learner resulting in a test that is tailored to each individual distance learner and computer technology is a viable tool for performance assessment in different subjects and a potentially powerful tool for replacing traditional product oriented paper and pencil tests.

MEANING OF EVALUATION

Evaluation is an integral part of the instructional process. It involves three steps. They are:

i) identifying and defining the intended learning outcomes,

ii) constructing or selecting tests and other evaluation tools relevant to the specified outcomes; and

iii) using the evaluation results to improve learning and teaching.

The above steps emphasise that evaluation is a continuous process. It is essential in all fields of teaching and learning activity where judgments need to be made. The teaching and learning process involves a continuous and inter related series of instructional decisions to promote student learning.

Our main contention here is that the effectiveness of the instruction depends to a large extent on the quality of the evaluation data/information on which the decisions are based.

Generally, most of the people engaged in the educational system (mainly teaching) are interested in ascertaining the outputs of an educational programme. Output is counted in terms of test results. Naturally, the results are expressed in quantitative indices, say scores or marks. For obtaining those scores a device consisting of a set of tasks, called a test is used. Tests may consists of term-end question papers, assignments, interviews, group discussions, projects and so on. On the other hand, an act of measurement is done when we award marks, say 60 out of 100 (or 60%) to an answer paper or a project report. Thus, we obtain the measurement of an individuals objectivity in quantitative or numerical indices when we administer a test. Sometimes confusion arises when another term evaluation is used alongwith the term measurement for the same process. But there is a clear cut difference between these two terms: measurement and evaluation.

In case of measurement we express an individual's ability in numerical indices or scores, in evaluation we express it in qualitative indices (say, good, excellent). By doing so we attach a value judgment to our measurement. When we say Ms. Angela has secured 75% marks in term end examination we talk about 'measurement'. But we 'evaluate' her ability by saying that she has done very good (value judgment) and stood first in the examination. We provide a qualitative description to Angela's ability.

The above example distinguishes evaluation as qualitative descriptions of Angela's performance from "measurement" which is quantitative description (75% marks).

So, from instructional point of view evaluation may be defined as a systematic process of determining the extent to which instructional objectives are achieved by learners.

There are many definitions and explanations of evaluation in education. Let us see the definitions stated by Thorpe Cronbach:.

> "By the term evaluation, we mean systematic examination of events occurring in and consequent on a contemporary programme – an examination conducted to assist in improving this programme and other programmes having the same general purpose." "Evaluation is the collection, analysis and interpretation of information about any aspect of a programme of education and training, as part of a recognised process of judging its effectiveness, its efficiency and any other outcomes it may have".

Wottawa and Thierue made an attempt to explain the concept of evaluation which can serve different purposes. They are:

- Evaluation has something to do with valuation.
- Evaluation serves to help in planning and deciding and thus has something to do with assessment and valuation of alternative ways of acting.
- Evaluation is oriented towards aims and purposes. It primarily has the aim of checking practical measures, of improving them or of making decisions concerning them.
- Evaluation measures reflect the current state of techniques and research methods.

Difference between Assessment and Evaluation

The terms 'assessment' and 'evaluation' are not synonymous. Assessment is distinct from evaluation in the following way:

Assessment	*Evaluation*
Focuses on the learning of the students. Focuses on the performance of the students (grading or marking).	•Focuses on the way the various components of a course perform—e.g. the syllabus, the teacher, the resources, and so on.
Assessment results may be used as a source of information for evaluation.	•Focuses on the performance of the provider and the provision.
	•Evaluation results have no direct bearing on students'assessment.

Purposes of Evaluation

The main purposes of evaluation are the following:

- *Proving*: to demonstrate conclusively that something has happened as a result of learning or training and that this may also be linked to judgements about the value of the activity; whether the right thing was done, whether it was well done, whether it was worth the cost, and so on.
- *Improving:* to ensure that either the current or future programmes and activities would be better than they are at present.
- *Controlling:* to use evaluation data to ensure that an individual learner or trainee is performing upto the standard or that subsidiary learning/ training establishments are meeting targets according to some centrally determined plan.

Evaluation in an Educational Programme (EIEP)

The modern concept of evaluation has assumed wider meaning and scope than the traditional role of evaluation that was concerned only with the end of the course measurement of the quantum of learning possessed by the learners. The modern role of evaluation encompasses a wider scope in the whole educational programme.

Any educational programme consists of three components:

- educational objectives;

- learning experiences; and
- evaluation procedures.

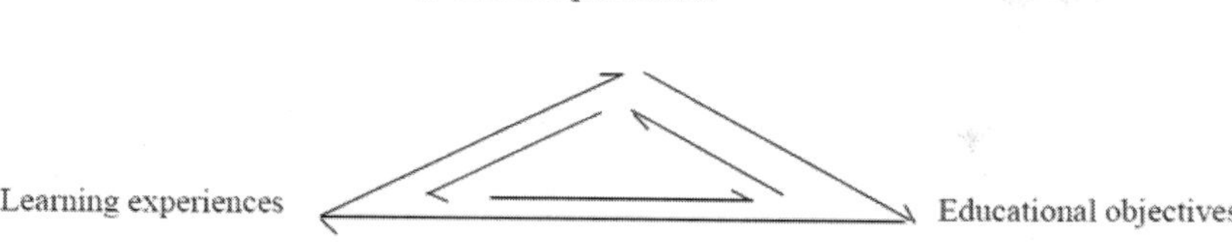

Evaluation in an educational programme

These three components must support one another to achieve the desired effectiveness of the programme. The function of evaluation procedures in this triangular relationship is dual:

- to examine to what extent the pre stipulated learning objectives of a programme have been achieved in terms of learners' academic achievement; and
- in an on going process, to provide continuous feedback, after evaluation (i.e., the above function), to the planners of the programme to suitably revise/modify either the programme (educational objectives), or the programme activities (learning experiences) or even both for achieving improved effectiveness of the programme.

Evaluation procedures have their respective functions at the beginning, during the process and at the end of the programme or course. At the initial stage, the programme planners use pretests to study the existing knowledge of learners about the proposed programme before they enter it, so that learning experiences, appropriate to the concerned learners can be suitably designed and effectively presented. At the mid process stage, they help monitor the progress of the learner and the teacher, and provide feedback to improve upon the process of learning. And, at the end of the programme, they help in the measurement of the learning outcomes.

Within the process-product relationship in an educational programme, the process of evaluation may help in:

- diagnosing weakness in learning;
- predicting learner's aptitudes and abilities;

- selecting suitable persons for a course or career through entrance tests;
- grading learner's abilities through tests/examinations;
- providing guidance for course choice and subject choice within a course; and
- evaluating the effectiveness of the whole programme, i.e. programme evaluation.

Evaluation of an Educational Programme (EOEP)

Evaluation within an educational context or training programme can be described as a systematic activity involving the analysis or documentation of programme related components and processes, the measurement of variables associated with the programme, and the elaboration of recommendations based upon the collected information. This activity provides opportunities for feedback, accountability, and cost-benefit information.

Evaluation in Distance Education

Evaluation has significant implications for distance education both in terms of evaluating learner's progress and attainment, and evaluating the effectiveness of the whole programme. The former refers to "evaluation in distance education", and the latter to "evaluation of distance education programmes".

In distance education, we depend on both the continuous assessment of learner's progress on the course with the help of both commenting and grading the assignment responses, and the term end examinations. In this context, assessment can be both formative and summative.

Going through the assignment responses of the learner and writing comments on them is formative assessment, for it not only identifies the weaknesses and strengths in learning, but also helps him/her to improve upon both the process and the attainment of learning. Assessment is also summative because of the fact that at the end of the course or the term, the attainment of the learner is graded on the bases of both the continuous assessment and the term end examination.

Grading or scoring may be done in formative assessment too. So, grading or scoring at both formative and summative assessment lead to award of final grades and certification of what has been achieved by the learner. Assessment in terms of both commenting and grading the assignment responses of the learner gives him/her the necessary feedback to know not only the weaknesses in his/her learning but also how to overcome them. Further, they suggest the relative position of the learner in the peer group. The knowledge of the relative position in his/her group of learners helps him/her considerably to do self assessment which is an important means of learning at a distance. Moreover, assessments (both continuous and terminal) in terms of grading lead to final award of a certificate/diploma/ degree to the learner. In an open and of distance education system, the individual learners proceed at their own pace, and sit for examinations when they feel they have successfully learnt what is to be learnt in a course. This may create problems to the distance teaching institution in making arrangements for individual assessment/evaluation. Besides this, because of heterogeneity in the test taking behaviour of the distance learners, there may be problem of constructing different items/questions for different learners. These problems call for a large question/item bank (with reliable and valid questions or items) from which questions/items are picked up to constitute tests as and when needed.

Reliability and Validity in Distance Education

Reliability and validity assume greater significance in distance education with special reference to commenting and grading the assignment responses. Comments on assignment response are considered reliable if the distance teacher/tutor has similar reaction to the same response and writes nearly similar comments when he/she goes through that particular assignment response for the second time or even for the third time. Not only that, the contexts/occasions of commenting by one tutor must also be nearly similar to those of the second tutor if both go through the same assignment response. Similarly, in case of grading the assignment responses and answer scripts, there should be higher inter reliability. The same logic is also applicable to the validity of both commenting and grading

Reliability of a Test

Reliability of a test refers to the "accuracy" or the "consistency" of measurement of what the test purports to measure. To understand it more clearly in terms of our day-to-day experiences of life, perhaps a good example may be the weighing machine at the railway station. Let us suppose that the machine for all time to come weighs constantly 2 kg. less than the actual weight of persons. So if a person gets his/her weight as 62 kg in the first trial, also gets the same weight in the next trial the next minute, the weight is constant at each trial. Though the actual weight of that person is 64 kg (because the machine due to some defects always weighs a constant of 2 kg less than the actual), the machine can be relied upon because of its consistency in measuring weight.

In academic situation, a test is reliable if a learner, for instance, takes the same test at two occasions (say, with a gap of fortnight) and secures more or less the same score at both the occasions. In this context, Gronlund points out that it is more appropriate to talk of the reliability of the test results rather than the test itself, for a test may have different reliabilities at different occasions/situations with different groups of subjects. Further, the obtained scores on a test are said to be reliable on the basis of certain criteria. These are called the estimates of reliability. Generally there are five methods to estimate reliability coefficients on the basis of which reliability may be expressed. They are:

i) stability,

ii) equivalence,

iii) stability and equivalence,

iv) internal consistency, and

v) scorer reliability.

- Stability refers to the consistency of test results over two occasions. Test-retest method is used to estimate stability. The same test is administered twice to the same group of subjects with a time interval of, say, a fortnight or a month, and the two sets of scores (obtained at two different occasions) are correlated. A higher coefficient of correlation indicates greater stability, and vice versa.
- In case of establishing the estimate of equivalence of a test, two different versions of the same test equivalent in terms of content and the level of difficulty are administered to the same group of subjects on the same day with very little time interval. The two sets of scores obtained on the two versions of the same test are correlated, and the coefficient of correlation gives the measure of equivalence. The measures of stability and equivalence include two purposes: to predict the long-term reliability of the test, and ii) to infer one's knowledge in a subject area.

- The split-half method (i.e., correlating the two sets of scores obtained on the odd and even items of the same test separately) is used to establish the estimate of internal consistency.
- Variations exist in the scoring/marking/grading patterns of more than one scorer/examiner/evaluator. Two examiners may award different marks or scores to the same answer script. To estimate the reliability between evaluators/scorers, product moment correlation and Spearman-Brown prophecy formula are used.

Validity of a Test

Validity of a test refers to the "duty" or "truthfulness" of the test. Does the test measure what it is supposed to/purports to measure? Before establishing the "truthfulness" of its measurement or assessment, it is necessary to define "what" it is going to measure/assess. It is very difficult to achieve the situation where the test "fully" measures whatever it purports to measure. So there is always a gap between the purposes of a test and the extent to which they may be achieved.

There are mainly four types of validity corresponding to four aspects of establishing test validity:

i) *content validity* — related to the content of the test items;

ii) *concurrent validity* — related to the extent to which the test under consideration matches with other tests with similar purposes;

iii) *predictive validity* — related to its prediction of other related variable(s); and iv) construct validity — related to the extent of its inference of the constructs of the theory on which it is based.

In the above discussion we have focused upon the definition of evaluation in distance education, role of reliability and validity in distance education. Even though the definition is comprehensive enough to include different approaches, concepts, tasks and methods of evaluation, we thought of presenting, in this section, a variety of evaluation tasks in distance education. These tasks are:

- Tasks of Evaluation
  - Student assessment/evaluation
  - Course evaluation
  - Evaluation of the effectiveness of media

   - Student services
   - System evaluation and social impact analysis
   - Social needs analysis
   - Policy evaluation
   - Organizational evaluation
   - Market analysis
- Evaluation Methodology

The variety of evaluation purposes and the above tasks correspond to the diversity of the methodological approaches, procedures and methods that are used in evaluation. They are:

- Qualitative approach
- Rating procedures
- Retention tests
- Survey method
- Face to face interviews
- Methods of observation
- Methods of content analysis
- Cost benefit analysis
- Experimental studies

References

Dynan, M.B. and Cliford, R.J. (2001) Eight years on: implementation of quality management in an Australian university. *Assessment and Evaluation in Higher Education* 26(5), 503–515

El Khawas, E. (2006) Accountability and Quality Assurance: New Issues for Academic Inquiry. In *International Handbook of Higher Education*, vol. 1 (Forest, J.J.F. and Altbach, P.G. eds), pp. 23–37, Springer Verlag, Berlin.

Jordan, S. and Swithenby, S.J. On-line summative assessment with feedback as an aid to effective learning at a distance. Proc of 2004 ISL Symposium Diversity and Inclusivity (Ed C. Rust) Alden Press, pp 480-485.

Kimura, T., Yonezawa, A. and Ohmori, F. (2004) Quality assurance and recognition of qualifcations in higher education: Japan, In *Quality and Recognition in Higher Education: The Cross Border Challenge* (Larsen, K. and Momii, K., eds), pp. 119–130, OECD, Paris.

3

Program Evaluation Methods

During the 1990s of professional program evaluation in higher education, the most probable task for a program evaluator would have been to document and report "program fidelity" between an approved proposal for program services and actual services delivered and whether program activities were in accordance with legislation or regulations. Funding agencies and program administrators focused on questions about use of resources and program implementation: Were program resources used as intended? Was the program implemented as proposed? What was the number of products or services that were delivered? How many clients were served? Were clients satisfied with the deliverables or services? These types of questions, which were more research-oriented than evaluative in nature, directed evaluation efforts in that era.

Today, professional program evaluators are asked to do much more. Program evaluation is increasingly being used to meet the demand for information about the performance of public and nonprofit schools as well as private, for-profit educational programs. Institutional leaders, elected officials, funders, and citizens want to know about the quality and value of programs and services they support. Professional program evaluators are now asked to systematically conduct evaluations that have either a learning orientation emphasizing program improvement or development, or a results orientation emphasizing accountability for achieving intended results and determining impact.

What difference does the program make, for whom and under what circumstances? Is the program a justifiable expense? Does the program contribute to achieving the core mission of the organization? What is being developed in the program, and what are its merits? These questions require evaluators to think and work in ways that necessitate understanding institutional and departmental missions and goals, identifying program stakeholders and engaging them in exploring and articulating a program's rationale and theory, and specifying stakeholder evaluative-information needs. If answering such questions is to usefully inform individuals with vested interests in the program, then understanding the nature of program evaluation is necessary for identifying evaluative questions that are critical for planning, designing and conducting a useful evaluation.

The reality is that higher education administrators and program managers need to manage the meaning (why they exist and how they work) of their programs just as much as they must manage program information, e.g., to support resource allocation and other policy decision making. Therefore, the role of the professional evaluator must be not only to enhance the quality and accuracy of evaluation data through systematic social science methods but also to help build the capacity of program executives to *think evaluatively and critically and to be able to appropriately interpret findings to reach reasonable and supportable conclusions.* Understanding why a program works or does not work is essential for making informed decisions, and making sense of evaluative program data is no easy task in a rapidly changing environment. Our institutions of higher education are very complex, dynamic systems encompassing multiple academic and developmental programs, some working independently, yet side by side, others in collaboration across their various disciplines. Today's evaluators must be professionally competent, possessing the necessary knowledge and skills to conduct such complex program evaluations, and they must be sensitive, perceptive, analytical and dedicated, as well.

In the *Handbook of Practical Program Evaluation, 3rd Edition*, by Wholey, J. S. et al, a program is defined as:

> …a seto of resources and activities directed toward one or more common goals, typically under the direction of a single manager or management team.
>
> (Wholey, J. S., et al, pg.5)

Further, in *The Program Evaluation Standards*, it is emphasized that programs entail more than just activities. They consist of multiple components, including:

a. Contexts and how they interact with programs and program components;

b. Participants and other beneficiaries as well as those who encounter costs or loss of benefits;

c. Needs, problems, and policy spaces in programs and their contexts;

d. Goals and objectives;

e. Resources and costs of all kinds, including staff, facilities, materials, and opportunity costs;

f. Activities, procedures, plans, policies, and products;

g. Logic models, beliefs, assumptions, and implicit and explicit program theories explaining why and how programs should work; and

h. Outputs, results, benefits, outcomes, and impacts (p. xxiv).

In Michael Scriven's *Evaluation Thesaurus, 4th Edition*, evaluation is defined as "*...the process of determining the merit, worth, or value of something, or the product of that process*," the purposes of which are to make improvements in whatever is being evaluated or to determine the overall quality of what is being evaluated. The 2nd edition of *The Program Evaluation Standards* similarly defines evaluation as: "*...a systematic investigation of the worth or merit of an object.*" Here "object" refers to the program under review. These notions of merit, worth, value and quality are expanded upon in the recent *3rd Edition of The Program Evaluation Standards* by combining the two terms, program and evaluation, rendering a definition for program evaluation that includes:

- the systematic investigation of the quality of programs, projects, subprograms, subprojects, and/or any of their components or elements, together or singly
- for purposes of decision-making, judgments, conclusions, findings, new knowledge, organizational development, and capacity building in response to the needs of identified stakeholders
- leading to improvement and/or accountability in the users' programs and systems, and
- ultimately contributing to organizational or social value.

Clearly, then, professional program evaluation is to be methodologically systematic, addressing questions that provide information about the quality of a program in order to assist decision making aimed at program improvement, development or accountability and to contribute to a recognized level of value. Such evaluations may include guided monitoring of a program or services by program personnel, building the capacity of program administrators and staff to understand the value of evidence and to conduct their own evaluations. Good professional program evaluations help key stakeholders answer specific evaluative questions necessary for sound decision making about their programs and/or services.

Concept of Programme Evaluation

An academic programme in open and distance learning consists of a few courses offered at a distance. It might involve print, audio and video materials, other modern technologies, assignments with tutor commenting and grading, project work, extra reading materials, face to face academic counselling, workshops and seminars, training, learning from resource centres, home kits, students' own study, term end examination, etc.

The programme has certain broad objective(s). For example the PGDDE programme of IGNOU has the following objectives:

- Promoting awareness about the concept and utility of open and distance education in India and other developing countries; and
- Developing the much needed human resources for the existing open universities and correspondence/distance education centres, and many more that may come up in the near future.

The PGDDE programme is designed and developed to provide education and training which is of benefit to both distance learners and the distance educators. The PGDDE programme is evaluated to help the institution in meeting both internal and external needs for information, feedback and insight into the nature and quality of the teaching and training provision.

"Programme evaluation is necessarily concerned with the specific programme that has already taken place, i.e., it fairly deals with the retrospective findings. On the other hand, the results of such evaluation certainly feed to the long term decisions of the programme and looked this way, a programme evaluation obviously contributes to planning of the programme. Therefore, this is necessarily an on going process and there is certainly a starting point for both the first planning and the first evaluation of a programme.

Secondly, such evaluation might adhere to either an accountability perspective (i.e., to examine especially the efficiency of a programme so as to report to the funding agency/authority) or a managerial perspective (i.e., to assess the effectiveness of the programme so as to provide feedback to the programme manager or the programme team regarding the effectiveness of programme delivery and management, and the programme itself). In the former situation, the focus is on the ultimate objectives of the programme. The evaluation methodology is scientifically objective. The data gathered are mostly quantitative. And the purpose behind such an exercise is to decide whether to retain the programme or reject it altogether. On the other hand, the latter type of evaluation is concerned with the immediate or intermediate objectives. The methodology followed is rigorous to the extent that sound decisions can be derived. Collected data are both quantitative and qualitative in nature. And the purpose of such evaluation is to improve the programme along with its delivery. In our discussion on programme evaluation, both the perspectives have been thought as necessary and therefore have been considered, though the stress has been on the managerial perspective so as to increase the effectiveness of the programme".

Based on the works by Jenkins, Gooler, Rumble, Feasley, an evaluation perspective/approach has been formulated as given below.

Programme Evaluation in Distance Education

Output

This is concerned with the overall evaluation of the system that has more cultural or national connotation with an accountability perspective (accountable to the government or some funding agency like the public in general/the parents of the students in particular) where the evaluator acts as an adviser and has control over the entire process of evaluation. Some of the dimensions/parameters at this level include the following:

- Equality of educational opportunity.
- Access or quantity.
- Student grading/marking.
- Relevance to needs and expectations.

- Impact on other open universities/distance learning systems, and traditional learning systems.
- Overall efficiency: cost not only to the system but importantly to the nation because many of the cost components like broadcasting, infrastructure at regional and study centres, etc. include expenditure by public authority and/or private institutions.

Process

In fact, this includes both the process, the input, and a part of output put together (i.e. operation of the sub systems) that has more system connotation with a managerial perspective (with the intention/objective of improving the effectiveness and efficiency of the functioning of the subsystems so as to increase the overall system effectiveness and efficiency) where the evaluator acts within a democratic collaborative style at every stage of the evaluation exercise(s). The following are some of the dimensions/parameters at this level:

- Quality of programme(s)
- Generation of knowledge (teaching methods and learning processes in general)
- Student learning (pace, style, strategy, attitude, satisfaction, student feedback, etc.)
- Curriculum development and implementation
- Instructional design and development; course design and self instructional materials print and non print (audio/video), and their openness
- Assignments (two way communication, commenting, grading, etc).
- Support system (the system, academic counselling, other supports) perceived by the students, the ACs, the faculty, etc.
- Course team
- Student entry characteristics (age, sex, residence, caste, previous educational experience, economic status, study skills, language proficiency, course needs, attitude to the system, occupational background, spare study time, etc.)
- Student dropout/dropdown: background characteristics, social integration, academic integration, goal commitment, institutional commitment, course/personal/socioeconomic problems, etc.

- Subsystem(s) efficiency: costs; subsystem(s) effectiveness
- Student administration and related student affairs
- Material production and distribution
- Admission system
- Evaluation system (with special reference to course objective vis à vis testing and grading/marking)
- Quality control and decision making subsystems; evaluation of the line managers and their efficiency and decision making; evaluation of decision making processes/mechanisms, etc.
- The logistical systems: personnel, finance, establishment, administration, etc.
- The coordination system, especially among the important instructional functionaries like course writers, academic counsellors, media producers, paper setters, evaluators, etc.
- The system of staff development: orientation and training
- Staff attitude towards and satisfaction of teaching (materials, tutorials, commenting and grading, etc.)
- Academic freedom and its utilisation
- Users' perception of data base
- Staff progress report vs. actual performance/programme management
- Graduate placement/employment
- Employers' perception of the programme."

The above model might be misinterpreted that if the output (for example, the students) is up to expectation, there is no need to study the system operation and, therefore, only when output is not satisfactory against certain criteria (id at all pre fixed), then only one may go for evaluating the system operation. But it is construed that this may not always be the case. What if the students at entrance to the system were very weak or dull? If they do not succeed, the system may not necessarily be non functional. The argument can be that if the courses/programme(s) are based on learner needs and characteristics, the question of non functionality may not arise, though this ideal is rarely achieved.

So in this model of programme evaluation, both the final product as well as the process of teaching learning including the logistics are simultaneously evaluated on a continuous basis so as to increase and maintain subsystem efficiency.

Types and Purposes of Program Evaluations

There are many reasons for conducting a program evaluation. Sometimes debated, but generally agreed upon by most evaluators, are three broad categories of evaluation that generally describe the nature and purposes of program evaluations: *formative* program evaluation, *summative* program evaluation, and *developmental* program evaluation. Each type of evaluation has a unique focus and within each lies its own rationale as to why program evaluation is valuable and important.

Formative program evaluation has as its purpose *improvement by providing constructive feedback* to program implementers and clients. This type of evaluation is aimed at helping a new program "get up to speed" or "find its feet," or it may be aimed at helping a mature program try out new strategies to improve its performance. In other words, formative evaluation informs program managers about ways to improve program quality or the delivery of program services. Formative evaluation asks how well the program meets the needs of its intended program recipients or how the initial outcomes achieved for program recipients compare with outcomes achieved by others in similar programs elsewhere. Some designs for conducting formative evaluation include *implementation evaluation*, *process studies* and *evaluability assessment.*

Summative program evaluation has as its purpose *measuring program performance in terms of outcomes and impacts* during ongoing operation or after program completion. It determines the overall quality or value of a program. Summative evaluation asks whether the program was worth what it cost in terms of time, money, and other resources, or it asks, compared to other similar programs, was this program the most cost-effective. A main reason for conducting a summative evaluation is to inform decision-makers (administrators and funders) about whether the program was successful, which may lead to decisions about continuing or discontinuing the program or about implementing the program more widely.

Developmental program evaluation has as its purpose *informing social program innovators* who intend to bring about major change through development of new program models. It asks what is getting developed and with what implications, and it facilitates knowledge generation, that is, the focus is on exploring the nature and effects of a program as it is being developed, so as to contribute to the existing knowledge base.

Developmental evaluation is intended to facilitate innovation by:

> Helping those engaged in innovation examine the effects of their actions, shape and formulate hypotheses about what will result from their actions, and test their hypotheses about how to foment change of uncertainty in situations characterized by complexity.

As Patton tells us, developmental evaluation is aimed at holding social innovators accountable as they explore, create and adapt new program models *before* there is a program which can be improved upon or whose performance can be measured. The role of the evaluator in developmental evaluation is to become part of the program innovator team, facilitating team discussions by suggesting evaluative questions, data and logic, and assisting decision making during the developmental process. Developmental evaluative questions may include: What's being developed? How is what's being developed or what's emerging to be judged and valued? Given what has been developed or has emerged, what is next?

Recapping the three primary types of program evaluation, then: formative program evaluation relates to gathering information that is useful for improving existing programs; summative program evaluation relates to gathering information useful for reporting on a program's intrinsic merits or determining its worth to participants or the associated organizations or institutions; and developmental program evaluation relates to the continuous gathering of information useful for making adaptations in the course of developing a program.

Designing and Conducting a Program Evaluation

The overarching goal of evaluating a program is to create an evidence and information data base through which administrators and managers are informed so as to allow them to identify aspects of the program that require improvement in order to achieve intended strategic goals or to communicate the value of their program to key vested stakeholders. To these ends, much has been written about the processes for planning, designing and conducting program evaluations.

The process of designing and conducting a program evaluation can be condensed into six necessary areas for reflection:

1. Learn the institutional context of the program under study;
2. Clarify the program's theory;
3. Identify stakeholders;
4. Clarify the purpose of the evaluation;
5. Identify evaluative questions and criteria;
6. Locate, collect and analyze data; and
7. Report evaluation findings.

Area 1: Learn the Institutional Context of the Program

The organizational, political and social context of a program matters. Socrates has been credited with the saying, *"before we start talking, let us decide what we are talking about,"* and Yogi Berra is credited with, *"If you don't know where you are going, you won't know when you get there."* Useful program evaluation practice must begin with an understanding of *why* the program is thought to be necessary and *what* needs are being addressed. Both the *why* and *what* are intrinsic to institutional values and are (or should be) articulated in its mission and goal statements. Thus, in higher education, systematic program evaluation must begin with understanding the nature and purpose of the institution.

The difficulty and complexity of learning the institutional context of a program is expounded upon in an article titled, "The Art of the Presidency," by Frank H. T. Rhodes, well-respected President of Cornell University from 1977 to 1995. He wrote:

> The most important task, and also the most difficult one, is to define the institution's mission and develop its goals. That is the first task of the president. Everything else follows from that; everything else will depend upon it. The mission and goals must be ambitious, distinctive, and relevant to the needs and interests of campus constituents.
>
> The vision drives the goals, as the president establishes the benchmarks and articulates the values on which the day-to-day life of the institution will depend. Those goals, developed item by item, unit by unit, set the agenda, the blueprint for action, the mandate for change. This, too, is a joint effort: Trustees, provosts, vice presidents, deans, faculty, staff members, students, alumni, the public, advisors, and consultants — all have a role and a proportionate voice — actively influencing decisions, motivating effort, and channeling resources.

This is a keenly-decided statement. It is inclusive; it implies complexity in the process of achieving particularized goals, recognizes multiple perspectives, suggests a reality of organizational politics and competing administrative goals, invites various power relationships and has a focus on social change. As has been noted by Greene, evaluation is inherently a political activity and the evaluator is, whether he or she realizes it or not, part of that activity. As such, the program evaluator is not completely independent and must keep an eye on institutional purpose and organizational structures, so as to understand what programs and services are contributing in meaningful ways towards achieving institutional goals. The evaluator must recognize and reflect on various stakeholder positions and points of view. Alkin stresses careful listening and observing to ensure that the program and its issues are understood from multiple stakeholder perspectives. Where are they coming from? How do they view the program? Such understandings will promote better communication, professional collegiality and cooperation across all stakeholders. As Alkin states, *"programs reflect a political consensus – a compromise- and an accommodation of multiple views"*. The evaluator must be attuned to these multiple views.

An example illustrates the complexity and challenge of understanding the organizational and political context of a particular program under study. The University of Illinois, located in Champaign-Urbana, Illinois, is a large Midwest public research university. The campus has several "living and learning" communities, of which Weston Hall Exploration is one. Weston Hall Exploration is managed and operated by University Housing, which is itself administered by the University's Office of the Vice Chancellor for Student Affairs.

Let's assume for the sake of illustration that Weston Hall Exploration is being evaluated for the purpose of determining its quality and worth (i.e., is this program worth what it costs?). The evaluator has the complicated task of, first, determining who the primary stakeholders are and, then, deciding which of them should be engaged in the evaluation. Selection should be made by prioritizing according to both practical and political reasons. This means that the evaluator must be able to communicate effectively with key individuals at all four administrative levels. The evaluator must cross all four organizational boundaries wherein the Weston Hall Exploration program resides in order to obtain relevant information about the program's worth from key individuals. As one can surmise, there is no "one size fits all approach;" the evaluation of Weston Hall Exploration must be tailored to the University's unique organizational and political context and to its specific set of circumstances.

Table 1. Vision and mission statements at four administrative levels: University Level, Divisional Level, *Departmental Level and Program level (as posted on their respective websites)*

University of Illinois at Urbana-Champaign	
Vision:	Become the preeminent public research institution
Mission:	The University of Illinois will transform lives and serve society by educating, creating knowledge, and putting knowledge to work on a large scale and with excellence.
Goals:	Leadership for the 21st century; Academic excellence; Breakthrough knowledge and innovation; Transformative learning environment; and Access to the Illinois experience
Division of Student Affairs	
Vision:	Student Affairs successfully transforms the lives of students, preparing them for citizenship in a global community. Its programs and services will attain a preeminence that will serve as a model for other universities.
Mission:	Student Affairs transforms lives. We provide quality programs, services, facilities and living environments that create the Illinois experience at Urbana-Champaign which empowers students to achieve the greatest potential in their personal and academic development.
Goals:	Enhanced knowledge & appreciation of diversity; Environmentally sound and culturally relevant facilities; clarity and enhancement of the student experience at Illinois; and Creation and sustainment of collaborative partnerships
University Housing	
Vision:	Communities improving the world
Mission:	University Housing cultivates a safe space for the Illinois community to achieve its full human and academic potential.
Goals:	Stewardship of resources; Create and maintain exceptional facilities; Hire and retain a qualified, diverse workforce; and Create a leadership culture
Weston Hall Exploration Living and Learning Community	
Mission:	Weston Hall Exploration opened in Fall 1997 with the mission to bring together classroom and living experiences to provide opportunities for students to discover areas of interest and abilities and how they relate to academic majors and careers. Students entering Liberal Arts and Sciences General Curriculum may find Weston Hall Exploration a particularly supportive and stimulating environment in which to begin their Illinois experience. Weston students from all majors can utilize the resources to identify and prepare for careers.

Program context matters. The practice of program evaluation in higher education begins with knowledge and understanding of the institution's organizational structure and culture and the political context in which the program resides. A good starting point is to identify institutional values as expressed in stated vision, mission and goals. Fleshing out context, administrators and program managers must be purposive about the program information they collect and clear about how it will be used to inform decision-making at various levels, e.g., institutional, divisional and unit. During this phase, the program evaluator is a facilitator as well as participant in the evaluation process. The overall intent is to engage primary stakeholders in the creation of an evidence and information framework through which the evaluation questions can be answered.

Area 2: Clarify the Program's Theory

Kurt Lewin's famous maxim, *"...there is nothing as practical as a good theory"*, exemplifies the importance of program theory in evaluation. As it suggests, the intent is to integrate theory with practice, and the best use of theory is to facilitate an understanding of applied aspects of social science. In this sense, program theory can serve as feedback to inform and enlighten program administrators, policy makers and practitioners, as well as those who created and funded the program.

Programs are results of deliberate allocations of resources in support of specific strategies or activities to produce defined services or products. These services or products are intended to address strategic problems or issues and may be considered necessary to fulfilling the institution's mission. In other words, programs are intended to produce desired outcomes. Describing a program along a continuum of resources, program activities, outcomes and impact is a program's logic. This description of a program's "*logic*" has been referred to as an "espoused theory of action" or a program's theory of change. The theory then becomes a reference point against which progress towards achieving desired outcomes can be systematically assessed.

In the course of conducting an evaluation, it is difficult, at best, to interpret evaluation findings without a clear understanding of a program's theory. Program theory is inextricably tied to the evaluation questions about the quality of a program and to the value of its intended effects, that is, a level of performance required for satisfactory functioning. Thus, learning about and understanding the program's theory is essential before evaluation begins. In sum, the evaluator must learn about the purpose of the program, who the program serves, what the program intends to do, what it intends to accomplish, and what kinds of resources are needed to operate and manage the program.To accomplish this, the evaluator should seek out existing written documents and conduct formal interviews with program staff and administrators and knowledgeable observers or experts in the program area who can provide insights. Alkin suggests five types of documents that might be examined: the written program proposal materials, guidelines of the funding agency, program materials, management documents, and past evaluation reports. Prior research and monitoring reports are also good sources of information. Alkin suggests that the most important of these documents is the program proposal as typically it will contain the goals of the program and particular activities that are expected to lead to accomplishing those goals. The proposal will also describe the resources (personnel and materials) needed in order to operate and manage the program. Interviewing key stakeholders, such as staff, administrators and program developers also can provide important information on a program's "raison d'être," its goals and its strategies to reach those goals.

A useful graphic for presenting a logical understanding of the program's expected performance is the *logic model.* As McLaughlin and Jordon and Bickman explain, a logic model will help describe the program by presenting a plausible and sensible rationale for how the program will work, under certain conditions, to meet unmet needs and solve identified problems. The logic model presents a clear graphic of the program, depicting linkages between a program's resources, activities/components, and the change those activities/components are intended to produce in the targeted participants. The logic model tells "*why*" a program exists and "*how*" the program works, at the same time that it identifies *external factors* influencing, positively or negatively, program operations or achievement of intended and unintended outcomes. Program logic models may vary, but most likely would include the following elements:

a) *Resources*: Resources dedicated to or consumed by the program. Resources may include such things as staff, volunteers, time, money, facilities, etc. The guiding question is: *What must this program have in order to operate effectively?*

b) *Activities and components:* What the program does with the vested resources to fulfill its strategic intent. These include such things as conducting workshops, taking field trips, establishing partnerships, etc. The guiding question is: *What is to be done to achieve the intent of the program (e.g., its goals or outcomes)?*

c) *Outputs:* Direct products of program activities or components and typically measured in terms of volume of work accomplished. This may include such things as workbooks produced, number of training seminars held, participants reached, etc. Guiding questions are: *How much or how frequent and for how many clients?*

d) *Participants:* The individuals, groups, organizations or institutions that receive the direct products or services from program activities and functions. The guiding question is: *Who do we serve and why?*

e) *Outcomes:* The intended or unintended changes for individuals, groups, or organizations during or after participating in program activities. Outcomes may include changes in participants' knowledge, skills, or attitude; changes in behavior, practice or decision making; or changes in conditions. The guiding question is: *What changes in our participants or in a condition are we trying to effect?*

f) *External and Contextual Factors:* Constraints on a program or unexpected outcomes over which administrators or program managers typically have little or no control.

When we place these elements together in such a way as to show relationships between resources and program activities (*how* the program is supposed to work), between program activities and expected benefits or changes in program participants, or between benefits or changes in program participants and addressing a problem or issue (*why* the program exists), we can readily see multiple realities involving all these elements.

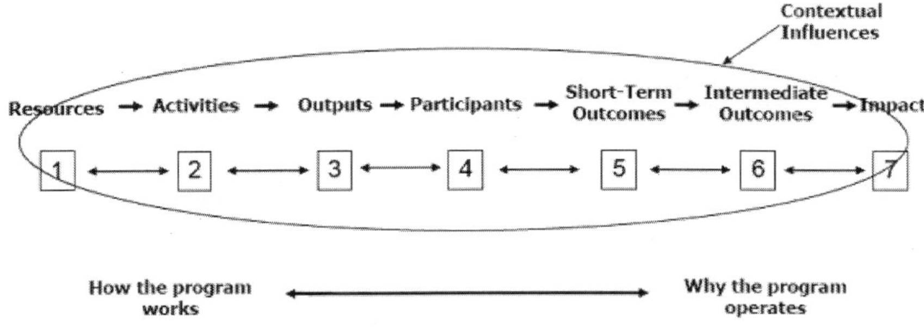

Figure 1. Generic Program Logic Model

As it is displayed, the logic model provides a narrative along the line of "we use these resources [#1] to do these things [#2, #3] for these people [#4] in order to change them in these ways [#5, #6] so as to achieve these ultimate program goals [#7]. More simply stated, a program logic model displays how resources are linked to results which address a major issue or need for the program.

To illustrate with a more descriptive program logic model, displays the basic elements with typical descriptors that tell the program's story of why the program exists and how it intends to operate. This illustration can be used to answer an essential question: *Can the program, with these resources, through these action plans, yield these products and deliverables, which meet the needs of participants (short term and intermediate outcomes), so that various deleterious conditions are changed or issues of concern are addressed (impact)?*

Describing such theories of action is actually a very common occurrence for many of us. Most administrators create budget or funding proposals on a regular basis. Each proposal describes a program or service that we think will address a certain problem, issue, or priority. Often, in other situations, we are asked to describe the strategic aim of a program or its purpose. Sometimes we are asked to justify the existence of a program, that is, we are asked to answer the question, "is the program necessary?" When we carry out any of these activities, we are describing program theory; we are saying, "if we do these things, we should get these results," and exploratory evaluation, e.g., evaluability assessment and rapid feedback evaluation, can help to test or validate the theory.

Developing a program's logic can yield benefits beyond those that accrue to the evaluation process. As was mentioned above, there are usually many individuals with vested interests in any particular program. Those close to a program, i.e., managers, staff, and participants, may have different understandings about how the program should operate. Engaging these individuals in describing the program and building its logical framework can lead them to a greater understanding and shared vision of the program. Further, as they gain understanding, they may well decide to make important changes in the program.

Summarizing Area 4, the logic model identifies the resources dedicated to or consumed by the program, describes what the program does with the resources to fulfill its mission and goals, identifies direct products or level of program activities, describes the benefits or changes for participants during or after program activities, and identifies the constraints on the programs, that is, external or contextual factors. Deciding which evaluative questions are to be addressed is facilitated by considering each element in the logic model as it relates to the intended use of performance-based information by primary users of the evaluative findings.

Area 3: Identify Stakeholders

Programs are about people: their values, behavior, relationships and attitudes. They work as individuals and in groups and they partner with other groups within and outside of their organizations. Every evaluation is political in that it is socially constructed, consisting of various interacting individuals and/or groups, each imbued with differing values, cultures, and intentions. Individuals may include but are not limited to: senior management, policy makers, community members, program managers, staff, participants, partners, advocates, adversaries, program sponsors and/or funders. At times, any of these may seek information helpful in making decisions or in understanding the program. For example, a trustee might need information to inform policy; a senior manager might have a strategic planning focus and need information that justifies allocating resources to a program; a program manager may seek ways for the program to run more cost effectively; a program staff person may seek information on how to improve program quality; and, funders may want to know whether the program is worth investing in.

Once a list of primary stakeholders has been identified, it is important to prioritize the list of stakeholders by whether they are critical to the evaluation's success and/or the use of findings. Practical or political implications should also be considered in determining who will be engaged in the evaluation process. Once a list of key stakeholders is established, they should be involved early in developing evaluation questions (focusing the evaluation). Further, stakeholders should be continuously and actively engaged in determining design and data collection methods, analyzing data and interpreting findings, and developing recommendations and action plans. A goal is to ensure that stakeholders feel ownership in and are committed to the evaluation, increasing the odds of evaluation findings being relevant, credible and useful. Perhaps more important, when you engage stakeholders, they learn about evaluation. Their active engagement increases their knowledge of evaluation, encourages them to value a culture of evidence, and builds their capacity to conduct evaluations themselves. As Patton maintains, along with completing evaluation themselves, a parallel aim of evaluation activities is to have an impact on those involved. Individuals who participate in the evaluation should learn to use and apply the logic, reasoning and values that underlie the evaluation process.

Area 4: Clarify the Purpose of the Evaluation

It involves practical and political strategies for communicating with primary stakeholders and engaging them in non-adversarial discussions to determine the purpose and focus of the evaluation. This is particularly true in complex situations and organizational structures where various primary stakeholders have competing evidentiary and informational needs.

The purpose of the evaluation is not always easily ascertained, but the evaluator must not begin the evaluation without a clear understanding of its purpose. As was described earlier, purposes may include: *program improvement* where the focus is on bettering the quality and operation of a program; *accountability* where the focus is on determining whether program expectations have been met; *program impact* where the focus is on determining whether the program made a difference and is worthwhile; and on *knowledge generation* where the focus is on exploring the nature and effects of a program as a way to contribute to the existing knowledge base or to develop a new program.

Area 5: Identify Evaluation Questions and Criteria

Program evaluations cannot produce relevant, credible and useful findings unless they have a set of good questions that can guide the evaluation process. Questions should be formulated in consultation with primary stakeholders and should solicit information that the stakeholder needs. In addition, questions should be evaluative in nature, addressing the actual merit, value or worth of a program. A set of carefully thought-out evaluation questions is the lynchpin upon which a professional program evaluation hinges.

Identifying, constructing and/or clarifying evaluation questions are by no means simple exercises. Questions must comport closely with the purpose of the evaluation. It is helpful to start by asking the primary stakeholders what type of information they will need as they make decisions about the program. Clearly articulated evaluation questions give structure to the evaluation, lead to thoughtful planning, and facilitate the choosing of appropriate methods to gather data to answer those questions.

If an evaluation's purpose is to judge the overall success of a program in order to make decisions about program continuation or expansion, criteria that will be used to judge the success of the program must also be identified. The evaluator should involve stakeholders in the identification of these criteria and should share with stakeholders the full evaluation plan in order to get their feedback, consensus and support for its implementation. In sum, good evaluation questions establish the boundary and focus of the program evaluation. They make clear to everyone concerned what the evaluation will and will not address. Further, good questions will be aligned with a program's logic providing actionable answers for program decision-makers.

Area 6: Locate, Collect and Analyze Data

Upcraft and Schuh describe [evaluation] assessment as "any effort to gather, analyze, and interpret evidence, which describes institutional, divisional, [program], or agency effectiveness". Once evaluation questions are identified, the next steps should be to determine where the information to answer those questions is located, how best to collect it, and then how to analyze it. As has been stated in multiple areas above, it is important to involve stakeholders in all these steps.

The evaluator will want to select evaluation methods that can generate the most reliable and useful information pertinent to the overall evaluation purpose and then identify the sources of such information. Relevant information may already exist in readily available form (e.g., existing evaluation and/or status reports, existing data collected for other purposes, other public documents and data bases, etc.).

Some of the more frequently used data collection methods include: one-on-one *interviews, focus groups* (a group interview or discussion), *surveys, observations* and *expert panels*. In some instances, data collection will consist simply of locating existing data files. There are many excellent texts on designing and conducting interviews, and on designing and conducting focus groups. Regarding observations, Creswell, and Stake, provide in-depth understanding on the nature and challenges in making observations of various programs under study.

It should go without saying that, in order to identify and eliminate bugs in the process of constructing a new instrument, one should pilot test the newly developed data collection procedures before full implementation. Usually, data collection procedures are piloted on selected segments of the program. For example, in conducting surveys with program staff, only one or two units in the program might be engaged to test meaningfulness and understandability of items. All data in an evaluation, whether quantitative or qualitative in nature, should be appropriately and systematically analyzed, so that evaluation questions are fully and effectively answered. Further, any conclusions reached should be explicitly justified by the data, so that stakeholders can assess their validity.

Area 7: Report Evaluation Findings

How evaluation findings are reported is just as important as what is reported. Often, *tables and pictures*, such as graphs or bar charts, are useful to present a concise and clear summary of findings. The goal is to present evaluation findings in such a way that they will be easily understood. Presentation of findings may not be in the form of a formal writing but, rather, findings may be presented orally or interactively depending on the intended use and/or intended users of the findings. Conclusively, as Patton cautions, it is important to realize that dissemination of findings is different from use of findings.

Lastly, as noted by Davidson, *"weave the findings together to create a cohesive answer to a real question"*. This weaving of findings is known as "triangulation" and is standard professional practice in both the field of applied social sciences and the field of evaluation. Triangulation is using different types of data and from different sources, the purpose of which is to get different perspectives on the answer to the same question. When this is done, weaving the data together in the analysis, the results should be a cohesive answer to an evaluation question. This is the ultimate aim in reporting program evaluation findings.

Performance Measurement

In planning evaluations intended to improve program performance, it is possible to begin by identifying the program's *performance spectrum,* i.e., the logical ordering of program outcomes, including immediate outcomes, intermediate outcomes, and impact-associated performance indicators (types of evidence) by which the program will be evaluated. Again, a program's logical framework can be quite useful for identifying performance measures.

According to Friedman, performance measurement essentially describes program achievements in terms of outputs and outcomes within a given time frame against a pre-established goal. It asks: Is progress being made toward achieving strategic goals? Are appropriate activities being undertaken to promote achieving those goals? Are there problem areas or issues that need attention? Are there successful efforts that can serve as a model for others?

Friedman also posits that all performance measures involve two sets of interlocking questions. The first set of interlocking questions relates to *quantity* (how much did we do?) and *quality* (how well did we do it?). The second set of questions relate to the work itself: *effort* (how hard did we try?) and *effect* (is anyone better off?).

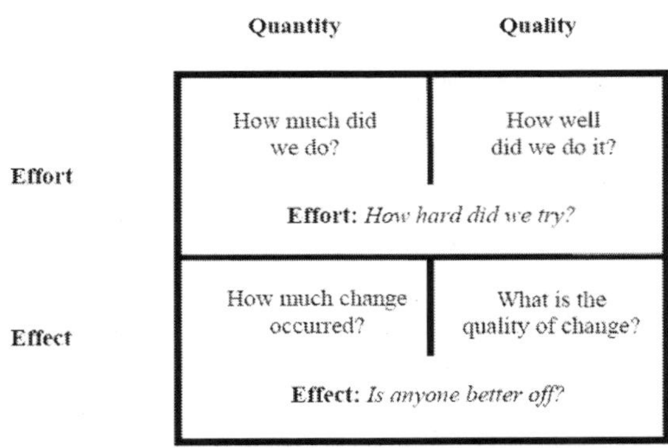

Figure 3. Quadrants of Performance Measures.

Using a program's logic model, as can be seen in the quadrants, if we focus on program activities and outputs elements in the logic model, we can identify indicators that describe volume (quantity) of work accomplished and quality of services delivered. This type of information can help us answer the questions, "*What are we doing and how much did we do?*" and "*How well did we do it?*" If we focus on the outcome elements, we can identify indicators that describe the effects of our program. This type of information can help us answer the questions, *"How much change or effect did we bring about?* and *"What is the quality of the change or effect we brought about?"* In summary, then, learning about institutional context, engaging stakeholders, identifying evaluation questions, and articulating a program's theory or logic are critical prerequisites to identifying performance indicators. Once these necessary pieces are in place, indicators by which the program will be evaluated can be identified, and data can be located, collected, analyzed and reported.

Programme Evaluation at IGNOU

Evaluation of Printed Coursewares

At IGNOU, programme evaluation of academic programmes comprises two components evaluation of the very planning of a programme/course and evaluation of materials that result from the plan. The activity involved in the former is to evaluate a programme/course in terms of the need for it, its marketability, its utility, its economic viability, adequacy and appropriateness of its content and media components. As an illustration, Koul elaborates on one of the above factors—the economic viability of a programme/course. For this, various criteria are used to indicate as to how much is to be spent on preparing a course and what might be the returns. These cost factors help in estimating whether a course is cheaper than the other, etc., and thus establish their relative cost effectiveness. However, it should be mentioned here that IGNOU is still at the experimental level with regard to evaluation of curriculum planning.

For evaluation of the materials produced, a checklist of the following type is generally used:

- Is the course content adequate?
- Is the language used appropriate to the level concerned?
- Is the material adequately self instructional?
- Is the media utilisation pedagogically rational?
- Is the material easily accessible?
- Is the course material considered useful by academics outside the university and are they using it in their systems?
- Does the material conform to the institutional norms of format, size, etc., as required by the university?
- Does the material help the student to get good grade in the examination?

- Does the material facilitate and help in effective and active student learning?

This discussion should suggest that programme evaluation is a two tier operation—the first consisting of those elements of evaluation which are a part of the general management process. For example, the rationale behind and the outline of a particular programme/course is looked into by an expert committee; modifications brought in at this stage are again discussed and reviewed with the course writers; in the process of course writing, the materials go through the hands of a language editor, a content editor, a format editor, etc., depending on the need, and at the post production level informal/ unsystematic feedback is obtained from students, counsellors and others who matter. All these stages are the components of programme/ course evaluation and a part of the management process — the establishment has not to put in any separate resources for this level of programme/course evaluation.

However, the second tier of course evaluation may or may not fall within the general management process. It may have any one or more of the following forms:

i) *Piloting of programmes/courses*: In this scheme the materials are tried out with the first batch of students and revisions brought in subsequently. This is a well known approach and very often the management takes to it almost without giving any thought to its utility in relation to its cost. The following are strong reasons why IGNOU should not depend on this approach for each and every course:

    - Given the constraints on the resources (financial as well as human), it will not be possible for all courses to follow this approach and then offer an improved course to the second batch of students.
    - It is also not within educational ethics to use the first batch of students as guinea pigs always and ever.
    - Correspondingly, the credibility of a course will be in question, should different batches of students get different kinds of courses and yet assessed by the same examination procedures.
    - Operationally, bringing in revisions immediately after the first launch adversely affects distribution and support services.
    - The cost of course design will be prohibitive and the rate of course production also gets adversely affected by this approach.

- If the first version of each and every course is prepared hastily, the image of the university will be affected adversely in the long run.

It is not, however, suggested that piloting a programme/course is entirely a futile task. Better ways of achieving similar results, nevertheless, should be explored. For example, the concept of 'quality assurance' may be inculcated in the production processes.

ii) *Routine evaluation*: This is best done as a part of the management process. The advantage of keeping this evaluation within the management process is that in doing so it will not demand high resource allocations. Besides, it will keep the institution in constant touch with the students and the materials, resulting in appropriate and timely feedback to the academic schools, course writers and academic counsellors. It will eventually feed into the process of course maintenance which can be carried out through supplementary materials and thereby saving the resources. Routine evaluation, thus, implies
   - evaluating each course within the year it is launched; and
   - evaluating assignment question and the term end examination question papers, in addition to course materials.

Evaluation of Non-print Media Materials

A few learning objectives, especially those concerned with acquiring skills and/or attitudes can not be realized by print materials alone. The use of electronic media within the total media mix of a programme is useful to achieve objectives pertaining to psychomotor affective domains.

To determine the worth of non print materials, we need to go for the description of its attributes. The attributes are the opinions and beliefs, needs, results and outcomes. The evaluator/teacher has to describe the physical conditions for conducting evaluation and the psychological attributes associated with a programme. For example, a video presentation of a theme related to specific unit may be described as 20-25 minutes long, in 16 mm format, with high quality colour pictures and sound. It may be described also as having four episodes at its conclusion in which learners are asked to identify interpersonal skills that the film purports to teach. The description might document that most counselors using the film think that it is effective, and that the skills it develops are important. It might indicate that 70 per cent of those viewing the film are able to identify at least three of the four skills demonstrated in the concluding episodes.

To describe the video cassette, assessments are made, some of these are quantitative, such as recording the time and percentage of viewers who can identify a given number of skills, etc., while others are qualitative such as collecting statements about effectiveness or monitoring individual perceptions, of picture and sound quality. This may by considered as example of how a non print media is evaluated adequately with the help of the descriptions of the attributes.

Evaluation of Student Support Services

Evaluation of student support services includes the following:

i) *Tutor evaluation*: Tutors/academic counsellors are essentially engaged in the activities of informing, advising and counselling students both in the face to face contexts and at a distance by post; meeting students in face to face situations for a number of sessions during an academic year; assessing assignment responses and helping distance learners to learn how they should learn on their own. These activities are the bases of evaluating the tutors. This evaluation, thus, consists of evaluating
    - the nature of communication between them and the students—through letters and/or in face to face situations,
    - the quality of their comments on assignment responses,
    - the reliability and validity of the assessment of the responses,
    - the turn around rate of assessed assignment responses.

ii) *Evaluation of face to face sessions*: As far as face to face sessions are concerned, IGNOU evaluates the academic counsellors' punctuality, regularity, nature of rapport with students, quality of the conduct of sessions, students' satisfaction, academic counsellors' motivation/enthusiasm, etc., through its regional centers.

iii) *Evaluation of continuous assessment*: This entails evaluating the validity and reliability of continuous assessment. This in effect means evaluation of assignments for their validity, their reliability and for their correlation with the questions set at the end of the term examination. A certain percentage of the evaluated assignment responses are further monitored by the concerned school faculty (sometimes, the regional center senior functionaries), every year.

iv) *Evaluation of support system*: Evaluation of the support system itself consists in evaluating the quality and quantity of support available to students in relation to various courses at various study centres. Such evaluation will have implications for recruitment of academic counsellors, providing support in terms of equipment and other support to counter issues relating to local and socio geographical constraints, etc.

In general, to evaluate student support services, IGNOU seeks answers to a few questions of the kind given here:

- Do these services cater to the information needs promptly, adequately and convincingly?
- Do these services provide for advice at pre course, on course and post course stages adequately and effectively?
- Are these services easily accessible?
- Are the staff involved in these services attitudinally tuned to the kind of work assigned to them?
- How do these students rate the support services?
- Do the support services make a pedagogically rational use of various media in operation?
- Do the support services help the learners get a good pass in the examination?

References

Alkin, M. C. (2011). *Evaluation essentials*: From A to Z. The Guilford Press

Bickman, L. (Ed.). (1987). *Using program theory in evaluation.* San Francisco, CA: Jossey-Bass

Colton, D., & Covert, R. W. (2007). *Designing and constructing instruments for social research and evaluation.* Jossey-Bass

Joint Committee on Standards for Educational Evaluation, (2011*). The Program Evaluation Standards: A guide for evaluators and evaluation users* (3rd Ed), Sage Publications, Inc

Patton, M. Q. (2011). *Developmental evaluation: Applying complexity concepts to enhance innovation and use.* Guilford Press

Upcraft, M. L., & Schuh, J. H. (1996). *Assessment in student affairs: A guide for practitioners.* San Francisco, CA: Jossey-Bass

Wholey, J. S., Hatry, H. P., and Newcomer, K. E., (2010). *Handbook of practical program evaluation*, (3rd Ed). Jossey-Bass.

4

Quality Assurance Instruments

The discussion on concepts of quality of teaching and learning in higher education was given boosts, first in the 1980s by the introduction of what can broadly be called 'new public management', with its predilection for management models developed in the business world, then in the 1990s by the fall of communism in Central and Eastern Europe, and most recently in the 2000s by the Bologna and Lisbon agendas in Europe. With each of these drivers went diferent instruments for quality assurance: starting from quality assessment for 'value for money', but also for quality improvement, a trend can be seen towards accreditation of study programmes and higher education institutions. While there is a relationship between the political concepts of quality and the quality assurance instruments chosen, the choice of instruments also has consequences for the concept of quality that is best served by it.

Concepts of Quality and Quality Assurance Instruments

Subject Delimitation

Matters around quality of research will not be addressed here themselves, although engagement in research may be part of the quality of individual staf members (in U.S. terms, these are called 'faculty', but I shall use 'staf', 'teachers' or 'academics'). In quality assurance of research, attention tends to centre on output and impact or on management of research groups. Also, I shall not go into institutional quality assurance, in which the focus is on developing institutional missions, capacity for change or, more mundanely, on the implementation of central services.

Concepts of Quality

A real simplifcation is not given in this way, however, as there is not an essential 'quality': words can be given any meaning, as the mediaeval scholastics already found out, and as novelist Pirsig repeated: "Quality... you know what it is, yet you don't know what it is....But when you try to say what the quality is, apart from the things that have it, it all goes *poof*! There's nothing to talk about. But if you can't say what Quality is, how do you know what it is, or how do you know that it even exists?"

Deductive Approaches

In a deductive approach, the meaning of a concept is derived from more general theoretical relationships. The main problem for deductive approaches to quality is that there is no theory of quality as such. The quote given above from Pirsig's novel is illustrative of what happens if one tries to deduce the meaning of 'quality' without having a pertinent theory. Where could such theories be found?

The first and main area where one would expect to fnd a theory on how to produce quality of higher education is pedagogy. More specifcally, the question that pedagogy would have to answer from our perspective is: how to produce quality of teaching, or rather of student learning? For it is agreed among educational specialists that, as a consequence of diferent characteristics of students (intelligence, educational, social and cultural backgrounds, but also learning styles), any single way of teaching does not produce equal learning results for all students. However, beyond this general insight, the production function remains 'opaque'.

Another area of knowledge in which quality is researched extensively is economics. Although the bulk of publications on quality is from the sub-area of business studies, it may be useful to think in terms of micro-economics of quality as a balanced outcome of demand and supply, connected to the price in a market. Yet even modern and neo-institu-tional economics have difculty handling quality in formal market models. Still it may be interesting to pursue some arguments from the perspective of economics, as they will assist in making some points about the concept of quality.

A fundamental question with regard to the economics perspective is whether education can be treated like a market good or service at all? The answer that should be given to this question is clearly of the 'Yes, but...'

type; the 'yes' applying to the element that education has the characteristics of a service, and the 'but' being that it is debatable whether education, and especially higher education, is not a public good that should be exempted from market perspectives. The term 'public good' is ambiguous. Do we mean a collective good, or do we mean a good that has to be provided from the public purse? From an economic point of view, the answer is simple: education is *not* a *collective* good. Collective goods are defined as goods where the consumption by one individual in no way prevents others from consuming the same good. Evidently, education does sufer from crowding efects, as, for instance, German students who have to sit in the aisles for lack of chairs can testify, and, even more, selection processes by universities make it patently clear that individuals can be excluded from consuming education.

However, education has positive externalities, i.e. other individuals beneft too if one individual attains better education (e.g. several jobs are created when one individual starts an enterprise, or many people can enjoy better-performed symphonies). Education therefore can be called a merit good. Merit goods may sufer from market failures, indicating that, for individual consumers, the investment in education provided at market prices may not be worthwhile given the limited benefts they themselves have of it, while, for society at large, the individual benefts plus the positive externalities may make a higher level of consumption of education very desirable. The merit good status, then, would be a valid argument for giving government a role in providing education. This seems to lead to the sometimes confusing result that, as public authorities are (legitimately) involved in providing the goods, they may be called public goods. Educational economists tend to agree that education has a merit-good character at least up to secondary education, in the sense that public benefts outweigh the private ones. That is to say societies have much beneft from having a well-educated labour force, while, for the individual, there is not much to gain in terms of, for example, income or job security from attending education up to the secondary level, since almost everyone does so.

Educational economists equally tend to agree, conversely, that private benefts outweigh public benefts for postgraduate courses. The moot question then would be on which side of the borderline between predominantly public and predominantly private benefts is higher education? The prevailing European point of view seems to be that higher education is a merit good.

In taking this point of view, I have the impression that European policy-makers and students, who are most vociferous in this respect, are thinking of undergraduate higher education. With the increasing proportions of populations going into higher education, one of the arguments for believing that the private benefits outweigh the public ones for initial higher education becomes increasingly weak. For that argument is built on the idea of having a higher education degree being a 'position good': position goods give benefts to their holders because others do not have it (a scarcity argument). Obviously, if having an undergraduate higher education degree is becoming common, they are not scarce anymore. At this level then, it may well be true that the collective benefits of a highly skilled workforce make up the most important part of benefts. On the other hand, graduate and postgraduate degrees remain relatively scarce, so that they still function as position goods, as may be shown by the signifcantly higher income that holders of master and doctorate degrees ofen earn. In summary, there is more reason to treat higher education as a marketable good for graduate and postgraduate degrees than for undergraduate degrees.

A second consideration with regard to the applicability of market mechanisms in higher education is that benefts appear only in the very long term. Whether one takes 'narrow' benefts in terms of income, or 'wide' benefts including personal growth, happiness, health, etc. (which all seem to be positively correlated with having a higher education degree), these are all benefts that appear afer a number of years, sometimes a large number of years. Future benefts are discounted, economic theory holds, so that they play a smaller role in prospective students' decisions than the size of these benefts warrants. Markets function better with short-term benefts. Student satisfaction is not a good proxy for the eventual benefts, because student satisfaction is an immediate reaction, not one based on long-term considerations.

The fnal consideration we want to address here is the 'transformation argument', explained in detail by Harvey and Knight. One of the core aims of education is to change the student, especially mentally; they are to learn new knowledge, skills and competences. Therefore their view of the world will change in the course of their education. As Harvey and Knight put it, education is not a service *for* a fxed customer, but something that is done to the students. As a consequence, students' preferences change during their education, including their preferences with regard to education itself. And that, in turn, means that standard market theories cannot be applied, because those assume fxed preferences. This argument may apply more to 'initial' higher education students (a student's first encounter with higher education) and to young students (adolescents are changing their views on life radically anyway) than to mature students pursuing second and further degrees. Accordingly, market approaches are more applicable to the latter category rather to than the former.

The conclusion of these economic considerations must be that education is a complex kind of service, which by its very nature is not easily amenable to market co-ordination, while that option is not completely precluded either. The previous arguments do not imply that it is more easily co-ordinated by planning mechanisms. Also, they do not answer the question of whether higher education should be funded (to an undecided extent, and through whatever mechanism) from the public purse; the merit good argument is one in favour of public funding. It does establish, I think, that higher education must be considered in the context of the political economy of a society.

Maybe surprisingly, the term 'quality' did not appear in the above, but it was implied, especially in the consideration of the long-term character of benefts from higher education: students do not value high quality of education as much as they 'ought' to if they took future benefts fully into account. In the short run, *consumption* motives (immediate satisfaction, enjoyable lectures, easy exams, comfortable facilities, nice town, etc.) outweigh *investment* motives (lifelong valuable competences such as analytical skills, 'learning to learn' and 'learning to earn'). Students may therefore overemphasize consumption arguments in their judgements on quality of higher education, while teaching staf put more stress on investment-associated aspects of quality. This is just one example of how diferent stakeholders have, understandably and legitimately, diferent views on what constitutes quality in higher education. Another may be that the teaching staf made careers in higher education itself, so that they tend to overemphasize the internal values of the higher education community, i.e. they stress 'academic excellence' over practical usefulness for the student in other career (and life) paths. For such reasons, I shall not try to give a once-and-for-all definition of quality: "there are (at least) as many definitions of quality in higher education as there are categories of stakeholders (such as students, teaching staf, scientifc communities, government and employers), *times* the number of purposes, or dimensions, these stakeholders distinguish". Briefy though, all definitions in the literature (e.g. ISO 8402/ ISO 9000 series definition) point to the link between the good or service under consideration and desires of customers as the essence of quality.

The complication in higher education may be that there are many diferent stakeholders rather than a single category of customers. Partly, this depends on a lack of clarity of focus or level in the discussion. If higher education is considered to be what happens between teachers and students in the classroom, laboratory, etc., then it is clear that the 'customers' are the students. If a macro perspective is taken, things are more complicated: higher education's 'business' is to deliver graduates to the economy, and then, at the highest level of abstraction, the employers (among them the public sector represented by the state) are the customers, or, taking a step back towards the micro level, the graduates are the customers, who have 'purchased' a package of knowledge and skills which they can trade for an income on the labour market. Much depends therefore on the theory applied to higher education (e.g. macro- compared with micro-economics, or economics compared with educational science) and the level of discussion. The only viable solution for political systems (in which higher education fgures) to handle quality of higher education seems not to make a choice for one level or theory, and go back to the multitude of stakeholders, each with their diferent views on quality.

Inductive Approach

In the above section, it appears that the deductive theoretical approach was not successful (yet), but led to contingency statements: quality may be diferent for diferent stakeholders, and, we may add, at diferent moments: the zeitgeist of 1968 demanded quite diferent qualities from higher education than the 1980s/1990s career-oriented students. Let me therefore approach the issue from the other end, inductively: what do we see when we look at existing schemes around quality in higher education?

Dimensions and Terms

Before looking at quality assurance schemes in detail, first a few words on terms. We shall use 'quality assurance' as the general term for these arrangements, emphasizing their function toward society. 'Quality control' and 'quality management' are used for the schemes within higher education institutions, the former stressing measurement and maintenance of current standards within the field of 'producing' education, and the latter stressing the connection of quality control with general planning and control cycles and thinking of possibilities of enhancement and change. 'Quality assessment' or 'evaluation' is used for external quality assurance schemes when focusing on the 'measurement' (quantitatively and qualitatively) of quality. 'Quality audit' is used in the jargon of higher education for an evaluation mechanism that investigates quality management arrangements within higher education institutions. 'Accreditation' difers from quality assessment and quality audit in that it leads to a brief formal statement of reaching certain quality threshold levels, giving the judged unit (programme or institution) an ofcial right to exist in a higher education system. These terms are defined here for working purposes, to cut short the complicated and tedious question of translation of ofcially used terms. The etymology of ofcially used terms ofen says more about political pathways in which quality of higher education has been involved, than about commonalities and diferences in substance.

Quality assurance schemes, then, appear in a confusing multitude of forms, with diferent aims, scope, foci, levels, etc. To add to the confusion, the diferent options per dimension are not (always) mutually exclusive. The aims of a quality assurance scheme, for instance, may be to support quality improvement in higher education institutions, but also for them to be accountable to society about the efectiveness and efciency of (tax) money spent on higher education, and to inform employers and/or future students about diferent qualities of diferent higher education institutions. A complication is the issue of what should be taken as valid statements about those aims: what the governments says, what the co-ordinator of the quality assurance scheme says, what staf say, what researchers about quality assurance schemes fnd as the aims in use? For diferent aims of analysis, diferent answers may be the most relevant.

Dynamics of Quality Assurance

A further complication in looking at quality assurance schemes inductively is that they are not stable over time; quality assurance displays changes, which can be analysed to uncover mechanisms driving dynamics. In our view, there are four main phases in the development of quality assurance schemes.

The mechanisms that explain development from one phase to another are internal and external. Internally, the mechanism is learning: parties learn their roles in a quality assurance scheme, which, on the positive side, implies increasing levels of awareness and capacity to handle issues of quality. On the downside, though, it implies that parties 'learn the tricks' so that, instead of a genuine quality assurance scheme, any system tends to become a bureaucratic routine replete with window-dressing behaviour, but without any impact on the actual education process. Positive learning opens the option of a higher phase; negative learning induces co-ordinating actors to change quality assurance schemes (probably without 'climbing' a phase, although a 'fight forward' could be a viable option in some cases).

The first mechanism of external dynamics is that solving one problem leads to the next one coming to the surface (hierarchy of problems; favours 'climbing' to next phase), but it is a recipe for failure to try to address problems of later phases unless the lower-level problems have been brought to closure. The second external mechanism might be termed the 'social dynamics', these are the exogenously changing views and politics, which may bring other roles of higher education to the fore in society, and therefore change the quality problems in the higher education system.

Its heuristic value may be high, but the empirical value of the mechanisms explaining dynamics is limited, because it seems that the social dynamics, i.e. the uncontrollable, exogenous, changes of policies and views, override them. Moreover, the consistency that we as researchers saw among the diferent elements within a certain phase may have been seen diferently in the political reality. For instance, in the situation of the new challenges posed by the Bologna Declaration of 1999, we found that, under the circumstances of present-day higher education with its modularization (further supported by Bologna) and concomitant individualization of curricula, the study programme was, as it were, 'deconstructed' so that quality assurance schemes ought to focus on the individual learner's competences and on reporting on aggregated measures of higher education institutions success in teaching learners under these new circumstances.

Two Decades of Quality Assurance History

The question of how quality assurance schemes and especially accreditation have spread across Europe since the early 1980s was the subject of a comparative study of 20 countries, published at the beginning of the 21st

Century. Quality assurance schemes were first introduced in some Western European countries just before the middle of the 1980s. In Central and Eastern Europe, they were introduced from 1990 onwards. The diferent timings already indicate that there were diferent aims and goals attached to quality assurance in Western and Central/Eastern Europe. Below, I give a schematic overview of the spread of quality assurance, and then go into diferent (social) dynamics and the concomitant diferent concepts of quality.

Main Quantitative Results and Main Drivers for Change

When looking at the number of countries where some form of quality assurance scheme is applied, it appears that, in the space of 20 years, this new policy instrument became well-nigh universal. In even less time, so did accreditation; however, as will appear below, these fgures should emphatically not be taken at face value! Especially when looking at accreditation, it has to be borne in mind that the authors only looked at the question of whether there was one or more supra-institutional schemes for some part of the higher education system. Tus, for instance, the fact that there are tens of professional bodies in the U.K. with accreditation power for a certain set of study programmes made them put the U.K. in the category of 'has accreditation', even though the main quality assurance scheme, afecting all of the higher education sector, is the institutional audit driven by the QAA (Quality Assurance Agency), which is not an accreditation scheme. Similarly, Austria is in the category of 'has accredi tation', even though the schemes apply only to private higher education institutions and non-university institutions, but not to the traditional public universities. As a third example, in Sweden and Norway, there is also accreditation, but that functions mainly on a one-of basis, namely if an institution wishes to be upgraded from college to university status.

The 'pioneer countries' with regard to quality assurance schemes in Western Europe were the U.K., France and The Netherlands. In the spirit of neo-liberalism that inspired new approaches in the public sector, e.g. labelled 'New Public Management', governments in these countries sought to make higher education more accountable for the tax money spent on them (a sum that was reduced, especially in the U.K. and The Netherlands), and to refrain from detailed regulation ('dysfunctional bureaucracy') by replacing regulation with market-like mechanisms. Quality assurance can be seen, on the one hand, as a policy instrument supporting transparent markets for students and graduates by making information about quality diferences public, and, on the other, as a safeguard against too blunt minimizing of quality levels in the free supply behaviour of higher education providers on (quasi-)markets. The latter would be induced by, e.g., performance-related funding where performance is in quantitative rather than qualitative terms, in particular numbers of graduates (invites lowering of standards in order to maximize graduation rates). Besides, quality assurance schemes were meant at least in some cases to stimulate quality improvement in the sense of making higher education institutions adapt more fexibly to the changing demands on graduates in the move from industry-based to service-focused economies, or to the emerging knowledge society.

In 1990, Denmark was the first follower of these pioneers, and, from then on, the 'quality movement' spread to the rest of Western Europe. An important event in spreading the diferent models of external evaluation was the EU (European Union)'s Pilot Project on external evaluation methodology of 1994. The basis for this pilot was the fnding that, on an abstract level, a common four-step model seemed to apply to most quality assurance schemes: a national co-ordinator, self-evaluation, peer review and some type of public report on the external evaluation outcomes. The pilot project consisted of evaluation exercises involving one or two programmes in two knowledge areas in all (then) EU countries and some other Western European countries. Years later, in 1998, it led to the EU's decision to establish a network of quality assessment agencies, ENQA (European Network for Quality Assurance in Higher Education). A further 2 years later, this became operational, and, afer some years, it gained a key position in the Bologna Process. Meanwhile, from two inventories made in 1998, it can be concluded that almost all Western European countries at that moment had a government policy to assess quality in higher education. The most notable exceptions were Germany, Italy and Greece. By 2003, of these three, only Greece was lef without a formal national quality assurance scheme. In Germany and Italy, the combined Sorbonne and Bologna Processes had given the fnal push for establishing quality assurance schemes.

Developments in Central/Eastern Europe had started later than in Western Europe, namely with the fall of communism in 1989. The first new higher education laws in the transformation era, those of the Czech Republic (at that time Czechoslovakia) and of Poland, showed diferent routes towards rapid institutional transformation. The Czech approach included an accreditation committee from the outset, to assess, among other things, all study programmes. In Poland, transformation was not couched in terms of evaluating quality, initially. Other countries in the area also followed their own routes towards renewal of higher education, but many included (semi-)independent, ofen academically controlled committees with a remit to accredit quality of institutions and/or programmes. In Romania, for instance, the new legal arrangements allowed for the rapid rise of multitudes of private higher education institutions as well as the creation of campuses associated with foreign higher education providers. The academic establishment reacted by introducing accreditation for new higher education institutions, focusing heavily on sufciency of input factors, especially staf numbers and facilities.

Only with the Bologna Declaration did the idea of accreditation move from Central and Eastern Europe to the West, as a way to enhance international transparency (compatibility) of the until then very diferent national higher education systems, and to assist in transforming, where applicable, old-style single-cycle study programmes to the newly required two-cycle structure. Accordingly, for some countries, such as Germany, it gave the push to end a decade-long discussion on quality assurance and actually to begin to implement it. In others, it led to a major revamp of the existing quality assurance scheme. For instance, in The Netherlands, the quality assessment scheme that afer more than a decade was beginning to show signs of wear, was 'topped up' with a programme accreditation organization which, as had been predicted by some, drastically changed the dynamics of the interaction between evaluators and evaluated units. In still other countries, by contrast, very little changed, as there was no wish within the country for change (e.g. the U.K. and Denmark).

Later, the Bologna Process became more institutionalized, especially once the European Commission gained a permanent position in the BFUG (Bologna Follow-Up Group). From then on, the process acquired its own dynamics, exerting force towards harmonization on all countries involved, and especially on those that joined the process later. Thus ENQA had been given the task by the ministers of developing common standards for quality assurance schemes, especially at the supra-institutional level although with ramifcations for internal quality assurance in higher education institutions (published as). Before that, the European Commission had already strategically supported informal initiatives of countries to develop common descriptors for undergraduate and graduate learning outcomes, what I called the 'Dublin Descriptors' when they were first publicly presented, in

Amsterdam in 2002. Similarly, it had supported the university-based projects to develop learning outcomes for several areas of study, i.e. the Tuning projects. These informal pilot projects quickly achieved (semi-)ofcial status as standards to be followed, not least thanks to the verbal support they were given by the European Commission.

Changes in Concepts of Quality in Use

Afer this brief overview, it may be useful to refect on the changes that have taken place with regard to the concepts of quality that are used in the European higher education systems. This refection is limited to the concepts used at the level of higher education systems as a whole, which is conditioned by the method chosen for this contribution. Had the level of consideration been the quality concepts used in (a sample of) the 4000 individual higher education institutions in Europe, things might have looked diferent. The contribution would then have looked at quality management systems based on EFQM (European Foundation for Quality Management) models, ISO-9001/9004 certifcation, and 'native' higher education models. However, from the literature, it appears that higher education institutions in their choice of models for their quality management systems and even more in the indicators and areas chosen for application in those systems, are driven by external requirements. And among the external requirements, the market forces are one important factor, but the state's (and other accreditors') demands are the most outstanding factor. Indeed, it has been hypothesized that institutional management styles (and presumably also the management instruments) parallel the governmental style of steering. Accordingly, it may be expected that the concept of quality used by the government has an important infuence on the higher education institutions.

A constant, rather than a change, in the quality concepts in use over the last two decades among European governments is, obviously, that the governments and/or their agencies retained a central infuence on the quality assurance schemes, notwithstanding statements about increasing autonomy for higher education institutions. The fact that governments have remained the main, if no longer the only, funding source for higher education institutions, together with the concomitant conviction that government is responsible for higher education on behalf of society, is the main factor for this constant position. It leads immediately to a second constant, namely that in the concept of quality, accountability to the government remained a main aim.

A major change has been that, whereas government approval used to be tied directly to the bureaucratic routines of establishing and funding higher education institutions in almost all European countries, there now are formal evaluation procedures tied to such decisions, i.e. there are accreditation schemes around. One can think of the upgrading of colleges to university status in Sweden or Norway, but also of the recurrent *habilitation* of study programmes in France that has become more evaluation-oriented in recent years.

Accreditation is meant to assure basic ('threshold') quality. I wish to make two remarks here. First, the metaphor of students as consumers has gained currency across many higher education systems; it is connected to accreditation in that both carry the sense that giving 'consumer protection' against malpractice of 'degree mills' is an important task for governments. Secondly, governments feel more responsible for assuring a threshold level for all students, rather than identifying excellence, which, by the way, is the most popular concept of quality among academic staf. In the political philosophies that characterized the welfare state's view of the role of government, but equally under the more recent neo-liberal state views, this is an understandable and condoned standpoint. Only when another state role is taken into account, namely to support its citizens in the international economic competition, does supporting excellence come to the fore. This is the agenda of the Lisbon strategy, but it does not seem to have much impact on the quality assurance schemes in European countries: quality assurance is for the basic level; excellence is pursued in other ways.

The fact, though, that quality assurance remains focused on the basic level of quality, implies that it does not in itself stimulate diversity in higher education. Although there may be diferent ways of reaching the quality threshold (e.g. through diferent didactical approaches, such as problem-based learning or distance education), still the single set of quality requirements is a homogenizing force in the higher education system. To what extent European co-operation with regard to standards will be a homogenizing force, or conversely whether the many translations of these European-level discourses through national policies and schemes will keep higher education systems separate, is an issue meriting further research. The infuence of ENQA and its guidelines, and even more of the register of quality assessment agencies that is to become functional for all of the Bologna area, is another case in point.

The question of Europe or the individual state is an important one. As appeared above, it was the European-level Bologna process that inaugurated a new phase for the quality assurance schemes in many European countries. The impact of Bologna on countries may have been diferent for each country, but at least the actors in the countries have had to address the question of how to react to this impulse. On the whole, the Bologna process has been instrumental in the rise of accreditation as the main type of quality assurance schemes in Western Europe. As a consequence, the general approach to external scrutiny of quality in higher education institutions has become more oriented towards assuring basic quality, consumer protection, accountability, summative evaluation, etc. The associated, unanswered, research question is what are the efects of changing the external evaluation scheme with a much more sophisticated internal quality management in higher education institutions. Do more sophisticated higher education institutions react diferently to the changing external pressure than when both institutions and external evaluators were still at the beginning of their learning curves?

Finally, I would briefy like to raise a fundamental question. It has been contended that external quality assurance schemes are policy instruments of 'organized distrust'. In that light, the spread of quality assurance and the hardening of external quality assurance into accreditation both point to a further decrease of trust. At the same time, policy-makers and higher education managers deplore this situation and want to efect a shif in the system back to a high-trust situation, but with some form of quality assurance, as this has proven to be an advantageous instrument for them. The fundamental question here is whether it is possible at all to shif back to a high-trust situation. Who coined the one-liner: 'Innocence once lost cannot be regained'?

Multiple Functions of Evaluation and Quality Assessment

Some form of quality assurance or assessment system is a part of the working environment for most people working in universities these days. Its rise is a function of higher education's massifcation, its diversifcation and its internationalization, and of the changes in its relationship with state and society. Quality assessment is implicated in developments such as marketization and managerialism. And it receives both the blame and the praise attached to such developments. Quality assessment has its enthusiasts, who see benign intentions and real benefts to higher education, and it has its sceptics and antagonists, who see attacks on academic freedoms and much else.

But what precisely are we talking about? Definitions can be found, but much of the terminology on quality in higher education relates to local systems and their nomenclatures. For some, much is imported to higher education from industry and the quality gurus of management theory. The externality relates only to the boundaries of what is being assessed. Thus it might include an 'internal' institu- tional assessment of the quality of a particular department or programme, i.e. externality in this case refers to the department/programme rather than the institution. On this conception, quality assessment does not necessarily imply the existence of a national, probably state-sponsored, quality agency, although, in practice, at least in most European countries, such a body probably does exist.

Learning to live with quality assessment in universities is about appreciating what it is really about and understanding its potential consequences for our working lives, our students and our institutions. Above all, we shall suggest that learning to live with quality assessment is about learning to use quality assessment, about avoiding undue defensiveness or obsessiveness about it, but seeing the mechanisms and procedures of quality assessment as tools which we can use to achieve things.

We shall also argue that quality assessment is as much about power and values as it is about quality. And it is about change. The practices of quality assessment both refect and can alter relationships, both within HEIs (higher education institutions) and between these institutions and other parts of society.

Multiple Actors

Who are the 'we' referred to above as the potential users of quality assessment? The implementation of quality assessment in higher education can be seen as an example of what has been referred to as a process of 'regulatory intermediation', whereby the ofcial purposes of a regulatory system become transformed into something rather diferent by the people who have a central stake in it. In a recent study, King et al. have focused on the roles of, on the one hand, assessors or auditors who undertake the assessments of quality, and, on the other, the senior institutional managers who receive and process the assessments locally. We would like to extend the notion of mediation by pointing to a much larger list of actors, or potential 'mediators', i.e. students, teaching staf, course leaders and heads of department, educational administrators ('quality' and 'other'), institutional leaders, quality agency staf, quality agency consultants (assessors/auditors), staf of other national bodies, ministries etc., politicians, employers, civil society etc.

Nor will there be much homogeneity within these groups. There will be institutional and subject diferences in perceptions, interests and responses. There will also be diferences according to what is perceived to be at stake. A prestigious institution or department might perceive greater reputational risk and hence threat from quality assessment than a more middle-ranking institution or department. Yet an institution with even greater prestige might have the confdence (even arrogance) about its reputation to treat external quality processes with some disdain. More marginal institutions and departments, i.e. those with little reputation to lose, might perceive their very existence to be at risk from a negative quality judgement. At the same time, they may also perceive the prospect of signifcant reputational gain from a 'good' assessment. Either way, it is probably those institutions and units at either extreme of a reputational hierarchy that have the most at stake from certain kinds of quality assessment procedure; i.e. from those types that result in a numerical or other form of summative judgement. Thus responses to quality assessment cannot be 'read of' as refecting a particular institutional position or stakeholder perspective. Interests and responses will be viewed diferently in diferent places, refecting local circumstances and perceptions. As part of an OECD (Organisation for Economic Co-operation and Development) project some years ago, we described the very diferent responses of some 30 HEIs (higher education institutions) from diferent parts of the world to the requirements of quality assessment.

It is worth noting, however, that the alternative to some formal quality assessment system tends to be evaluation by reputation. This can be a function of all sorts of things: history, size, location, as well as serious achievements in education and research. There is also, of course, a reciprocal infuence between reputation and quality assessment, the former being dented or enhanced by the results of the latter, but the latter being infuenced (sometimes unduly?) both consciously and unconsciously by the former.

In the above list of potential mediators, we have assumed the existence of something called a national 'quality agency'. The creation of such bodies in the vast majority of European countries is a central feature and driver of quality assessment practices within HEIs, but it is not co-terminus with them. For one thing, the agencies are frequently concerned only with the quality of *education*, leaving questions of research quality for others to determine. For another, they can draw attention away from the equally important *internal* processes of quality assessment. These have become a familiar part of the inner lives of many HEIs. Nevertheless, quality agencies have to be contended with. The EU (European Union)-supported ENQA (European Association for Assurance in Higher Education) and the more voluntaristic INQAAHE (International Network of Quality Assurance Agencies in Higher Education) exert infuence on the practices of individual national agencies and signal, to governments and others, the pervasiveness of their functions and activities in (nearly) all higher education systems.

Contexts

The way people use quality assessment processes refects a number of things. The first is the *context* in which they are working. Here, I want to point to just two features of context: power and diferentiation.

Power

The first concerns where power lies. The most common alternatives are the following: autonomous subject communities; a powerful and controlling state; self-governing HEIs; and market competition.

Countries differ in their traditions in these things (e.g.). The Anglo-Saxon tradition has been one of self-governing institutions and latterly of market competition. Within this tradition, even relatively modest exertion of state power is perceived as a threat to academic health and autonomy, whereas in the Humboldtian and Napoleonic traditions of most continental European countries, the state has ofen been regarded as the protector of higher education's freedoms and well-being. And, of course, things are not always what they seem. In some countries, academics have ofen quite successfully colonized the ministries and other bodies that apparently control them, with ministers drawn from among the ranks of the senior professors and national advisory committees comprising academics playing important roles in the exercise of state power. It is the relative weakness of individual institutions rather than the weakness of the academy as such that has tended to be the characteristic of continental higher education in contrast with the Anglo-Saxon tradition.

We can also point to diferences in the inner worlds of HEIs. The traditional autonomy of disciplinary 'basic units', in the terms of Becher and Kogan's model, is challenged both by changes in the forms and organization of knowledge, with the growth of increasingly interdisciplinary programmes and research endeavours, and by the exercise of greater central or managerial power within institutions. But institutions difer considerably in the current balance of power within their organizational structures, to say nothing of the strength of the cultural resistances to the exercise of such power.

Power is not, of course, all in one place and it may be shifing, arguably most commonly these days away from subject communities and the state towards self-governing institutions and market competition. Quality assessment may be helping these shifs to occur.

Differentiation

The second point of context is the character of the higher education system, whether it is diferentiated or standardized, unitary or binary, hierarchical or fat, large or small.

These are matters which are central to the functioning of quality assessment. The balance This is not to suggest that other contextual features are not also important, but it is suggested that the above are particularly signifcant when thinking about the functions of quality assessment. Thus is the purpose of the quality assessment system to ensure that quality is the same everywhere or to demonstrate that it is diferent? To what extent does it depend upon (or is it obstructed by) the local and informal knowledge and relationships which particularly characterize small systems and to what extent is it able to draw upon the wider expertise, greater neutrality and availability of comparison in large systems?

This discussion of contexts has assumed a national setting. But, increasingly, universities relate to a larger international academic community and marketplace. In some fields, international quality assessment processes already exist and are important sources of reputation and competitive strength. Various unofcial rankings and league tables of universities receive considerable attention. Internationalization does not remove the importance of quality assessment so much as add an additional tier to the evaluation processes involved. Thus national quality agencies within Europe are now expected by the European Commission to meet criteria set for them by ENQA.

Nevertheless, it is still generally local and national quality requirements that have the most direct impact on HEIs. According to the nature of the national and institutional contexts, I want to argue that quality assessment will refect diferent distributions of power and values and that it may have diferent efects.

Approaches

As well as diferences in context, I also want to consider diferences in *approaches* to quality assessment. Here, I want to distinguish between (i) whether it is external or internal (to the object of the assessment); (ii) whether it is undertaken primarily by methods of peer review, performance indicators, procedural compliance or client feedback; (iii) whether it is *holistic* or *segmented* (i.e. looking at teaching and research separately); and (iv) whether the level of assessment is a subject, an organizational unit, a course (and so on).

All of these things will infuence what is likely to happen in practice and, in particular, who are likely to be the winners and losers from quality assessment.

A predominantly internal approach is more likely to be linked to action, to making changes in some area of an institution's work. Otherwise, why do it? However, increasingly, internal quality assessment has an external driver and reference point. In some contexts, it serves as a 'dress rehearsal' for the 'real thing' of external assessment. In other cases, while not directly linked to a particular external assessment event and judgement, internal assessment takes place as an act of compliance to the requirements of an external (national or institutional) authority. In the latter case, it may be the absence of an assessment that would result in consequences for the institution rather than the assessment itself. The 'compliant' assessment would probably be characterized by ritualistic and symbolic behaviour. The purpose of the assessment would be 'to do the assessment'. There is quite a lot of such behaviour about in higher education these days!

The method or methods of assessment also have consequences. Classic notions of peer review embody the authority and the values of academic, usually subject, communities. They can be important ways in which that authority and independence are exercised and maintained and they can provide 'protection' against the intrusion of values and interests from outside the academy. However, it is also increasingly common to fnd a more 'managed' form of peer review where reviewers work to criteria and procedures which are set and managed from outside the peer group. In such cases, the peers receive 'training' and 'support' by quality professionals and become something of the 'hired help' of the assessment agency rather than the ultimate source of authority. It is also questionable how far assessment at anything other than the subject level can genuinely be regarded as 'peer review' if such review is assumed to imply a shared knowledge base and values.

Performance indicators can be neutral and independent of expert peers and hence are ofen regarded as managerial tools. However, peer-review processes, e.g. refereeing of publications or grant proposals, ofen lie beneath the metrics which produce the indicators. The interpretation and the credibility of performance indicators can also be dependent on their acceptance and endorsement by peer communities, which may be provided either cynically or enthusiastically.

Procedural compliance can occur as a feature of most forms of quality assessment, but it is probably most ofen found when the focus of the assessment is at the institutional level and where there is an external obligation to carry it out. It may also be linked to managerial forms of peer review, as discussed above. Thus codes of practice and guidelines are created and those undergoing the assessment must demonstrate that they are complying with them. The assessors will come and check or 'audit' whether practices conform to the codes and guidelines. While the notion of compliance carries with it rather negative connotations, it is of course perfectly defensible if the behaviours that compliance requires are desirable ones and benefcial in their outcomes.

Client feedback is frequently seen as part of increasingly consumerist and marketized trends in higher education. Students are transformed into 'customers'. Research has 'users' whose needs should be met. And academics fnd themselves attempting to prove that their activities are meeting the needs of a client or client group beyond the walls of higher education. These processes may themselves be largely compliant, i.e. the important thing is to demonstrate that the feedback has been collected rather than to do anything as a result of it. But they can also be used to promote market behaviour, as when the results of 'student satisfaction' surveys are published on websites in order to inform the decision-making of future generations of students (clients) on what and where to study.

Another element of the approach taken to quality assessment is whether it is holistic or segmented. In the latter, separate functions of teaching and research will be assessed separately and there may also be separate assessments of administrative. At five types of 'value' underpinning diferent kinds of quality assessment system. They can be regarded as providing diferent answers to the question of 'what is quality'?

The 'academic' type is the most traditional and is still pervasive in most forms of research assessment. The 'managerial' type tends to be associated with greater institutional autonomy. The 'pedagogic' type is associated with the professionalization of academic teaching, which is evident by increased amounts of staf training and monitoring. 'Relevance' draws attentions to societal expectations and the greater public expenditure associated with 'mass' higher education. 'Consumerism' comes with a growth in competitive behaviour and a faith in markets.

There is no very tight relationship between the methods used and the diferent criteria of quality. Methods of peer review, student surveys and performance indicators are commonly used across all types. But the way they are used may difer by type. Peer review under 'managerialist' types will tend to give less autonomy to the 'peers' than under 'academic' types. In the latter, the peers may be promoting their own interests and values. In the former, they are meant to be promoting someone else's, e.g. government or institutional management.

National, Institutional and Individual Perspectives

National purposes of quality assessment frequently refer to accountability for the use of public funds. There is certainly a belief within government and its agencies in England, for example, that higher education's share of the public fnances definitely requires the existence of evidence from evaluation and quality assessment that expenditure on higher education is put to good use. In more recent years, with neo-liberal ideologies emphasizing markets and consumer choice, it has become important that national quality assessment can support and justify diference and hierarchy. The benign justifcation for this is that it helps bring more funding into higher education. The critical view would be that the processes of quality assessment serve to distort and to damage the very things which they seek to assess. In some other national contexts, however, the job that quality assessment appears to do is to indicate membership of an international club.

Thus the countries of Central and Eastern Europe rapidly developed higher education quality systems and agencies as part of a much wider process of creating the public institutions thought to constitute the infrastructure of modern Western democracies. There, the important thing sometimes appeared to be the existence of these institutions rather than anything they actually did. This arrangement was rather compatible with the interests of academics whose top priority was generally to be 'lef alone'.

Other national objectives concerning quality assessment can be the production of more employable graduates, greater social equity, greater international competitiveness and so on. The nature of the objectives will afect the approaches to assessment and the potential threats and benefts to individual academics and institutions.

If we look at quality assessment from the institutional and individual perspectives, being 'lef alone' is frequently viewed as the preferred state of afairs. But reality ofen suggests otherwise. Quality assessment can sometimes be a source of scarce reputational capital, for both individuals and institutions. Where quality assessment ofers reputational prizes, few individuals or institutions are unwilling to compete for them. But the approach and the values of the particular quality assessment system are important in determining who is most 'at risk' or has most to gain (i.e. the rules of the game and the likely winners and losers). Where prizes are fnancial as well as reputational, the enthusiasm for the competition increases accordingly!

A peer-review approach which emphasizes research and curriculum content carries with it the most reputational prizes and risks for academics. The exercise of control over the assessment process, or at least an intimate knowledge of the 'rules of the game', is something to be valued in these circumstances. It may be a way that those who already possess considerable reputational capital, and hence have more to lose, can best hang on to it. By setting the criteria for quality and participating in the peer-review processes of its assessment, academics can best ensure that existing reputational hierarchies are reproduced.

Conversely, the interests of those who come out relatively badly from existing criteria and the values they embody have more to gain from changing those criteria and the overall approach to quality assessment. Criteria of employment relevance or customer satisfaction may result in diferent winners, but, unless the new criteria and methods are in tune with the values of the stakeholder groups, their potential for providing reputational gain may be limited.

Therefore for all parties some level of engagement with quality assessment may seem the wisest course of action. 'Join your local quality committee' may be strategically sensible advice, for both individual and institutional interests.

Diferent approaches to quality assessment empower (and threaten) diferent groups within institutions. Subject communities have the greatest control over peer-review subject-based assessments. Managers and administrators may feel their positions strengthened by quality arrangements that emphasize compliance with institutional codes of practice and procedures. Academics may regard such procedures as a nuisance, but are hardly threatened by them. Students may feel that neither have much of value to ofer them and governments may prefer the hard evidence of performance indicators.

It follows from all this that changes to quality assessment arrangements may subtly alter the balance of power, both within institutions, and between them and the organs of the state. And in so doing, they ofer some mechanism of steerage over the changes taking place in higher education.

Assessment and the Improvement of Quality

The absence of clear-cut evidence for these claims should not stop us from taking them seriously. There are a number of reasons to suppose that real benefts can accrue from assessment of quality.

First, there is the motivational argument. This assumes that without some form of monitoring and accountability, some academics will do little research and/or care little about their teaching. This is not just about threatening the lazy, but more of rewarding and recognizing the excellent. The threats and rewards inherent in quality assessment provide motivation for all, individually and collectively, to 'do better'. The downside to the motivational argument, however, is that quality assessment systems ofen reward the wrong things (the quantifable and the procedural) and have the efect of distorting academic work away from its intrinsic qualities. Moreover, the time spent on quality assessment procedures themselves is time no longer available for teaching and research. It has also been argued that the absence of trust that the motivational argument implies is itself damaging to relationships and behaviour within higher education. Nevertheless, the motivational efects of quality assessment using methods of performance indicators, student surveys and the like provide one of the arguments for using these particular methods.

Secondly, there is the information argument. Quality assessment can both identify and disseminate 'good practice'. By seeing what is working elsewhere, academics in their peer-review role can take new ideas 'back home' as well as to other institutions as part of the review process. Several national quality agencies also make explicit attempts to publicize good practice through the publication of reports, organization of conferences, etc. This is perhaps one of the stronger arguments in favour of peer-review processes, especially at subject level, and it is less clear how audit, performance indicators and surveys identify and spread information of 'what works' and, by extension, what does not. Thirdly, there is the argument that quality assessment can lead to improved relationships and more and better collaboration between academic staf. In particular, processes of self-assessment can bring a more collaborative approach to course design and teaching than would otherwise be found.

In research, a better knowledge of the interests and experiences of colleagues may stimulate collaboration and team working. It is argued that people can achieve more by working together than alone. Again, the counter-argument is that such potential benefts are too ofen undermined by the rules of the particular 'assessment game'. That even where people do, in fact, collaborate in order to 'get a good assessment result', this does not necessarily lead to improvements in either teaching or research. And, indeed, rather than improving relationships within the university, it can be argued that many forms of quality assessment work to undermine the trust that is essential to productive collaboration. Fourthly, there is the argument that, by simply disturbing the status quo, quality assessment can lead to change and innovation. There is some evidence in support of this, especially from the relatively early years of quality assessment when the processes of self-assessment did appear to lead to change and innovation in many places, but the difculty becomes how to maintain innovation if and when assessment becomes routinized and indeed professionalized. The sheer volume of assessment activity in some systems works against the achievement of its potential for innovation.

Fifhly, there is the argument that the 'threat' of external quality assessment can be utilized by managers within an institution to drive through changes that would not otherwise have been possible. This is really a variant of the anti-status-quo argument. The disturbance of existing ways of doing things, or at least the questioning of them, can be an opportunity for institutional leaders and managers to pursue their own agendas for change. In other words, quality assessment can be aligned with manage-rialism as a way of disturbing the conservatism and defensiveness of the academic profession. However, the extent to which such change agendas are genuinely 'improvements' to the quality of anything is likely to be a matter of judgement and values.

In their major review of the factors that afect what and how much students learn from their higher education, Ernie Pascarella and Patrick Terenzini accorded rather low importance to the efects of quality mechanisms. This is not to say that quality assessment has not done much good in disturbing existing and rather tired practices, through praising the good and admonishing the bad and in simply broadcasting the news that 'things can be diferent'. But it does suggest that precise measures of these changes still remain hard to come by. Nevertheless, the tools of quality assessment should rightly remain in the armoury of those committed to change and improvement in higher education.

Uses of Question Bank

The number of questions needed for a course/programme which runs for a number of years is likely to be very large in a distance education institution. Course team members, in open and distance learning system, therefore, might consider gradually introducing a system whereby they could develop questions, question types, and a number of different types of questions based on specific objectives. All the questions would be vetted by course team members for quality, then they would be indexed and banked. These questions when pooled in a bank, is called a question bank. Such banks allow a great deal of flexibility into assessment practices and distance teaching. For example, 'parallel' questions can be generated from the bank which would allow students who were ill for an examination or due to some urgent work remained absent to take up the examination later. The advantage of question bank is that questions which work out well in practice can be reused on a number of later situations. Thus, new questions do not have to be generated at the same rate from year to year and the quality of questions gradually improves.

The question bank is, thus, a planned library of test items pooled through co operative efforts under the aegis of an institution for the use of evaluators, academics and students in partial fulfillment of the requirements of the teaching learning process. It is, therefore, a systematic collection of a number of questions. The question bank is designed to fulfil certain pre determined purposes. Its efficient functioning demands co operative enterprise. Its clientele is specified depending upon the nature and scope of questions that constitute the bank. It is a utility service with an in built feedback mechanism for improvement of its questions.

Purpose of a Question Bank

A question bank can serve two purposes: i) to enrich the instructional aspect, and (ii) to judge the distance learners in terms of instructional efforts. On the instructional side, questions can be used by the teachers at the pre-testing stage for the development of a unit and for revision purpose. These questions can be used for self assessment questions (SAQ) as assignments and for term end examination. A pool of test questions can be used to frame a unit or a topic and to test for formative evaluation which is an integral part of distance teaching. Such a stock of questions can also be made use of in preparing question papers at the end of a term or a session for summative evaluation. Questions for mastery testing can be used for diagnosis of the student's difficulties while going through the learning material..

Keeping in view the place of evaluation in distance teaching, it is obvious that every teacher is supposed to prepare a larger number of quality questions on different topics of the prescribed course/programmes for various purposes. Because of lack of adequate know how and the limited time at his/her disposal, a teacher cannot be expected to develop a question pool of reasonable magnitude and quality. That is why preparation of quality questions in different subjects has to be entrusted to experienced teachers who are well conversant with the content and technique of framing questions. Under these conditions, it is necessary that a readymade stock of questions is built up and made available to teachers and testers. Such a pool of test materials can be of immense use if developed according to predetermined objectives.

Planning a Question Bank

In order to run a question bank efficiently it should be established after due planning. At this stage it is essential that the objectives of such a bank should be clearly visualised. The two major objectives can be:

a) To increase the value of measurement.

b) To increase the pedagogical value of evaluation.

Further details in terms of more specific objectives can be worked out by the institutions establishing the question bank.

Where should such a bank be located? To begin with, the Association of Indian Universities (AIU) has established question banks in various subjects. Apart from this, individual universities (state of central) can also have their own question banks. This, of course, would mainly depend on the materials received from the key institutions of the State, besides some materials developed in the institution itself.

Wherever the location of the bank may be, it should be managed properly to provide utility services to all those who are interested. For this, suitable place and equipment for storing, vetting or screening, sorting and classifying of questions are required. For efficient maintaining and up keep, subject wise assistance has to be arranged under the overall guidance of an academic manager who directs the activities of the question bank.

Development of Question Bank

What type of questions make up the bank depends entirely on the total framework of reference envisaged at the planning stage whether only the written examination questions, oral examination questions, practical exam questions or the questions of all three are to be kept in mind for developing the question bank. This development will involve the following guidance.

Blue Printing for Developing Question Bank: The blue print in question bank may be thought of as a two dimensional grid:

i) the behaviour/objective aspect; and

ii) the content/subject area aspect.

The objective aspect refers to the expected learning out comes in terms of abilities like recall, recognition, translation, extrapolation, application, analysis, synthesis, evaluation and any other abilities. The content aspect connotes the unit, sub unit of topic through the medium of which the above mentioned abilities are developed or tested. A good question pool will be one that contains questions on all the topics in a subject testing all abilities. A mere collection of a large number of questions will not constitute a question pool of quality, unless all such items fit into a pre determined structure. A sample of blue print for developing a question bank is given below. Before going through the blue print kindly perform these two activities given below.

In accordance with the blue print, questions are written or collected from various sources as under:

- Ready made questions may be collected from old question papers set in various examinations, from standardised tests and some from the review exercise of good text books. Such questions may need pruning from the point of view of their format before they are accepted as such.
- In the case of new questions, these may be invited from experienced teachers, examiners and paper setters. Such questions should, invariably, be accompanied by a key and outline answers, besides indicating the objective and the content area.
- Apart from the above techniques, it is still better to get the questions prepared by practicing teachers, invited to a workshop for the purpose. Such questions should be prepared by the participating teachers in their area of excellence and discussed in details before finding a place in the bank.
- Help of sister agencies may also be sought in enriching the bank as well as expertise.

Screening of Questions

After the questions are written, the question sheets are passed onto other members of the group for their comments. Though it is a time consuming process, it is educationally more potent and pedagogically sound. Not only the quality of questions improve but it also provides good training to the participants for framing good questions.

The second level screening may be done with the help of a group of three subject experts, all conversant with the technique of test construction. Such a group may consists of subject specialists who are in a better position to pass judgement on the authenticity of the subject matter. A teacher who has the experience of teaching that particular class for which the question is written, should also be associated. S/he is in a better position to judge the suitability of the question for a particular grade level. The third person may be an evaluation expert who can help in improving the format of the question in the light of the objectives to be tested. Further refinement is possible only after try out of the question. One of the main purpose in trying out of the question is to obtain valid, reliable and useful information about a question. This involves determining what is to be measured and then defining it in such precise terms that test items can be framed that call forth the desired performance. It also involves specifying the achievement domain in such a manner that the sample of test tasks will be representative of the total domain of achievement tasks and that the results will be appropriate for the intended instructional uses.

The possibility of preparing valid, reliable and useful questions is greatly enhanced if a few basic steps are followed. They are:

- Determining the purpose of testing
- Developing the test specifications
- Selecting appropriate questions
- Preparing relevant questions
- Assembling the test
- Using the results

There are certain factors which influence the validity, usability and reliability of test items. These factors are:

- Clear instructions to respond to the questions
- Sentence structure of a question

Test items appropriate for the outcomes being measured.

- Ease of scoring
- Ease of interpretation and application
- Cost of developing items.

Nevertheless, the questions are now ready for transfer to question cards for proper record.

Preparing The Question Cards

The finalised questions may now be transferred to cards made of thick chart paper cut into a post card size. Cards with different colours may be used for different objectives. For example, we may use the following colour scheme in preparing cards for different objectives and various forms of questions:

Objectives Form of Question/	*Knowledge*	*Comprehension*	*Application*	*Skill*
1. Essay type	Dark Yellow	Dark Green	Dark Pink	Dark Blue
2. Short answer type	Yellow	Green	Pink	Blue
3. Objective type	Light yellow	Light Green	Light Pink	Light Blue

In case we are interested in having one colour, we may use white for all cards with top margin of about one inch coloured strip on the same pattern. Such a colour scheme facilitates the identification and sorting of questions arranged in cabinets. Each card will carry the question data on it. A sample question card is given below:

Question Card (Front Side) Obverse

Objective........	Topic... Form...	Estimated difficulty level....S.No...
Specification:	Sub topic....	Org level..... Estimated time... Code No.
Questions:		

Question Card (Back Side) Reverse

Class for which suitable....... Date of accession ...... Date of try out
Difficulty level .... Discrimination value..... Place of try out
Key/outline answer:

Estimated difficulty level may be indicated on a three point scale, e.g., A for difficult, B for average and C for easy. The actual difficulty value can be calculated only after the try out of the questions and, therefore, may be entered after the try out.

Coding of Questions

After the cards are prepared, they are to be coded and classified in a manner that facilitates their use. This is necessary for quick location and sorting of cards just like books in a library. It is also advised that a system like that of Dewey's Decimal System of cataloguing the books is followed here to handle thousands of cards containing the questions.

Filing and Storage of Questions

A drawer/almirah/file cabinet with four or five cabinets each may be procured to hold the cards. It is easier to get the question cards typed as and when these are finalised. In case of unit tests and question papers, the questions may be typed on sheets of paper or even cyclostyled when more copies are needed for circulation. When a pool of unit tests full of question papers, diagnostic tests, standardised tests etc. are to be stored, almirahs of desired specifications may be procured to file such test materials. All question cards and other materials may be stored in duplicate so that one copy of that may be issued to the users as and when required. Original copy may be kept intact for official use and reference. Computer facilities are the latest additions to these aspects.

Using the Question Bank

When a sufficient number of questions, unit tests and question papers are ready in the pool, these can be used for the following purposes:

- A judicious selection of questions can be made for instructional purpose. Different types of questions selected from a question bank may be used for pre testing, development, review and revision of a lesson.
- In the preparation of textual material a question pool can be utilised for preparing review exercises in text books. Of course, the caps are to be filled in by the authors. Likewise, the preparation of teaching units or resource units also involve the use of evaluation materials which may be picked up from the question bank.
- For evaluating pupils' progress the question bank can be used most efficiently. Individual questions can be stored and grouped for use in topic or unit testing in periodical test. Individual questions, unit tests and question papers can be profitably used by the examining agencies by making the question bank available to their paper setters.
- When question banks are established in institutions, students can use them for self evaluation in their spare time. As an outline answer or key is provided in such questions, students can check their response against such keys and answers, especially in case of short answer and objective type questions. When questions on all topics of the prescribed syllabus are available pupils can revise their lessons. Even teachers can make use of such cards for quick revision. Like quiz cards, these cards can be used for an inter section/class competition by apportioning a particular subject area for students to learn through healthy competition.

A question bank may become a store of outdated material after some years, if not evaluated at regular intervals. At least once in three years, the question pool must be screened to discard the obsolete questions. Dead wood, therefore, must be continually removed and new material added. Curricular changes also put new demands from time to time. Enrichment of questions by updating, replacing, discarding, modifying, adding new questions, regrouping and classification is to be an ongoing process to give the question bank a dynamic look.

References

Fulton, O. (2003) Managerialism in UK universities: unstable hybridity and the complications of implementation. In *The Higher Education Revolution?* (Amaral, A., Meek, V.L. and Larsen, I.M., eds), pp. 155–178, Kluwer Academic Publishers, Dordrecht

Hulpiau, V., Masschelein, E., Van der Stockt, L., Verhesschen, P. and Waeytens, K. (2005) *A system of student feedback: considerations of academic staf taken into account*, 27th Annual EAIR Forum, Riga, Latvia, 28–31 August 2005

Dynan, M.B. and Cliford, R.J. (2001) Eight years on: implementation of quality management in an Australian university. *Assessment and Evaluation in Higher Education* 26(5), 503–515

van den Berg, R., Vandenberghe, R. and Sleegers, P. (1999) Management of innovation from a cultural-individual perspective. *School Efectiveness and School Improvement* 10(3), 321–351.

5

Quality Assessment

Compared with most of the many international meetings that have been held recently in the field of quality assurance, the Pavia conference "Quality Assessment in Institutions of Higher Education in Europe: Problems, Practices and Solutions" was original in several ways: it focused on quality assessment instead of generally referring to quality assurance; it covered both teaching and learning, and research assessments, which are usually addressed separately; and, being organized by the Academia Europaea, it was not driven by the political or corporate interests of governments, quality assurance agencies or HEIs (higher education institutions). The European dimension was well served by the attendance: 21 European countries were represented, with on average one or two participants per country (with, naturally, many more from Italy, the host country). Among organizers, chairs and speakers, Western European countries were predominant, and some emphasis was given to the Dutch, Flemish and British cases, since, in these countries, evaluations have become large-scale standard procedures, while they are hardly adopted in other European countries. Yet, from one country to another, even when the same words are used (assessment, evaluation, review, validation, accreditation, etc.), external quality assurance schemes, as well as their level of development, are rather diferent, and, moreover, they all change regularly and rapidly. Thus a certain degree of 'confusion' is present.

In the discussions, as well as in the preceding presentations, more or less all forms of assessment were referred to: assessment of learning and research programmes, of institutions (centres, institutes, departments or universities) and of individual academics and researchers, and of assessment systems themselves, serving to highlight both the complexity and instability of the present situation.

Selected some issues that to us seem to be perceived as the most crucial by conference participants, in both their presentations and their debate reactions, to ofer a state-of-the-art overview of quality assessment in higher education. This refection tries also to ofer some theoretical interpretation of the selected phenomena and issues, because we think that such interpretations are still implicit. As El Khawas noted, "despite a large volume of published work on quality assurance, the development of theory has fallen behind"; she also underscores that most analysis is policy-directed and thus has an evaluative, normative and prescriptive stance and aim, rather than an interpretative one.

Institutionalization: Processes, Actors and Degree Achieved

During 1980–1990, the word 'quality' and its related concepts, tools and goals, gained more and more prominence and difusion in almost all sectors of organized social life. It is embedded in the reductionist anthropology linked to market ideology and rhetoric with its view of social networks in terms of client–supplier relationship, where the former has interests, demands and needs that the latter must fulfl and satisfy at best. The reductionist view, in the end, is a general model of social actors and social relationships basically grounded on an instrumental and materialistic view.

Reform processes of the last 20 years in education and especially in higher education are triggered, inspired and based on such rhetoric and tools. In the first instance, higher education reforms have been embedded in the national contexts and their primary goals are to restructure both systems and institutions on the basis of larger autonomy from the State to achieve a greater efciency as well as cost savings. This restructuring entails that the higher education sector and institutions are reorganized as a quasi-market in which operate quasi-enter-prises, witnessing a thrust toward entrepreneurali-zation and competition. Autonomy of systems and institutions had to be balanced with their accountability towards the State and society at large. This need was generally deemed to be achieved by means of evaluation, quality assessment, quality assurance and, more recently, by accreditation schemes.

Thus quality assessment in the higher education sector is deemed to be useful to stimulate, attain and increase systems' and institutions' efectiveness, efciency, cost savings, quality and transparency towards users/clients/stakeholders interested and involved in it.

In the last few years, quality assessment and assurance have gained, especially in the EU (European Union) on the wave of the Bologna Process, a supranational dimension, legitimization and thrust. But similar processes seem to characterize regions other than Europe.

One of the main themes emerging from both the literature on quality in higher education and from the contributions collected in this book, is that quality is a product of a wide social process that can be conceived of as a process of structuration of an organizational field, where a plurality of institutional and collective actors are playing some roles in this process. The concept of an 'organizational field' refers to a set of heterogeneous organizations that in aggregate constitute an area of institutional life: suppliers, clients, regulatory agencies, stakeholders and other organizations providing similar, or the same, products or services. Thus this concept draws attention to the totality of relevant actors operating in the field with diferent degrees of mutual interconnect-edness. Given these characteristics, the boundaries of an organizational field cannot be conceived of in geographical terms, but in functional ones: its units are functionally interrelated, even though they may be geographically remote. Thus an organizational field is a delocalized institutional area. 'Structuration' is a concept drawn from Giddens used to account for the process of institutional elaboration, building and definition of an organizational field.

Between the 1980s and the 1990s, quality entered the higher education sector on the wave of State restructuring linked to market and New Public Management ideologies. In this first phase, the process was mainly nation-based, albeit that supranational institutional actors such as OECD (Organisation for Economic Co-operation and Development), World Bank and IMF (International Monetary Fund) played a relevant role in the elaboration, definition difusion and legitimization of the new institutional patterns. In particular, OECD was very active in legitimizing, supporting and stimulating reforms in the education sector and especially in the higher education one, incorporating the new rhetoric of enterprise and its contents, of which quality is part. In the late 1990s in European higher education reforms, thrust stemmed from the supranational level of the EU through the so-called Bologna Process, while, in general respects, the action of the international agencies cited above was growing, and, more recently, they have been joined by WTO (World Trade Organization) and GATS (General Agreement on Trade in Services). Higher education has thus entered an international dimension, where national governments and HEIs are more and more infuenced by, pressed by and, to some extent, dependent on this wider dimension. Higher education policy-making, as well as higher education activities, are no longer an 'internal afair' of individual national governments or institutions.

As an integral part of these internationalization and structuration processes, the issue of quality in higher education has grown in importance and elaboration, up to confguring itself as an international subfield of activity. As El Khawas has underscored, individual national quality evaluation and assurance programmes are to be complemented by international understandings and recognition, as a part of internationalization of higher education. The most manifest clue is the construction of international organized network ties among quality assurance and assessment agencies such as INQAAHE (International Network of Quality Assurance Agencies in Higher Education), gathering 80 agencies in over 50 countries; ENQA (European Network for Quality Assurance), with 36 organizations and 30 government members; EAU (European University Association), whose task is measuring the quality of international programmes and strategies of institutions; and ASEAN (Association of South East Asian Nations) programmes for quality evaluation of university education. Moreover, OECD, the European Commission and the EAU have launched and sponsored several international projects in quality assurance, assessment and institutional review. Finally, academic journals of higher education studies and research have dedicated monograph issues to higher education quality, and, since 1995, there is also a journal devoted to this theme, *Quality in Higher Education.*

On the whole, these networks, projects, publishing initiatives and the individual national policies in quality are creating a new infrastructure for quality in higher education. In other words, there is an ongoing structuring process of the organizational field of quality in higher education at both a national and an international level. As a result, while in the 1980s no industrialized country had a higher education quality assessment system and policy and almost none had any kind of accreditation scheme, in 2003 almost all have both, yet still with some diferences in their scope, arrangements and practices.

Regarding the consequences and the likely outcomes of the field's structuration process, it is possible to highlight three aspects. First, concerning institution building and the interorganizational relationship dynamics, it is possible to highlight the four aspects that follow.

1. *Increase of interactions among unities in the field.* There is a growing number of organizations participating in the quality assessment and assurance field and, above all, a growing interconnectedness and relationships among them: individual institutions, national governments and quality agencies, supranational agencies, authorities and networked organizations.
2. *Emergence of structures of dominance and patterns of coalition.* As El Khawas underscores, quality assessment has produced, or is producing, asymmetric relationships among governments, quality agencies and HEIs, even in countries where the higher education sector is dominated by universities with strong academic traditional values. Governments play a role of prominence in both quality agencies, since they have to be authorized and legitimized, and institutions, since they have to be evaluated by governments via quality agencies. Besides, quality agencies play the dominant role in the relationship with HEIs, since the latter cannot negotiate, contradict or renege on the agencies' evaluations and recommendations, because of government's legitimization of the agencies and their role. In Europe, this structure of dominance could gain a supranational dimension through the role played by the EU in building the common space of higher education and research in connection with ENQA and EAU, pressing national governments to incorporate the European frameworks for quality in higher education and to impose them via policy-making to respective higher education systems and institutions. EU, ENQA and EAU, on the whole, also represent the coalition supporting and difusing quality assessment in higher education.
3. *Increase of information circulating in the field.* All of the collective actors are engaged in eforts both to disseminate information about quality schemes, procedures, methods and practices, and to deal with all the information in order to structure and pursue quality arrangements

and requirements. In particular, the main organizations afected by the information load about quality are governments and individual institutions, in their eforts to elaborate policies, structures and practice in quality assessment and assurance. Besides, the dissemination of information, at least in the academic field, is also supported by journals whose articles provide examples, templates, theories and critical as well as supporting insights.

4. *Awareness of being involved in a common enterprise*. The most manifest indicator of such an awareness is the growing process of network-building, spreading to the international dimension. HEIs are also more and more concerned with quality in the context of their growing internationalization: being involved in quality movement, incorporating quality assurance structures and being assessed means for them the possibility to attract funds, students and researchers, to gain social prestige and legitimization, and to compete efectively for them in the international and national higher education marketplace.

Secondly, although, at present, there is still a rather high degree of heterogeneity in quality assessment schemes, the processes analysed are likely to produce, at least in the long run, a process of isomorphic convergence in higher education systems with regard to quality assessment and assurance. The role of supranational and international networked agencies for quality are the primary actors in the elaboration of similar, if not common, schemes for quality, as well as the primary source of difusion acting as normative carriers of them. These outcomes are more likely to occur if we consider that higher education is getting more and more embedded in an international dimension and competition, and this could trigger a growing need for similar (or common) comparable quality schemes, evaluation practice and parameters to use as comparative benchmarks for institutions as a whole, their study programmes and research capabilities. It is worth noting, in the EU context, that the European Commission in 2004 presented a proposal regarding accreditation for a recommendation about it to both the European Council and Parliament. The proposal is intended to create a supranational agency for the accreditation and recognition of the national and international, public and private accreditation agencies operating in the EU. If it will be pursued and achieved, this means a more homogeneous structure and thus a convergence at least in the accreditation criteria and activities.

Thirdly, it is possible to make a first appraisal of the institutionalization of quality assessment and assurance at the present stage, using the interpretative framework of the institutionalization process elaborated by Tolbert and Zucker:

1. *Habitualization.* A pre-institutionalization stage where there are relatively few adopters and, moreover, a greater variability in the way the innovation is adopted and implemented.
2. *Objectifcation.* The innovation starts difusing through organizations in the field by imitation and normative processes (but also coercive ones triggered by State). At this stage, there is also a high degree of theorizing about the innovation and its evaluation in term of positive outcomes that it produces or could produce. As theory develops and becomes more precise, the variance in the innovation's implementation declines. This stage is labelled semi-institutionalization.
3. *Sedimentation.* It refers to the full institution-alization of the innovation, when it is taken for granted and reproduced by actors in the field. Sedimentation could be undermined by opposition by a set of actors who are adversely afected by the innovation and able to mobilize against it, or by the lack of evidence that innovation actually works efectively, bringing positive results to organizations.

By the reconstruction made so far, we can say that quality assessment is achieved at the second stage of institutionalization, albeit with some clarifcation needed.

First, 'supportive' theorizing about quality assessment is getting more precise in relation to its necessity as a governance tool, while there is still a certain degree of variance in contents, procedures and arrangements of the practice. This is refected by the heterogeneity of national quality assessment schemes and structures, which are in turn explained by the diferent historical and institutional trajectories of structuring national higher education systems. As two examples, derived from a European context and constituting two opposite extremes, we can use Italy and The Netherlands. The former has only recently reformed higher education, and, moreover, its structure of governance, evaluation, quality assessment and accreditation are still at their first stages of development and their tools, practices, scope and purposes are still under debate and elaboration. The latter had started structural reforms and had introduced the issue of quality and its evaluation almost

20 years ago. In The Netherlands, quality assessment is in a very advanced stage of structuration and institutionali-zation.

Secondly, and more generally, beside supportive theorizing, there are also critical concerns, fears, resistance and vested interests' defences towards quality assessment practice enacted by academics, which can be labelled as 'critical' theorizing or counter-theorizing. To this second kind of theorizing, we must add scholars whose research and refections on quality assessment (like those in this book) highlight the unintended outcomes, more or less perverse efects, rhetorical and ceremonial uses, contradictions, ambiguous outcomes, interpretative translations, domestications in the implementation and in the concrete practices of quality assessment.

Practising Quality Assessment: Problems and Difficulties

The presence of heterogeneity of quality policies, schemes and their diferent degree of structuration in the various national contexts, the semi-institutionalization of quality assessment that exposes it to a certain degree of contention and, above all, the emphasis placed on systems' and institutions' accountability give rise to some problems, tensions and contradictions in the practice of quality assessment.

In particular, accountability produces some contradictions and hindrances in relation to institutional autonomy and quality improvement processes, since it appears as a new mechanism of control, replacing centralized regulative and bureaucratic arrangements, over systems, institutions and academics with which they have to comply. OECD explicitly recognized these aspects, stating that "Government is generally withdrawing from direct management of institutions, yet at the same time introducing *new form of control* and infuence based mainly on *holding institutions accountable* for performance via powerful enforcement mechanisms including funding and *quality recognition*". This shif from improvement to control through accountability exerted by the State was highlighted a decade ago by Trow who underscored that, under the new institutional conditions, there is a process of growing distrust towards academia and this distrust is tightly coupled with accountability.

It shows how the introduction of accreditation in Flemish Belgium and The Netherlands, although it was presented as merely the addition of a formal decision to the previous systems, actually initiated a thorough change: the ownership of quality assurance shifed from the institutions to the State, and the improvement dimension almost vanished. But self-evaluation, peer review and academic standards of quality linked to them are tendentially at odds with the need of the State to make academia accountable in order to allocate fnancial resources efectively, to pursue cost savings and to ensure that an institution will operate in the way it wants them to operate. In other words, there is a contradiction between two deeply diferent conceptions and logic of quality assessment.

1. The professional-based quality of academia, is grounded on standards elaborated by the academic community as a professional body, sharing a number of core assumptions and values about quality, its assurance and assessment, and deals with intrinsic, substantial and normative aspects of quality. Thus the only competent and responsible body to evaluate quality in activities, work and 'products' of individual academics and institutions is the academic community itself.
2. The new quality framework that combines extrinsic and formal aspects of quality (i.e. formal requirements, as in the bureaucratic model), intrinsic aspects (i.e. how systems, institutions and academics work, what they do and what kind of results they produce), with a prominence of the former, and above all substantial and normative aspects defined and imposed externally from academia (i.e. how systems, institutions and academics should work, what they should do and what results they are expected to produce), which are elaborated, defined and imposed externally to systems, institutions and academics.

The contradiction and tension produced by these opposite kinds of quality assessment conception and logic have a practical backlash: from the point of view of an institution, how to use an external agenda in such a way that it is internally benefcial? Moreover, the term 'improvement' itself, its content, goals and pursuing are contended on the grounds of the two diferent conceptions of quality and quality assessment. But there are other problems linked to that tension.

Since quality assessment is based on external evaluation of performance indicators, it is paralleled by an increasing reduction of the role and of the power of academics to define quality standards of their activities and to evaluate them. Furthermore, since quality assessment is based on quantitative parameters and indicators, it is perceived, represented and lived by academics as a bureaucratic procedure. One must note that it is also the way by which these quantitative parameters are conceived and the practices nested in that conception that make quality assessment resemble more a bureaucratic scheme with which institutions have to comply.

Finally, the emphasis on the quantitative side of indicators and parameters with which to evaluate institutional and individual performances obscures and neglects the qualitative side. This is manifest in criteria such as the number of graduates 'produced', the ratio between teachers and students, the amount of published research and the use of citation index scoring as an indicator of quality in research. As these examples show, the qualitative side of quality is largely, if not completely, lef out. Those quantitative indicators do not say anything about the quality of graduated students, or the quality of teachers and their teaching, or about the quality of research. Although quantitative criteria are useful and necessary as an 'objective' basis, or premise, for evaluation, yet they also seem not to be sufcient, and, above all, they could generate contradicting decisions such as in the case of Imperial College, which got the best results along with Cambridge, but decided to close down the departments with little research, although they were necessary for teaching and learning purposes; or as in the case of citation index parameters, as highlighted by Blockmans, which penalize research in non-English languages and in some disciplinary fields such as humanities and also in mathematics.

So far, we have highlighted some problems, contradictions and their consequences related to quality assessment practice. One could wonder whether these critical aspects are intrinsic to quality assessment schemes and practices, or are the product of social relationships that shape, or try to shape, quality assessment in a certain way. The second is the answer, to the extent that those problems are the refection of some conficting cleavages involving diferent actors, with their interests, dispositions and definitions, operating in the quality assessment field.

Logic of Quality Assessment

The organizational field is not only a social environment that exerts pressure on organizations, but is also a social space where individual and collective actors occupy diferent positions in it and thus are characterized by diferent dispositions, interests and power that could be and actually are in confict. This conception of the organizational field as a field of struggle is derived from work by Bourdieu and it was used by DiMaggio to account for the emergence of a diferent definition of art and its social use in the art museum field.

Quality assessment in higher education is not an exception. In the previous sections, we have seen that: (i) it is at the semi-institutionalization stage and thus it is, to some extent, an ambiguous and contended concept, hence it may have diferent meanings for diferent actors; (ii) consequently, its purposes, scope, tools and uses may be thought of and conceived of diferently in relationships of diferent interests and contexts; and (iii) fnally, it is a contended and contentious terrain where diferent actors, with diferent positions, interests and power, struggle to shape the form, the scope and functions of quality assessment. In other words, the stake is what kind of quality assessment is to be institutionalized. Tus, from this point of view, what are defined as *problems* in quality assessment actually are the refections of diferent definitions of its meanings, contents and purposes that diferent actors with diferent positions, dispositions and interests carry in the field. Hence, 'problems' are not only a matter of difculties in translating principles such as quality assurance and assessment in higher education, or that quality is a concept which has uses, meanings and purposes that are contingent to contexts, people and time. Surely they are, but it is also a matter of social definitions and of struggles for them.

There are several relational dimensions that structure this confict arena and the positions of actors inside it that could be conceived as lines of cleavage crossing the field. We number some of the most manifest which are also present:

1. State–higher education relationships
2. Society–higher education relationships
3. Academics–institution relationships
4. Interdisciplinary relationships

The first two identify external cleavage, and the second two identify internal ones.

Starting from State–higher education relationships, which is probably the most important structural relationship concerning quality assessment, we can fnd two main cleavage and tension lines. First, the policy of autonomy is awarding wider degrees of freedom to HEIs, but, at the same time, this freedom has not to be too wide, otherwise institution could pursue their own (private) interests in their own (self-established) ways, in spite of public interests and policies. Quality assessment is one of the most important control and steering tools in the hand of the State in order to secure that institutions will operate in the way in which it wants them to operate. Accountability replaced bureaucratic controls, performance evaluation replaced the conformity-to-rules principle and economic sanctions replaced the administrative ones. But the basic purpose still remains the control of the institutions. In this perspective, it becomes manifest the sense of loss of autonomy is sufered by academics and institutions, upon which they then enact responses characterized by manifest and latent strategies of resistance, aimed at weakening the impact of quality assessment on them. For example, the enactment of ceremonial, cosmetic and formal compliance behaviours is to be viewed more as a resistance and decoupling strategy than a consequence of the intrinsic property of the quality assessment procedures, or at least as a strategic use of its bureaucratic features as a resource to decouple quality from daily activities and to regain some room of autonomy. Concerning that, to some extent, the bureaucratic drif of quality assessment could be explained as an outcome of such defensive responses of institutions and academics.

Secondly, since quality assessment is based on performance indicators, the balance between intrinsic and extrinsic dimensions of quality is shifing more and more towards the latter. That means that performance evaluation cannot be pursued only by the academic community through a peer review mechanism. Intrinsic and extrinsic dimensions of quality not only relate to improvement and accountability respectively, as noted, but also to whom is in charge to evaluate it. The growing importance of external evaluation is paralleled by an increasing reduction of the role and of the power of academics to define quality standards of their activities and to evaluate them. Furthermore, since quality assessment is based on quantitative parameters and indicators, it is perceived, represented and lived by academics as a bureaucratic procedure, and thus they enact behaviours contradictory with such, as a demonstration. Again, the bureaucratic drif of quality assessment could be seen as linked to academics' perceptions and behaviour.

As far as higher education and society relationships are concerned, their dynamics are far more complex, given the heterogeneity of actors and interests involved, and this has a direct impact on quality definition, its ends and the tools to evaluate it. For example, on the one hand, students and families are interested in the quality of study courses and of teaching, since they consider higher education to be an investment that they undertake for their future cultural and, above all, economic gains. On the other hand, economic actors are interested in the quality of formative supply and didactic and applied research, because all of them are linked to the competitive advantages, in terms of a highly skilled labour force and innovative knowledge that they are expected to produce for enterprise. In brief, both students and economic actors bring mainly an instrumental conception of quality which should be evaluated on the basis of outcomes and gains that HEIs are able to generate. HEIs are not indiferent to such problems, but they have diferent conceptions. First of all, the quality of education and research that they provide cannot be assessed solely in instrumental terms. It is also highlighted that outcome evaluation cannot be assessed in a short time span, but requires a long-term perspective both for the graduates' working careers and scientifc knowledge-generated gains for industry and society at large. Secondly, societal actors are not deemed to be able to define and to assess what 'good' teaching or research is, since their quality is embedded in the professional knowledge, practices and standards institutionalized in the academic field. The tension here is between laypersons' conceptions of quality and the ones held by competent professionals, who perceive the external demands for quality as an undue interference. Thirdly, and linked to the previous point, there is a strong divergence (at some times manifest, at others implicit) on the definition of education, research and knowledge ends, that opposes instrumental and interested perspective to the expressive, curiosity-driven and non-interested (or knowledge for its own sake) one. All this produces tensions and sometimes confict between society and higher education. One of the most manifest clues is, on the one hand, resistance and manipulative strategies of institutions and academics to reduce the risks to be co-opted by the societal environment and, on the other, the growing eforts of societal actors to infuence and induce institutions and academics to be responsive to their needs and interests, basing their strategies on the growing economic power that they have on higher education. The balance between these two opposing views and behaviours is very difcult and, for higher education, it is ofen represented as a hard trade-of between conserving their autonomy, but at the cost of their social irrelevance, and following the market, but at the cost of losing their autonomy.

Coming to the internal lines of cleavage, the first one is related to academics–institution relationships. In systems where the institutional leadership, in managerial terms, the policies for quality and the entrepreneurial model are developed to a relevant degree, the relationship between academics and institutions are characterized by a tendential divergence in the way institutions are managed. Institutional leaders are pressed by State policies and societal demands to make their institutions responsive to them, to demonstrate that the institutions that they lead are responding to quality imperatives, or at least that they are working in such a direction. This is due both to legitimacy and social support concerns and to raising and securing the economic resources for their institutions. In this framework, institutional leaders are pressed to adopt an extrinsic and instrumental view on quality assessment and thus to enact institutional evaluation policies and tools consistent with that view. This ofen clashes against the academic community's values, by which the necessity of such institutional policies, what those policies are aimed at measuring and evaluating and, above all, how they do that are contended. In short, the tension is between a managerial view of quality assessment and a 'corporate' one expressed by academics. What is explicitly or implicitly assumed in academics' view of institutional quality assessment is, again, that their autonomy is under attack. Thus defensive and resistance strategies are enacted by academics against this 'institutional aggression' and, at the same time, they struggle to demonstrate and highlight the inconsistency of quality assessment tools, procedures and goals with the nature of their work. Moreover, there are two kinds of critical and complaining remarks on the academics' side. The first concerns their feeling to be overassessed; the second is that quality assessment activities are a further burden encumbering on their already overburdened work. These two kinds of overload again trigger defensive and resistance strategies in the professorate.

The last internal cleavage is related to interdisciplinary relationships. Disciplines could be conceived as specialized subsystems of the more general academic profession system. Thus they are very diferent not only in the research objective, methods and epistemology, but also in the standards that each of them sets as definition of appropriate scientifc work. In other words, disciplines are structured around diferent assumptions, conceptions and norms defining how research and teaching activities are to be carried out and what purposes they aim towards. As an example, Becher has highlighted ideal-typically these diferences among disciplines structured by two dualistic couples: hard–sof sciences and pure–applied sciences.

These diferences cannot but be refected in diferent assumptions and conceptions of what quality assessment is or should be. For example, quality standards in the humanities are rather diferent from those in hard science fields and the same holds for diferences that we can fnd in applied disciplines compared with pure ones. It is manifest that some disciplines react negatively to attempts to provide and use homogenous and homogenizing quality assessment standards and procedures in spite of their peculiarities, because such attempts menace their territories and their jurisdiction on them and thus their control over the definition of quality criteria. Quality parameters such as the citation index, borrowed from hard science fields and generalized as a quality assessment tool for all disciplines, could work well for sciences, quite well for some social sciences (such as economics and, to a lesser extent, sociology and psychology), and quite badly for humanities and social sciences such as law. This means that, in some disciplinary fields, the citation index criteria for quality assessment are perceived as something extraneous, improperly imposed and as an expression of hard science's 'imperialism' in those fields. Furthermore, there is also a perceived risk by some disciplines, linked to such a kind of assessment, of being marginalized both in their cultural importance and in their possibility of gaining access to research funds. Finally, the citation index has at least two more 'structural' biases. First, it only considers publications in the English language and not those written in other languages. This drives to underestimate a high portion of the production of research published in national languages and in non-Anglo-Saxon national contexts. But this is also linked to a discipline's characteristics, since some of them (think again to the humanities) are not suited, for the knowledge objects with which they deal, to have a relevance for the international academic audience and debate and thus to be published in English. Secondly, the citation index is a quantitative measurement scoring the number of citations an author's publication receives. In this kind of measure, there is an unrecognized short-circuit between quantity and quality, i.e. the more a work is cited, the higher its quality. Obviously, this correlation is wrong, since a work could be higly cited in a critical sense, to demonstrate its inconsistencies and fallacies, or also just as a ceremonial homage without any theoretical and heuristic repercussion.

A Balance and some Perspectives

Two main aspects of quality assessment in higher education can be highlighted: first, its growing degree of institutionalization as a part of the restructuring and governing of higher education systems; secondly, its contended and disputed features that undermine its legitimacy and then its fully fedged institutionalization. As noted above, this tension is typical of the semi-institutionalization stage of an innovation where it is, at the same time, difused and debated, practised and questioned. From this tension, I draw some remarks or, playing on words, assess quality assessment.

The first remarks concern the necessity of quality assessment in higher education. In the current landscape characterized by the mass (if not universal) access to higher education, the changes in economic sector and in the labour market demands the rationalization of public expenditure and the growing internationalization of higher education, it is manifest that quality assessment based on peer review is no longer an appropriate mechanism. Given its self-referring nature and its tendential closure towards societal demands, it cannot but reproduce a detachment of higher education from society and its developments. Society and, above all, higher education systems and institutions cannot aford to run this risk. Quality assessment is therefore an important leverage to stimulate HEIs to pay attention to the social environment dynamics and changes. On the other hand, it is also legitimate that the State and society at large, since they both contribute economically to and are interested in higher education, have the right to ask HEIs to be accountable for what they are doing and how they are doing it.

Considered in this perspective, many, if not all, would agree with quality assessment. But there is also the other side of the coin. Quality assessment cannot be just another word for control and another tool to centralize the governance, reducing both the institutional and academic autonomy. Many of the complaints of academics and institutional leaders about quality assessment are not simply the reaction of traditional, conservative and corporate attitudes in and of the higher education sector. Many of the critics are as entitled as the States and 'clients' to call for accountability. The problem is to balance properly autonomy and accountability; currently, there is an imbalance toward accountability as control. The fact that quality assessment arrangements and tools are, for the most part, currently used as a controlling mechanism by the State and as reporting procedures by institutions instead of as an evaluation mechanism to improve them, is the most manifest clue of this imbalance. This is the grounds for the ofen noticed drif toward ceremonial, window-dressing, cosmetic and compliance behaviour, detached from and without any practical consequences for improvement.

This last point brings us to some remarks on how quality assessment frameworks are structured and operate concretely. There is nothing to contest about this measure that is undoubtedly important, but does it tell us anything about the *quality* of the publications? Another example from the teaching side: questionnaires ask students about their satisfaction, utility, difculties and so on, regarding a course that they attended. Ofen the answers printed on the questionnaire are organized as a numerical scale grading the satisfaction, utility, etc.; if they are not organized on numerical scoring, they are structured in a way that they can be converted into numerical values and treated as such. At the end, we have a quantitative measure of the course which is important but not complete. How can a student tell if the course was useful for him/her? Maybe it was not at the time of the survey, but it could be 1 year later or at the end of his/her studies or when he/she enters the labour market. Thus is the *quality* of that course good or not? Even more importantly, this kind of measure favours bureaucratic and compliance behaviour which is the antipode of quality, not to say of improvements.

At the end of the conference, Ulrich Teichler proposed some conclusions and follow-up orientations in the form of questions to investigate further. We quote them here as perspectives for quality assessment in the near future.

1. The basic assumption is that quality assessment is here to stay, for it is indispensable or even desirable.
2. Why is it so? Because we need specifc procedures for quality improvement and for accountability, since, currently, the academic self-regulation, the supervision exercised by ministries and the market control cannot fully achieve these ends.
3. Looking at quality assessment developments and trends, we see that we are not moving towards an integrated system, but, on the contrary, towards multiple systems.
4. In the last 15 years, we cannot perceive any kind of optimization or a positive trend towards more satisfactory systems. Conversely, we observe increasing disinformation, as well as a pressure for uniformity.
5. It is therefore worthwhile to try to improve quality assessment systems, especially with regard to information.
6. Since there are multiple systems, it is necessary to tend towards an overall system that works properly, i.e. that serves teaching and research

appropriately, and also to see that the diversity of systems is adequate to the specifc conditions in which they operate.

7. Do certain countries need certain systems in order to counteract some forms of specifcity?.
8. Do quality assessment systems have hidden agendas? For example, ranking systems. What are the political agendas?
9. How can quality assessments serve quality assurance? What kinds of actions are appropriate? How do we limit the management burden?
10. In Europe at present, we see mainly national schemes, but also international accreditations and rankings. Are we moving towards pan-European systems? Or towards an exponential growth of quality assessment systems? Are we moving from a predominant national system towards a predominant supranational system?

Quality Assessment Systems: A Problem of Ownership

It is well known that quality assessment can have multiple and sometimes contradictory objectives, the most usual ones being quality improvement and accountability. Quality improvement addresses what van Vught calls the intrinsic dimension of higher education quality, which is mainly a concern of institutions, while the government pays special attention to accountability, which addresses the extrinsic dimensions of higher education quality, i.e. the qualities found in the services provided to society by HEIs. More recently, the increasing role played by markets in higher education and the obvious need for information to allow consumers to make rational choices have created a new role for quality assessment, as provider to parents and students of information about the quality of educational provision.

To use the market as a regulation mechanism for higher education, governments were forced to confer at least some degree of autonomy on to HEIs, allowing them to have some 'market-like' freedom as providers of higher education. The rules of the market demand that producers have decision-making freedom to compete and to adapt to the competitive environment. However, this has created difculties for the government's steering capacity and efectiveness, as institutions have acquired some freedom to define their own strategies under conditions of market-like competition. Quality assessment might be seen as a government tool to regain some degree of control over institutions, if necessary as a compliance mechanism. On the other hand, the emerging New Public Management policies have directly attacked the power of the professionals, and one may argue that quality assessment has led to micromanagement techniques that were used at local level (faculty and/or department) to control the behaviour of academics in an intrusive way.

At last, the European Community is promoting the implementation of a European accreditation system that may result in a highly stratifed European Higher Education Area.

When discussing quality assessment systems, a fundamental question is their ownership. There is a whole spectrum of possibilities, ranging from one extreme where the system is owned by the state or a state agency to the other where the system is owned by the institutions themselves. The consequences are obvious, and, when the owner is the state, the accountability function in general prevails over the improvement function; the reverse being observed when the institution is the owner.

It is interesting to notice that, when the first national quality assessment systems were implemented in Europe, there were cases where institutions were able to beat the government at its own game to gain ownership over the quality assessment system, a good example being provided by the Dutch case. By claiming that the major responsibility for quality lay with the institutions themselves, and that trust in the supportive character of the quality assessment exercise was a necessary condition for open and critical self-assessment (a fundamental tool for improvement), Dutch universities were able to convince the Ministry that they should control the quality assurance system through an 'independent' agency, the VSNU (Vereniging van Samenwerkende Universiteiten). The Portuguese universities have followed the same road, and the Evaluation of Higher Education Act (Law 38/94 of 21 November 1994) has given the ownership of the quality agency to 'representative institutions', which, in the case of public universities, was the 'Foundation of Portuguese Universities', similar to the Dutch VSNU.

Ewell already recognized in 1987, apropos of the American accreditation system, that assessment had moved more and more from education improvement to institutional accountability. At present, one observes a recent tendency in Europe for a shif in the balance between the two distinctive objectives of quality assessment, quality improvement (of higher education) and accountability (of HEIs), towards the second objective, which reopens the debate on the ownership of the system.

Quality Management

Academics have always maintained that the noblest objective of quality assessment is quality improvement, a concern that was expressed in the coining of new rhetoric expressions such as quality care and quality assurance. In the U.S.A, Dill et al. support the idea that institutions should keep the main responsibility for quality and suggest that the route to quality assurance must combine "a mutually reinforcing system of institution-based quality assessments of teaching and learning and a co-ordinated regional system of external academic audits". And Martin Trow contends that the role of outside supranational, governmental or quasi-governmental agencies should consist of "monitoring and encouraging the emergence of this culture in institutions of mass higher education, but not through 'evaluations' based on uniform criteria and linked to funding", and that accreditation should be transformed into "searching audits of each institution's own scheme for critical self-examination, its own internal quality control procedures".

However, the shif of the decision-making responsibility to producers of higher education resulting from increased institutional autonomy has had "substantial implications for institutional governance and management". Starting in the 1980s, and especially at the political level, several voices were raised against the traditional model of governance and management of HEIs, considered to be inefcient and outdated to face the new challenges confronting these organizations.

In fact, almost everywhere, higher education has been under pressure to become "more accountable and responsive, efcient and efective and, at the same time, more entrepreneurial and self-managing". Over the last two decades, we have assisted in the intrusion of the rhetoric and management practices of the private sector into higher education, which has led to important changes in the operation of HEIs. This phenomenon was interpreted using concepts such as 'managerialism', 'new managerialism' or 'new public management', being associated with the emergence of market or quasi-market modes of regulation.

It is within this context that the traditional criteria of social and cultural relevance of higher education are increasingly seen as obsolete and inefcient, being progressively replaced by criteria of economic rationality. HEIs are forced to demonstrate explicitly to society that they make efective and efcient use of their resources and that their activities are relevant to the economy and the labour market. “Governments have espoused managerialism, whether as ideology or as practice, to diferent degrees or not at all, and institutions have responded in very diferent ways, largely infuenced by their historical, economic and social backgrounds”. Despite considerable resistance from the academic community, some private sector management practices have, to a variable extent, intruded into the higher education world. However, so far, HEIs have been able to avoid most of what Birnbaum calls the ‘management fads’ that Hinchclife lists: “We have experienced a string of fads proclaiming the same institutional success including Statistical Process Control, Long-Range Planning, Strategic Planning, Management by Objectives, Zero-Based Budgeting, O & M (Organization and Methods) Teory ‘Z’, Teory ‘K’, Job Enrichment, the energetic Management-by-Walking-About, the Management Audit, Value-Added Planning, Work-Place Reform and the various other theories through which scholars and practitioners have earned their fame, their theses, their MBAs and their consultancy fees”.

There are reasons explaining why it is not easy to transfer many of the private sector management practices to universities, which one can analyse using as an example the application to higher education of TQM (Total Quality Management), one of the most popular management tools, at least in terms of marketing eforts. For Williams, this application is a “product of the market ideologies of the 1980s and of the managerialism that accompanied it”.

The resistance of HEIs to TQM begins with its own terminology. Terms such as product, client, empowerment or even strategy, not to mention TQM or re-engineering, do not echo easily in HEIs. Massy states, “the greatest resistance to quality process improvement comes from professors who think it’s just another business-oriented fad. The language of some TQM advocates contributes to this view… Customer, scientifc method and removal of all forms of waste are sure to raise the hackles of academics”.

Birnbaum considers that the most relevant barrier has also to do with the need for a compromise between TQM and what are the traditions, values and purposes of HEIs. However, he recognizes that TQM probably has been the first management tool capable of provoking a serious discussion not only about its technical merits and demerits, but also about its educational and social implications. Williams, although being aware of the difculties of implementing TQM in universities, defends that a number of TQM’s principles could be useful in higher education, such as continuous quality improvement, quality consistency, participation of academics, students and non-academic staf, satisfaction of the clients' needs and the existence of management procedures that reinforce quality.

For David Dill, there are also some important lessons that HEIs can learn from TQM, the most relevant being the central place that the social capital should occupy inside organizations. He defends that the assurance of quality in academic programmes requires "weaving the collegial fabric of academic communities, the collective mechanisms by which faculty members control and improve the quality of academic programmes and research".

Harvey, although considering that TQM is not applicable to HEIs, admits that one should "determine the worthwhile aspects of TQM and relocate them in the higher education context, stripped of alienating managerialist jargon and linked frmly to existing quality processes".

HEIs are facing demands for increased societal relevance of teaching and research and the government's attention to the extrinsic qualities of higher education to the detriment of its intrinsic qualities, which includes the progressive emergence of accreditation mechanisms. In this new context, it is possible that HEIs will assume a defensive attitude by adapting the more palatable, for academics, components of some private sector management fads, as Harvey and Dill suggest.

Quality Assessment as an Information Tool

Over the last few decades, markets have become an increasingly important regulation tool of the public sector, as governments are trying to improve the efciency of public services through the implementation of market-like competition mechanisms. Governments are more and more assuming that competition is the miraculous ingredient that will suddenly transform hardened bureaucrats into brave private entrepreneurs. Even the Bologna Declaration, "redefining the nature and content of academic programmes, is transforming what were once state monopolies over academic degrees into competitive international markets".

However, the efcient use of market regulation presents several problems. For the allocation of goods and services to be "optimally efcient for the larger society", the market needs to be perfectly competitive, which implies a number of conditions that are difcult to fulfl. Indeed, both government and market regulation may lead to inefcient action as is well documented in the literature.

Non-market or government failures are related to the fact that sometimes the government and its agencies are incapable of perfect performance in designing and implementing public policy, because of defects of representative democracy and inef-ciencies of public agencies to produce and to distribute goods and services.

Market failures are the shortcomings of markets when confronted with certain goods and conditions, namely the production of goods that show large externalities, as in the case of education. As the market is a means of organizing the exchange of goods and services based upon price, additional social benefts (externalities) will tend to be ignored or be too little taken into account by market mechanisms. Other sources of market failures are the tendency of a free market to build monopolies resulting in inefcient outcomes (in general, government regulation outlaws this kind of development in order to protect consumers) or the so-called "market imperfections", such as prices not refecting product scarcities and insufcient or asymmetric information.

However, in many cases, the relevant information is not available (imperfect information) or the producer has a much more detailed knowledge than the consumer (asymmetric information).

The information problem is very acute in the case of higher education, which has three simultaneous characteristics. First, it is an experience good, meaning that its relevant characteristics can only be efectively assessed by consumption, as it is only afer a student starts attending a study programme that he/she gets a real idea of what he/she has purchased in terms of quality, professors and the general value of the educational experience. Secondly, it is a rare purchase, as, in most cases, a student enrols in a single study programme throughout his/her professional life and cannot derive market experience from frequent purchases. Finally, opting-out costs are high, as it is, in general, rather expensive to change to a diferent study programme or institution.

The simultaneous presence of these three characteristics makes a strong case for government intervention to protect consumers, which may take diferent forms such as licensing, accreditation and the public disclosure of the results of quality assessment activities, all of them aimed at increasing consumer information, which justifes the increasing role of quality assessment for market regulation purposes.

However, Dill still considers that, from the strict point of view of "rational economic choice", "students lack sufcient information about the quality of academic institutions or programs to make discriminating choices", as what they need is the measure of prospective future earnings provided by alternative academic programmes and not "peer review evaluation of teaching processes, nor subjective judgements of the quality of a curriculum".

On the other hand, even if this kind of data were available, many students (or their families) would not use it, which questions the validity of the hypothesis of rational economic choice. This is what David Dill calls the problem of immature consumers and provides the ground for "the implementation of quasi-markets, rather than consumer-oriented markets, for the distribution of academic programmes". The state or a state agency, acting on behalf of the fnal consumers, can get a better bargain from the providers as it has a much stronger power of the purse than any individual client, a logic that is reinforced when (immature) clients do not make rational choices. The state is no longer a provider of higher education, but assumes a role as principal, representing the interests of the consumers by making contracts with competing institutions, which creates a quasi-market in which independent providers compete with each other in an internal market.

Quality Assessment as a Compliance Tool

Neave and van Vught have described the changing pattern of the relationship between HEIs and the state and society that started to emerge in Europe afer the early 1970s as a shif from the model of state control to the model of state supervision. The state was supposed to refrain from detailed scrutiny of the daily life of institutions and to steer the higher education system from a distance.

Van Vught refers to the cybernetic behaviour of institutions using his cat as an example: when the freplace is lit, the cat adjusts its distance to the fames until it fnds a comfortable temperature, thus behaving like a cybernetic animal. In the same manner, HEIs would adapt their behaviour and strategies until they were comfortable under the environmental conditions created by the government through distance steering. In an ideal system, the government should be able to ensure that institutions will perform in compliance with the government's goals and objectives in the pursuit of public good.

Despite the increased level of autonomy conferred on institutions, the state is still in control, and Neave and van Vught recognize that "the musicians are still marching down the broad highway of detailed plan and control". Roger Dale also uses a musical allegory to refer to the restrictions to autonomy under conditions of fnancial stringency: "So, while he who pays the piper always in the end calls the tune, he can specify more or less broadly what kind of tune he wants, but only with far greater difculty exactly how he should be played. Under 'licensed autonomy' the teaching profession was given what amounted to a negative programme by the paymaster: 'play anything you like but Russian music and folk songs'. Under regulated autonomy the requirement is much more positive: 'play only modern German music, as far as possible just like the Germans do, and we'll be listening to make sure you do'".

More recently, at least in some countries, neo-liberal governments have come into power and a new political rhetoric has become popular. Increased privatization of higher education has been observed in a variety of forms, which include the establishment of private HEIs, the use of market mechanisms and the increased contribution of students and families to the higher education costs. Neo-liberal politicians proclaim that the state should decrease its activity as service provider, that state regulation should retreat in favour of market regulation, and that competition among institutions is a necessary ingredient to ensure that institutions become more responsive to society and more efcient in the use of public funds.

Ben Jongbloed uses a trafc metaphor to make clear the diferences between the traditional government system of centralized command and control (similar to trafc signals) to co-ordinate their higher education systems and the adoption of market-based policies (similar to a roundabout). In this metaphor, trafc lights condition drivers' decisions heavily, the same way that government regulation conditions the behaviour of institutions. On the other hand, a roundabout, while infuencing trafc behaviour, delegates decision-making authority to the drivers: "Drivers in a roundabout are awarded greater discretion (and more immediate forms of accountability!) than when trafc is controlled centrally by signals. This co-ordination by 'mutual adjustment' supposedly increases the efciency of the trafc fow. The challenge confronting those experimenting with market-based policies in higher education therefore is to discover the institutional framework of rules and incentives that produces welfare maximizing competition among (mainly) publicly subsidized, but autonomous, academic institutions".

Despite neo-liberal claims that governments should not interfere with markets, several authors argue that the social benefts of markets cannot be realized in the absence of regulation defining the boundaries for market transactions. However, despite this state oversight of market operation, there was hope that institutions would become freer from state interference and have more freedom to define their strategies under the new mechanisms of market-like competition.

This raises a fundamental question of how more autonomous institutions will behave in a market-like competitive environment. Will institutions still uphold the primacy of public good or will they promote their own 'private good'? How will more managerial rectors and presidents view the traditional role of the universities?

Public universities receive at least a signifcant part of their budgets from the state, under the argument that they further the public good by contributing to economic development and by advancing the life prospects of citizens by increasing their 'employability' potential, to use the new European terminology. Public universities are non-proft organizations that are, by law, forced to reinvest any surplus in the organization itself, instead of providing private benefts for their members. This ofers the state some guarantee that the organization will not digress from its obligation of upholding the public good. And it explains why the state, at least in most European countries, mistrusts private HEIs, and either forbids them or tries to control them more closely that it does public institutions.

Massy, in two very interesting papers, argues that "the way institutions currently respond to markets and seek internal efciencies, lef unchecked, is unlikely to serve the public good", a danger that is exacerbated by excessive competition or by retrenchment operations. Massy considers that when competition is excessive, or when the state cuts public subsidies, thus curtailing the institutional capacity for discretionary spending, non-proft institutions may behave like for-proft ones, ignoring the promotion of the public good inherent to their missions. This forces the state to intervene by changing the rules of the market to ensure the fulflment of its own political objectives.

When quasi-markets are implemented, the government agencies making the purchases in the name of consumers face the classical principal– agent dilemma: "how the principal [government] can best motivate the agent [university] to perform as the principal would prefer, taking into account the difculties in monitoring the agent's activities". This problem is obviously exacerbated when providers have considerable autonomy. Therefore one observes an evident contradiction in neo-liberal policies. On the one hand, it is claimed that government intervention is the mother of all sins and that institutions should be allowed to operate freely under the rules of free market competition. On the other hand, the government realizes that autonomous institutions competing in a market may behave in ways that are contrary to public policies and the public good.

This leads to the arbitrary intrusion of the government to change the rules of the game in order to force the institutions to follow strategies that in some cases are even self-defeating from a pure market perspective. Dominique Orr suggests that the new relationship between the HEIs and the government is portrayed by the 'roundabout model', but with an increasing number of (government) trafc lights restricting the allowed routes. This is consistent with the idea that an efective delegation of 'public-interest decision-making' authority to institutions requires "an afrmative desire to interpret and serve the public good, the will to hold institutional self-interest at bay, and the fnancial strength to balance intrinsic values with market forces". However, the unchecked behaviour of institutions, especially under conditions of strong competition and fnancial stringency, may not correspond to the best public interest, which paves the road for government intervention.

That is why governments have been introducing an increasing number of mechanisms to ensure that institutions will behave as the government wants them to behave. Among these mechanisms, one fnds an extensive array of performance indicators and measures of academic quality, be it called quality assurance or accreditation. Therefore one sees the use of quality assessment as a compliance tool. A special case occurs with 'weak states', where intervention is, in general, more sporadic and occurs when a crisis is already well underway. In South Africa, the move to state supervision is part of the redefinition of the relationship between the government and civil society, and needs the services of the Ministry to "shif away from the traditional opposition between state and civil society to negotiated co-operation arrangements". Kraak considers that, for this change to be successful, it "requires leadership by the government, the only actor with powers of political co-ordination in society" that should become the beacon setting the direction of institutional activity on behalf of the nation.

The NCHE (National Commission on Higher Education) had a clear vision of the essential ingredients for success and suggested that, for the state to be able to play this leadership role in relation to higher education, four central capabilities were absolutely necessary: "organizational capacity (a corps of competent 'planning' civil servants); a long-term growth orientation (the development of a coherent socio-economic and human resource development plan); autonomy and independence from powerful private social interests; and being the honest broker in co-operative relations across public and private domains. Co-operative governance can succeed, only to the extent that the state acquires these capabi The conditions mentioned by the NCHE are not present in the weak state, which, being incapable of efcient steering, resorts to "a bureaucratic weak and arbitrary form of intervention based on prescriptive fat and rigid rules and procedures". The weak state is viewed as: "weak and unable to attain the sophistication required for 'steering', and, as a consequence, necessitating a reversion back to a conception of the state as bureaucratic and prescriptive. This is the only perceived route in which the (weak) state can gain some control over what is perceived to be a crisis-ridden and highly dysfunctional sector".

For instance, in some Eastern European countries, afer the demise of communism, there was an uncontrolled development of private higher education that came to an end when the state intervened drastically and sporadically to rescue the remains of a crisis-ridden system, by implementing accreditation systems.

Quality Assessment as a Substitute for Trust

Today, any specifc discussion of higher education management needs to be set within the broader context of New Public Management and related concepts, such as new managerialism and reinventing government, which have dominated public sector reform over the last two decades. As Denhardt and Denhardt note, "the New Public Management has championed a vision of public managers as the entrepreneurs of a new, leaner, and increasingly privatized government, emulating not only the practices, but also the values of business".

Under New Public Management, the public are clients of the government, and administrators should seek to deliver services that satisfy clients. In higher education, too, students are referred to as customers or clients, and, in most higher education systems, quality assurance and accountability measures have been put in place to ensure that academic provision meets client needs and expectations.

One of the consequences of the New Public Management policies appears to have been a strong attack on the professions, including the academic profession. Reed states: "By imposing market competition through political dictate and administrative fat, the ideology of 'new managerialism' attempted to destroy, or at least weaken, the regulatory structures that had protected unaccountable professional elites and their monopolistic labour market and work practices across the full range of public sector service provision throughout the 1980s and 1990s".

The academy no longer enjoys great prestige on which higher education can build a successful claim to political autonomy. One observes the gradual proletarization of the academic professions; an erosion of their relative class and status advantages. Academic capitalism also made faculty more like all other workers, making faculty, staf and students less like university professionals and more like corporate professionals whose discoveries are considered to be work-for-hire, the property of the corporation, not the professional.

The 'de-professionalization' of academics has been coupled with a claim to professional status by administrative staf. Thirty years ago, administrators were "very much expected to operate in a subservient supportive role to the academic community, very much in a traditional civil servant mould", and, in the meetings of the academia, they were expected to be seen, but not to be heard. Today, managers see themselves as essential contributors to the successful functioning of the contemporary university. agement mechanisms to respond to outside pressures, promoting the new values and demands of "economy, efciency, utility, public accountability, enterprise and various definitions of quality". Management control technologies include systems for evaluation and performance measurement of research, teaching and some administrative activities, particularly those linked to fnance. The implementation of these systems occurs in basic units, which are internally made accountable for budget expenditure (eventually decentralized) and for the results of evaluations of teaching and research activities. The infuence of the recommendations (or sanctions) from those evaluations is one of the most important aspects determining the selection and concentration of activities in HEIs, as well as the degree of autonomy of professionals.

In the U.K., for instance, control mechanisms included an extremely detailed framework of devolved performance criteria against which operational efciency and efectiveness at the unit level would be monitored and assessed. Sets of indicators were selected for diverse public services such as health, social security and education. And Reed states: "Within the context of much more intrusive and pervasive performance management, a consistent emphasis on the detailed monitoring and evaluation of 'quality' standards in service delivery and outcomes emerged as the overriding priority".

The emergence of the New Public Management and the attacks on the efciency of public services, including higher education, resulted in loss of trust in institutions and professionals. For Martin Trow, every institution is linked to its surroundings through some combination of accountability, market and trust. Accountability is the obligation to report to others, to explain, to justify, answering questions about how resources have been used, and to what efect; the link of higher education to society through the market is visible when support is provided to a college or university in return for the immediate provision of goods or services; trust is visible in the provision of support, by either public or private bodies, without the requirement that the institutions either provide specifc goods and services in return for that support, or account specifcally and in detail for the use of those funds. The laws of autonomy or envelope budgeting are examples of trust.

For Martin Trow, accountability is an alternative to trust, and eforts to strengthen it usually involve parallel eforts to weaken trust, and he adds that accountability and cynicism about human behaviour go hand in hand. The U.K. under the premiership of Margaret Tatcher is a classic example of the withdrawal of trust and increasing demands for accountability.

Quality Assessment as a Supranational Policy Tool

The new European Higher Education Area that the Bologna Process aims to implement will be a complex system of very diverse institutions, ofering a wide range of quality. It can be observed that the more neo-liberal model that occasionally becomes visible in European policies tends to emphasize the importance of the efciency of the system, as can be seen from a document by the European Commission entitled *Making the Best Use of Resources,* where one can read "The necessary level and type of investment and their consequent impact on efciency depend on the development level of the country as defined by its proximity to the technology frontier (i.e. relative to the technologically most advanced countries). Countries far from the frontier should focus on primary and secondary education (imitation process), whereas countries close to the frontier should invest primarily in higher education (innovation process)".

When simultaneously one observes other developments, such as the recent report *Institutional Profles: Towards a Typology of Higher Education Institutions in Europe* supported by the European Commission that proposes a European higher education typology (even if it states that it should be emphasized right away that the European higher education typology is not an instrument for ranking HEIs) and the interest of organizations such as UNESCO (United Nations Educational, Scientifc and Cultural Organization) and the OECD (Organisation for Economic Co-operation and Development) in rankings, one may well guess that something is coming.

It is true that massifcation of the European higher education systems has created new problems. Trow recognizes that "the growth and diversifcation of higher education, along with associated changes in pedagogy, will require that a society and its systems of higher education surrender any idea of broad common standards of academic performance between institutions, and even between subjects within a single university, ministerial assertions to the contrary notwithstanding".

This is a criticism of the stubborn attitude of many European governments in considering that all HEIs ofer similar quality, an attitude that clearly contrasts with that of the Americans who "never made (or could make) any commitment as a nation to the maintenance of common standards across our thousands of colleges and universities". These developments can be linked to the eforts of the European Commission in the area of accreditation.

In February 2001, the CRE (Conference of European Rectors) [now EUA (European University Association)] organized in Lisbon a validation seminar, 'Towards Accreditation Schemes for Higher Education in Europe?', where the main conclusions of an exploratory project on accreditation as a tool for promoting the internationalization of higher education were presented. Those conclusions were challenged by a wide majority of the participants. However, the written conclusions of the seminar conveyed to the Salamanca Convention of European HEIs just stated that "representatives of HEIs, as well as student organizations, quality assurance agencies, national higher education authorities and intergovernmental bodies discussed accreditation as a possible option for higher education in Europe, particularly as a contribution to the completion of the European Area of Higher Education, ignoring the controversy.

At Salamanca, accreditation was once more presented as a component of the European Area of Higher Education, but the majority of the universities present at the Convention rejected it. The international press present at Salamanca reported that accreditation was a hot topic of debate and the Report to the Ministers of Education assembled in

Prague states that no consensus on accreditation had been possible: "The question of who is responsible for setting the reference standards has proved to be a delicate and controversial one, especially if it is considered at European level. Alongside those that frmly believe in accreditation, even at European level, there are those that fear externally imposed European standards, as inadequate to their national system or reality and a restriction to the institutional capacity to innovate".

However, the fnal conclusions of the Salamanca Convention of European HEIs conveyed to Prague state "the way into the future will be to design mechanisms at European level for the mutual acceptance of quality assurance outcomes, with 'accreditation' as one possible option". On the contrary, the fnal Communiqué of the Higher Education ministers assembled in Prague avoids any reference to a European system of quality/accreditation.

Despite the opposition of a large number of HEIs, the idea of European accreditation has survived all difculties, and, in 2004, the Commission has presented a proposal for the recommendation of the Council and of the European Parliament. According to the proposal, there will be multiple accreditation agencies, public and private, national and international, that need to be recognized by a central agency. HEIs should be allowed by their governments to choose any agency they prefer. This is consistent with the idea of a stratifed European Area of Higher Education, as institutions would be allowed to choose an accreditation agency adequate to their quality level. One may foresee that some accreditation agencies will address excellence at an international level, while others will be more appropriate to regional or local institutions, some will accredit research universities, while others will specialize in teaching-only institutions. Therefore one may conclude that quality assessment can also be used as a tool for the implementation of supranational policies.

References

Dale, R. and Robertson, S.L. (2002) The varying aspects of regional organizations as subjects of globalization of education. *Comparative Education Review* 46(1), 10–36.

Dale, R. (1999) Specifying globalization efects on national policy: a focus on the mechanisms. *Journal of Education Polic y* 14(1), 1–17.

De Wit, K. and Verhoeven, J.C. (2001) The higher education policy of the European Union: with or against the member states. In *Higher Education and the Nation State: the International Dimension of Higher Education* (Huisman, J., Maassen, P. and Neave, G., eds), pp. 175– 231, Pergamon, Oxford.

van der Wende, M. (2002) *Hoger Onderwijs Globaliter: naar Nieuwe Kaders voor Onderzoek en Beleid*, Universiteit Twente, Enschede.

Verhoeven, J.C., Kelchtermans, G. and Michielsen, K. (2005) *McOnderwijs in Vlaanderen: Internationalisering en Commercialisering van het Hoger Onderwijs*, Wolters Plantyn, Mechelen.

6

Assessment of Assignments

Distance learners' responses to the assignment questions sent to them by the distance teaching institutions form an important instrument of teaching learning at a distance. Long spatial distance may exist between the distance learners and the distance teaching institution, but non contiguous communication through assignment questions, responses to these by the learners, and subsequent comments by the distance teacher on those responses minimise this spatial distance and increase academic and psychological closeness between the two. Meaningful and constructive suggestions through comments written on assignment responses can effect successful distance learning. So, assessment of assignment responses of distance learners as a part of continuous assessment in terms of both commenting and grading is an activity that needs careful analysis, discussion and understanding on the part of the distance teachers.

Types of Assignments

Assignment is an important device through which two way communication takes place in a distance education system. This is a learning task. This enables the learners to ensure that they have learnt what they are expected to learn from the course materials and their response to it give their distance teacher an opportunity to help them by commenting on their performance.

Generally, two types of assignments are used in distance education system: (i) Tutor Marked Assignments (TMAs) and (ii) Computer Marked Assignments (CMAs).

Tutor Marked Assignments (TMAs)

These assignments are marked/evaluated by the distance teacher/tutor. Thus, these are called tutor marked assignments. These assignments comprise a variety of questions such as essay type, short answer type, problem solving exercises etc. These assignments are generally used to assess the higher order cognitive objectives such as analysis, synthesis, judgement, comprehension, application, etc.

Examples of TMAs

1. *Essay type:* Answer the following in about 1500 words. Imagine that you have been asked to plan and organise a training programme for the academics in a newly established open university in your country. In which area will you give training first, and why? Prepare an outline of your training programme.
2. *Short answer type*: Write short notes of about 250 words each of the following:
   i) The wild life of Himalayas
   ii) Seasonal marketing
3. *Practical type exercises:* Answer the following in about 1200 words. Prepare a self learning unit on a theme of your choice incorporating a unit structure, two sections, SAQs, Summary and check your progress possible answers.

Sometimes these assignments comprise of objective type questions also. There are generally seven major types:

a. True false
b. Fill in the blanks
c. Completion of sentences
d. Matching
e. Multiple choice
f. Sequencing
g. Graphical/pictorial type.

We assume, all of you have either designed or evaluated these kinds of questions and their responses in several occasions. So, here we will not discuss these in detail.

Computer Marked Assignments (CMAs)

These assignments are marked/evaluated by the computer only. Thus, these are called computer marked assignments. These assignments are generally comprised of objective type questions, preferably the multiple choice questions, which are most versatile amongst all objective type test items.

Tutor Marked Assignments (TMAs)

A few criteria for designing useful tutor marked assignment questions are:

- Is the assignment question clear and unambiguous?
- Does the question directly relate to stated objectives?
- Does the assignment as a whole test the main things the learner needs?
- Does the assignment begin with fairly easy questions?
- Does the assignment include a marking scheme?

In a computer marked assignment the distance learner responds to multiple choice questions. The writer of computer marked assignment is the best person to decide exactly what message should reach the distance learner. So human skills and experience are needed for designing CMAs.

Assignment Response

Assignment is a learning task. The learners make an attempt to respond to the assignment after going through the study materials. This he/she does according to the instructions written on the assignment. Thus, the answer written by the learner with respect to a particular assignment is called assignment response.

Commenting on Assignment Response

Passing comment is a natural habit of human being. You have observed your friends, relatives, colleagues passing comments on several occasions. You may have also done the same in several occasions. But here, we are talking about 'comments' which have special significance in teaching learning. These comments mean your reactions to the assignment response the learner expressed through written words that promote his learning. These comments should have a special significance while you are commenting on an assignment response of a distance learner. These written words should provide academic support to the isolated learner. As a teacher of a conventional system of education you use spoken words, gestures, etc. to affect classroom/face to face learning, similarly as a distance teacher you should use written words with varied styles and in different ways to enhance learning at a distance.

Tutor Comments

You have learnt that some assignments are marked/evaluated by the distance teacher/tutor which are called tutor marked assignments. Similarly, comments written by a distance teacher/tutor on assignment response are called 'tutor comments'. This word is popular in distance education system. A 'tutor' is a person who helps the distance learner to learn on his own. He is a facilitator. He facilitates learning by providing academic counselling, guidance, etc. and also writing comments on assignment response of the learner. In other words, writing comments on assignment response is primarily the task/responsibility of the 'tutor' or 'counsellor' in a distance education system.

Importance of Tutor Comments

As a distance teacher/tutor you should know the importance of tutor comments first.

i) The distance learner is an independent learner. He/she may need continuous feedback to sustain and/or increase his/her motivation. Feedback in terms of fruitful comments increase the motivation of a distance learner.

ii) The distance learner is an isolated learner. He/she does not get frequent occasions to interact with peers and evaluate his/her position among the peers. Comparison with peer group provides indirect feedback that increases the competitive spirit of the learner. He/she can assess his/her mode of learning and make necessary modifications for better performance. But the distance learner does not have the facility of regularly meeting the peer group. Occasionally, he/she can meet the fellow learners at the study centres during face to face contact sessions. Through fruitful comments on assignment response, the distance teacher can remove the learner's feeling of isolation, and can also bring him/her closer to the peer group by making him/her see clearly his/her achievement, drawbacks etc. in relation to those of the peers.

iii) Through written comments the distance teacher can provide guidance, counselling and suggestions to improve the study habits of the learners, if necessary.

iv) Through written comments the distance teacher can clarify the ambiguities, if any, or difficult portions of a course unit.

In short, the tutor comments are a very important tool in distance education as they are both the content and vehicle of communication which effect learning.

Writing Comments: Some Important Steps

While writing comments on any assignment response you may follow the steps mentioned below:

i) You may go through the assignment question critically, understand what the assignment asks for and then build in your mind, the 'ideal response' which may be from your point of view, the best response to that question.

ii) You may identify the weakness, if any, in the assignments question and course unit(s) on which the particular assignment is based. Then, you may match these weaknesses with the pre determined 'ideal response'. This will help to reduce the bias in the assessment of assignment response.

iii) Next, you may go through the assignment response and evaluate its organisational aspects, viz., introduction, body or mid part, ending/ conclusion, etc., accuracy of information, content density, logical and critical analysis of concept, clarity in expression, language and so on. For assessment you may assign precise value to these organisational aspects of the response. At the end you may write the global comments.

iv) While writing global comments you may award the grade or mark/score to the particular assignment, as the global comments, among other things, justify the grade or marks awarded to that assignment response.

Types of Tutor Comments

If you randomly select a few evaluated assignment responses of any open university, you will find various types of comments written by the tutors. Some comments may be very effective for distance teaching, some may not. Because it is not so easy to write precise and pedagogically purposeful comments. Only the oriented or trained distance teacher/tutor can write pedagogically purposeful comments. Before we discuss the types of tutor comments we will suggest you to do the following activity.

Here, we will discuss various types of comments generally written by the tutors under three different sub heads: i) Comments: must be written for distance teaching, ii) Comments: may be written with caution for distance teaching, and iii) Comments: must be avoided.

Table 1. Broad Classification of Tutor Comments

Various types of tutor comments discussed as follows:

Teaching Comments	*Non Teaching Comments*
• Positive comments	• Harmful comments
• Constructive comments	• Hollow comments
• Global comments	• Misleading comments
• Personal comments	• Null comments
	• Negative comments

Note: Null comments and negative comments can be made effective distance teaching comments with suitable additions and modifications.

Comments: must be written for distance teaching

You must write those comments which help the distance learner to learn successfully. Consider the following comments:

a) "Your explanation with regard to information processing theory is very good. I appreciate your diagram number one."

b) "You could have discussed the factors of environmental pollution with examples and illustrations".

We have presented above two types of comments which are must for distance teaching. These are positive comment (a) constructive comment. We will discuss these very briefly.

Positive Comments

The first comment (a) approves of what the learner has written. Thus, it is called positive comment. It motivates the learner and encourages him/her to improve his/her future performance. It increases the frequency and improve the pedagogic strength of two way communication. So, you must support the right information, explanation, illustration, example etc. written by the learner. These comments are generally written in the margin against or opposite to the text of the assignment response you are commenting upon.

Constructive Comments

The second comment (b) offers constructive suggestion as to how the answer could have been improved. So, this may be called 'constructive' comment. This comment is very helpful in bringing about purposeful didactic communication. You must write this kind of comments for effective distance teaching. This should be written in the margins beside the relevant portions of the answer scripts.

Global Comments

This is another type of comment which must be written for increasing further effectiveness of distance learning. This is comprised of overall remarks made on an assignment response. This should be written on a plain paper or in a table/sheet specially prepared for writing such comments. The detailed comments on various aspects of answer or response are put together, and the inter related overall issues are highlighted in the global comments. Here you may mention about spelling, neatness, handwriting, etc. But do not forget to explain and justify the grade you have awarded to the learner. These explanations will help the learner identify both his/her weaknesses and the ways to improve the performance.

Comments: may be written with caution for distance teaching

There are some types of comments written by some distance teachers which cannot function as successful teaching comments. Only with suitable additions and modifications these can be made effective distance teaching comments. Consider the following comments:

a) "The first part of your answer is not clear. The second part is not relevant".

b) "?", "=", "??"

The first comment mentioned above is called negative comment. The second comment (zero meaning, non verbal remarks) is called null comment. We will discuss these very briefly.

Negative Comments

Through negative comment, the distance teacher/tutor points out the wrong presentations and interpretations in concepts, facts, explanations, examples, relevancy of content, etc. Such comments indicate whether the answer is incorrect, incomplete or inadequate, but do not indicate what is correct and how to make it complete and adequate. Thus, this type of comments do not serve the purpose of distance teaching. The distance teacher needs to indicate categorically what can be added or changed to make the answer correct/

complete/adequate. So, while evaluating an assignment response you may point out the weaknesses (which is necessary), but do not forget to suggest how these weaknesses may be removed.

Null Comments

Many teachers have the habit of putting non verbal remarks like question marks (?), underlining (_) etc. in the answer script of the learners. While going through the assignments some distance teachers/tutors tend to put this kind of signs and symbols.

Comments expressed through these signs and symbols do not convey any meaning to the learner. The distance teacher needs to indicate in writing what these signs and symbols mean.

So, while evaluating an assignment response you may put 'question mark' or 'cross', but do not forget to write a few words explaining why you have put these signs and symbols and also guide the learner to write the correct answer.

Comments: must be avoided while distance teaching

Sometimes, distance teachers write some comments which do not suggest anything meaningful to the learner, but on the other hand misguide the learner. Such comments disturb and even hurt the distance learner. Consider the following comments:

a) "Your answer is so so. You can improve your presentation. You may spend some more time in writing this answer".

b) "I am not going to tell you in which unit you will get this answer. Better you go through the whole block once again".

c) "Are you writing English for the first time? So many grammatical and spelling mistakes? How do you expect pass marks"?

Above we have mentioned three types of comments. Do you think any one of it can be used for effective distance teaching? Probably your answer is 'No'. You are right. These comments are not at all helpful in effecting didactic communication. The first type of comments may be called hollow comment, the second type is misleading comment and the third is harmful comment.

Hollow Comments

Some comments are only 'word salads'. These are written words which do not suggest anything meaningful to the distance learner. The learner does not get any benefit out of these comments. Consider comments (a) above. It says that the learner can improve presentation, but how? The learner can spend some more time in writing the answer, but what will be the benefit? He may commit similar mistakes. The learner will not academically gain anything from these comments. So, while evaluating assignment response you must avoid this kind of 'hollow comment'.

Misleading Comments

Some comments may misguide or mislead the learner. Consider comments (b) above. The comment reads "….go through the whole block again". The learner may go through the whole block again, but will it solve his/her problem? He/she needs some specific instructions and guidance to answer the assignment properly. He/she may be guided accordingly. He/she may be told the unit no. where he/she will get the answer. He/she should not be misled.So, never write this kind of comments which may mislead the learners.

Harmful Comments

Some comments are 'rude' by themselves. They build barriers between the distance teacher and the learner and consequently, all possibilities of 'communication' get blocked. Consider the comment (iii) in the previous page. This kind of comments may disturb, hurt and demotivate the distance learner. This may compel the distance learner to withdraw from the course. So, never write any comment which may cause harm to the learner.

Comments: to break the 'isolation'

As a distance teacher you may break the isolation of the learner and can provide extra incentive and help through communication at the personal level. The learner has no way of assessing his/her performance in relation to that of the other learners on the course. Thus, he/she may suffer from 'isolation'. Breaking this isolation is much more difficult than writing comments for effective teaching at a distance. You may write as many personal comments as possibly you can, but your comments should be properly worded. Consider the following personal comments.

- "Your answer is better than other answers I have gone through till today".

- "I appreciate your style of presentation. It is something new. No other student has presented the diagram on information processing theory. Carry on please. You will definitely be able to achieve learning objectives.
- I think you have faced some difficulties while responding to this assignment. Don't worry, most of the students have faced the same problem. Actually, you should have answered this based on your personal experience only. You have done well. While some students have done well, some haven't".

References

El Khawas, E. (2006) Accountability and Quality Assurance: New Issues for Academic Inquiry. In *International Handbook of Higher Education,* vol. 1 (Forest, J.J.F. and Altbach, P.G. eds), pp. 23–37, Springer Verlag, Berlin.

Scott, W.R. and Meyer, J.W. (1991) The organization of societal sectors: propositions and early evidence. In *The New Institutionalism in Organizational Analysis* (Powell, W. W. and DiMaggio, P.J., eds), pp. 108–140, University of Chicago Press, Chicago.

Hinagi, T. (2004) Networking of quality assurance agencies in the Asia-Pacifc region and the role of Japan University Accreditation Association. *Quality in Higher Education* 10(1), 37–41.

El Khawas, E. (2001) Who's in Charge of Quality? The Governance Issue in Quality Assurance. *Tertiary Education and Management* 7(2), 111–119.

Scott, W.R. (1995) *Institutions and Organization,* Sage Publication, London

7

Development of Accreditation Systems

Since the late 1990s, a certain type of scheme established for the assessment of the core functions and activities in higher education has spread rapidly in Europe: the accreditation scheme. The establishment of accreditation schemes has had quite a tremendous impact on the overall scene of evaluation in higher education in Europe. Terefore this development deserves special attention even though one might consider it premature to analyse the development of accreditation, to assess its strengths and weaknesses and to summarize its impact all over Europe.

In the subsequent text, éforts will be made to: (i) describe the character of accreditation in the overall setting of evaluation in higher education in Europe; (ii) discuss the causes for the rapid emergence and spread of accreditation in Europe; (iii) demonstrate the extent to which the accreditation systems emerging in the various European countries have common characteristics or difer from each other; (iv) summarize first experiences as regards proper functioning and desired outcomes of accreditation schemes according to their own goals; and (v) discuss the impact of the emerging accreditation schemes on the overall map of evaluation activities in Europe.

When accreditation became increasingly popular in Europe, I raised the question of whether accreditation was the single most relevant, suitable and useful instrument of system-wide systematic assessment of study programmes in Europe. In the meantime, a second sceptical working hypothesis might have been proposed: the establishment of accreditation schemes might have contributed substantially to the overcomplexity and overburdening of assessment exercises and it might endanger other schemes of assessment in higher education which are potentially more important to ensure the 'quality' in higher education in Europe.

These two cautious observations at the beginning set the agenda of the subsequent analysis in two directions. First, the scope of the analysis is not limited to the question of how a system of accreditation and its immediate impact on the 'right to be' of study programmes difers from other modes related to the 'right to be' of study programmes, notably from approval by governments in combination with various modes of public funding and public supervision of higher education. Rather, accreditation is viewed as one of possibly various activities of systematic assessment of study programmes and various mechanisms of ensuring the quality of study programmes.

This is appropriate because the establishment of an accreditation system is one of the possible options of assessment of study programmes and, as will be discussed, the establishment of an accreditation scheme has an enormous impact on previously existing assessment schemes. Secondly, the analysis focuses on Europe (cf. the overview in). Accreditation was developed in the U.S.A. under conditions that difer substantially from those in Europe today, and it is not the aim here to discuss the rationale of accreditation in the U.S.A., a country much more prone to any kind of formal assessment exercise, traditionally experiencing and only tolerating a weak 'visible hand' and traditionally not having any 'gold standard' of quality embedded in the steeply stratifed higher education system.

This analysis draws substantially from the first major substantial account of the development of the newly emerged accreditation schemes in about 20 European countries until 2003. This study was co-ordinated by two higher education researchers of the International Center for Higher Education Research Kassel (formerly the Centre for Research on Higher Education and Work of the University of Kassel) (Germany) and the Centre for Higher Education Policy Studies of the Twente University (The Netherlands). Stephanie Schwarz and Don F. Westerheijden jointly edited the book *Accreditation and Evaluation in the European Higher Education Area.* The comparative analysis and about half of the country reports were also published in the German language.

Concepts and Definitions

Accreditation is one type of decision-making-related, and thus practically relevant, assessment (i.e. analysis and valuation) exercise of the core functions and activities in higher education of HEIs (higher education institutions) and subunits.

'Quality assurance' became the most popular umbrella term in Europe for all types of assessment in higher education linked directly to activities of developing and improving the 'quality' of higher education. The term 'quality assurance', however, is dubious in three respects.

1. The criterion of practically relevant assessment of higher education is not only 'quality' in terms of the most common understanding, i.e. the level of standard of what is considered good in higher education. Rather, assessment in higher education tries to establish quality, relevance and efciency. If we define 'relevance' and 'efciency' as sub-criteria of 'quality', we play down the possible conficting nature of these three criteria.
2. 'Quality' does not tend to be viewed in terms of a scale from 'very high' to 'very low' or from 'very good' to 'very bad'. Rather, the term 'quality' underscores the positive end of the scale: the top is quality. Thus the use of the term 'quality assurance' contributes to a positive normative bias for the highest possible standards, thereby implicitly disregarding or treating pejoratively a high degree of vertical diversity within higher education which many experts consider the normal state of afairs as a consequence of the expansion of higher education systems.
3. The term 'assurance' links, in a fuzzy way, the analysis and the valuation of the status quo of higher education at the time of analysis with subsequent actions of rewards and sanctions or other actions aimed at improvement.

Terefore 'evaluation' can be considered to be the most suitable umbrella term for systematic activities of practically relevant assessment and valuation of the core functions and activities of HEIs or their subunits.

Admittedly, evaluation is used by many experts and actors not only as an umbrella term in this way, but also as term for supra-institutionally institutionalized schemes of assessment of the core functions and activities of HEIs or their subunits not closely linked to approval processes. In this way, the term was used in the 1980s in France and The Netherlands, and subsequently became popular in many other European countries.

Accreditation schemes difer from those specifc evaluation schemes, both in the type of judgement and its function. Accreditation schemes end in a "formal summary judgement" (e.g. 'yes' or 'no'), and they are linked to "formal approval processes" (of institutions, study programmes, etc.).

Approval means that a legitimate power grants "the right to exist". Or one should add that a power wishing to have the respective social control certifes the right to exist in the hope that institutions, study programmes etc. not being granted the right to exist would actually cease to exist or that the benefciaries of the non-accredited institutions or programmes would be stigmatized.

If the accreditation activities are managed by the institution granting the right to exist, approval is likely to be the inherent component of the accreditation process. If, however, the management of the accreditation process is dissociated from the power of granting the right to exist (this holds true for most national accreditation systems established in Europe since the late 1990s), there is room for two options: either the power of granting the right to exist foregoes any additional procedure, thus accepting the result of accreditation automatically as the basis of approval, or this power establishes a formal procedure in which it examines the result of the accreditation as well as possibly other information available and eventually makes an approval decision (or non-approval decision) on its own. With regard to the latter, for example, the Hungarian government, in establishing the first major accreditation system in Europe in the early 1990s, asked the Hungarian Accreditation Committee to assess the quality of study programmes and the Higher Education and Research Council to assess the social relevance, the economic needs and the feasibility of the programme, and eventually based the approval decision on both assessments.

Emergence of Evaluation Schemes in Europe

The sudden popularity of accreditation in Europe cannot be explained only by pointing at changes in the regulatory 'logics' of higher education systems emerging between the mid-1980s and the end of the 20th century (see, notably,), nor on the basis of a growing inclination to 'borrow' solutions from the U.S.A., but it certainly has to be viewed as well as a reaction to the state of national evaluation systems which had emerged and spread in

Europe during the same period. Terefore before discussing the character of this reaction, we first need to look at the understanding and the state of evaluation in Europe before the spread of accreditation systems.

Assessment in higher education is a traditionally well-established activity with respect to students: students' achievements are assessed frequently, and they are eventually awarded a degree which is conferred on the basis of assessments during the course of study and at the end of study. Grades or expressions such as 'with distinction' suggest that assessment to a certain extent is relative to the pool of students assessed. Decisions of 'pass' and 'fail' as well as the decision not to award a degree suggest, on the other hand, that assessment of students also has an absolute standard in mind as well. Assessment practices of individual teachers and within institutions and countries vary in the extent to which assessment is viewed relative to the pool of those assessed or is absolute according to perceived standards, but some kind of a compromise between these extremes is customary.

Also, academics are accustomed to frequent assessments of their 'performance'. They are assessed if they (i) apply for appointment and promotion, (ii) apply for resources beyond those granted to more or less every academic, and (iii) want to publish in prestigious publication outlets.

Retrospectively, i.e. afer we have experienced various evaluation systems, we might argue that assessment of 'performance' and 'achievement' in higher education in European countries traditionally: (i) was primarily linked to specifc occasions: assessment was undertaken if positions were to be flled and individuals looked for a position, if promotion was at stake, if scholars wanted to acquire grants and if persons wanted to publish in a highly reputed way; (ii) primarily addressed individuals, i.e. students and scholars, but hardly aggregates, i.e. study programmes, departments or institutions of higher education; (iii), in the case of assessment of scholars primarily directed to the above-average successful ones, was ofen only scheduled when scholars wanted to be promoted, to receive more grants than others and to publish with a mark of distinction; and (iv), in the case of assessment of scholars, was more strongly directed to research activities than to teaching activities.

In the mid-1980s, The Netherlands, France and the U.K. established national evaluation schemes in higher education. In subsequent years, many other European countries followed suit and established evaluation systems as well which refected the diferent approaches prevailing in the three 'pacemakers' of evaluation to a varying extent. Certainly, more or less all of the new evaluation systems difered from formerly existing schemes of assessing academic performance, notably in four respects.

1. Evaluation under the new schemes was undertaken regularly (for example every 5 years) instead of previously dominant assessments at specifc occasions (for example, on the occasion of asking for specifc research funds).
2. Evaluation schemes were all-embracing. Not only the high achievers were assessed (as in the case of application for research grants or for publication in selective publication outlets), nor only the low achievers, but also all levels of performance were included.
3. Evaluation schemes were systematic: criteria and procedures were to a certain extent general and known in advance. The systematic nature of evaluation was expected to guarantee a high level of quality of the assessment exercise.
4. Evaluation schemes, as a rule, addressed aggregates of scholars or other actors. Individual scholars or small relatively homogeneous teams were not assessed, but rather whole institutions of higher education, departments or study programmes in which the average and the interaction of a relatively heterogeneous set of actors belonging to an institutional unit were taken into consideration.

The evaluation was not used as a term to characterize merely any kind of assessment, but rather regular, all-embracing, systematic and aggregate-directed assessment.

Causes for the Establishment of Evaluation Schemes

Tere are various interesting explanations for the emergence of national evaluation schemes in Europe. They difer here and there, but we can easily draw from them a common core of explanations.

- Concerns had grown that the level of performance had been watered down at least in some sectors of the higher education systems in the wake of expansion and 'massifcation'.
- Governments, as the major funders of higher education, aimed increasingly at achieving efciency gains. They wanted to keep or increase the level of quality, even though they reduced the real per unit

expenditures in higher education (i.e. expenses per student and research expenditures per scholar).

- Afer a period of increasing involvement of governments in the planning and coordination of governments of the various European countries in the 1960s and 1970s, we noted an increasing loss of confdence in the 1980s and 1990s in the ability of governments to control and foster the quality, relevance and efciency of higher education through detailed means of control and supervision.
- Concurrently, there was an obvious loss of confdence in the academic profession that academics themselves would improve and safeguard quality, relevance and efciency in higher education through concentrating on their subject matter as such in their teaching and research activities, driven primarily by intrinsic motives and traditionally grown privileges.
- Hopes spread in the 1980s and 1990s that institutionalized refection of the processes and outcomes of activities in higher education, and increased managerial power within HEIs, would lead to advanced performance in higher education.

One has to add, however, that there is no full consensus among experts about the major causes of the establishment of evaluation schemes. Schwarz and Westerheijden argue convincingly that in the countries that were slow to introduce an evaluation scheme or have not introduced general evaluation schemes at all, the public trust in the academic self-regulation of quality was by no means higher than in countries that were at the forefront of introducing evaluation schemes.

Initial Disinterest in Accreditation

To a substantial extent, these changing views about defcits in the proper functioning of higher education systems in Europe were based on the assumption that the higher education system in the U.S.A. had been the most successful one for a couple of decades and that it would be valuable to copy some of its features in Europe in order to enhance the quality, relevance and efciency of higher education in Europe. Many features of higher education evaluation established since the mid-1980s in Europe had been borrowed from the U.S.A.

Why did Western European countries, when a need was felt to have all-embracing, regular and systematic assessment of HEIs or its subunits and areas of activities, not introduce accreditation systems? And why did Western European countries move towards the establishment of accreditation systems more than a decade later? Why did some Central and Eastern European countries establish only accreditation schemes or accreditation schemes prior to other evaluation schemes, and why did several of these countries introduce accreditation systems earlier than Western European countries?

We do not believe that we can explain the decisions of Western European countries not to introduce accreditation in the 1980s and 1990s by the peculiarities of the U.S.A. system of accreditation, i.e. a general, although decentralized, scheme of institutional accreditation alongside various separate schemes of professional accreditation, only if strong and highly organized professions existed, whereby accreditation remained ofcially 'voluntary' (, cf.). One could have assumed that these characteristics had been viewed as suitable for Western European countries. Such an explanation would not be convincing, however, because, when the Western European countries eventually introduced accreditation from the late 1990s, they did it distinctly from these U.S.A. peculiarities. Terefore one could argue that European countries could have introduced a distinct 'European' accreditation system earlier.

Evaluation systems such as the Dutch system introduced in the 1980s were considered to be more suitable in Europe and no need was felt for a long time to introduce accreditation of any kind.

First, a need was felt in Europe in the 1980s and 1990s to mobilize refection of the performance of higher education and to improve higher education through such a refection. This was considered in most European countries as being better served by an open system of evaluation rather than by a system linked to formal approval decisions.

Secondly, 'quality' improvement as well as decisions about the re-allocation of resources on the basis of quality assessment were viewed as necessary across all levels of quality. This need would not have been served well by an accreditation system putting a stronger emphasis on the minimum threshold of 'quality'.

Thirdly, on the other hand, no strong need was felt initially to move the quality assessment linked to the ofcial approval of the right to exist to some visible distance from the government. The key issue was not the infuence of government on the evaluation system, but rather government's use of information collected in evaluation activities in decisions of resource allocation.

Fourthly, no strong need was felt in the 1980s and 1990s to create substantial mechanisms in order to identify the 'black sheep' which should not have a right to exist. One assumed that more or less all government-funded programmes have the right to exist and that the identifcation of black sheep within the private programmes could be undertaken through other specifc means.

First Steps Towards Accreditation System

The establishment of accreditation schemes was first discussed and implemented in some cases in Central and Eastern European countries. Actually, the first major accreditation system was established in Hungary in 1993. This system could already be evaluated systematically before various Western European countries decided to establish an evaluation system.

Two reasons have to be named for why the introduction of accreditation schemes was more favourably viewed initially in Central and Eastern European countries than in Western European countries. First, when the old political regimes collapsed in Central and Eastern European countries, many representatives of universities and many academics hoped to gain substantial autonomy by becoming the visible prime actors of assessment of study programmes linked to approval. Secondly, a substantial expansion of higher education in the process of catching up with enrolment rates similarly to Western Europe was expected in Central and Eastern Europe; in this process of expansion, private higher education was assumed to be given a fairer chance, with the emergence of black sheep controlled not by the government, but rather by an accreditation system.

One might cast doubt, however, as to whether accreditation in Central and Eastern Europe really could fulfl the expected functions. The external evaluation of the Hungarian accreditation system, for example, which was undertaken 5 years afer its inauguration, is diplomatic in tone, but raises a few principal questions.

- For example, the accreditation system does not guarantee the autonomy of the decision-making process as a whole. The Hungarian Ministry not only asked the Accreditation Committee to assess the quality of the study programmes, but also asked the Higher Education and

Research Council to consider the needs and the fnancial feasibility of the study programme, and the Ministry eventually made an approval or non-approval decision, thereby taking into consideration the recommendation of both bodies.

- In addition, the standards for accreditation were viewed to be so high that a substantial expansion of the higher education system, and notably of the private sector, was by no means smoothly supported.
- Moreover, the workload involved in the accreditation system was generally viewed as being so high that it clearly discouraged the establishment of any improvement-oriented evaluation system alongside it. One could argue, however, that the advice for improvement might have been more important for the higher education system than the stigmatization of black sheep.
- Finally, it remained unclear how powerful the accreditation system would be for the actual provisions of study programmes. Experts agree that no public university would continue to ofer a non-approved programme and that programmes in many fields of study in the private sector would not survive for a long time. In the most fashionable programmes in the private sector, i.e. business study and computer science, non-accreditation would hardly be a threat for private HEIs ofering these programmes.

Having been a member of the external evaluation team of the Hungarian Accreditation Committee, I came to the conclusion that the majority of Hungarian actors involved were not sure whether one should introduce an accreditation system if one could decide again. But hardly anybody saw the possibility, once this system was established, of moving to any other logic of accreditation, evaluation and approval. In most cases there was room for minor improvements.

Recent Growing Interest in Accreditation

One might argue that there was not such a substantial change in the Western European higher education systems and their socio-political context from the 1980s and early 1990s towards the late 1990s that more or less 'necessitated' the shif from emphasis placed on evaluation schemes towards a preference for accreditation schemes. But there was a bundle of factors, each of which contributed towards a general change of public mood around

2000 in favour of accreditation schemes. Tree of these factors are outlined here.

- Tere certainly is a continuation of the shif in the public trust in the higher education system: a process of decreasing trust in government, declining confdence in the self-regulation of the academic community, growing emphasis on market forces, and fnally, increasing eforts to strengthen management power in higher education based on the hope that a strong university management could signifcantly improve the efectiveness and efciency of the higher education system.
- The notion spread that, in the wake of growing international competition of higher education and growing international mobility of students and graduates, those study programmes which had undergone a thorough systematic assessment process with a strong role of other forces than government in the framework of approval of study programmes were likely to have a higher reputation.
- The Bologna Process, i.e. the establishment of a stage system of study programmes and degrees all over Europe in a convergent manner, necessitated more intensive activities of curriculum development than ever found before. This was viewed by many actors as the right moment of moving towards a new system of assessment of study programmes, if one considered such a move preferable at all.

This list of arguments is similar to that presented by Hämälainen et al.: a growing emphasis on 'trust and accountability' in the spread of New Public Management concepts; the expectation that a common European labour market will emerge and that accreditation systems will serve to facilitate the mobility of students and graduates in Europe; and, fnally, that "borderless markets for higher education" are likely to lead to a "proliferation of accreditation systems".

One might add a fourth factor. Critique was increasingly voiced in Western Europe that the power of evaluation schemes with regard to subsequent reforms was too 'fuzzy'. This called for a system of programme assessment which does not serve either for most HEIs, even only as 'sof' advice, or for governments as a clear control instrument immediately linked with resource allocation. Accreditation was ofen viewed as a step towards a greater level of control, but not towards really threatening levels of control, because it denies the right to exist in extreme cases, but is not really threatening for the majority of evaluees. Such a new balance could emerge if one expected that the number of possible black sheep, for example through expansion of private institutions and study programmes, is somewhat on the rise in order to justify the establishment of accreditation systems, but the accreditation system as a whole was not a threat for the majority of study programmes.

It seems difcult as well to explain clearly the rush towards accreditation schemes according to a change of functions expected to be fulflled by major assessment schemes. Schwarz and Westerheijden, with reference to Weusthof and Frederiks, named four functions of assessment schemes: (i) accountability; (ii) quality improvement; (iii) validation; and (iv) information.

Accreditation schemes clearly serve validation more strongly than evaluation schemes. They might more strongly emphasize accountability and information as well, but this is by no means certain for all cases, because both evaluation schemes and accreditation schemes difer in their major thrust, and the borderline between these schemes is fuzzy in some cases. Altogether, it is not clear whether certain functions have gained so much weight over the years that they could be served better by accreditation schemes than by evaluation schemes such as those established in many European countries in the 1980s and early 1990s.

Actual Development of Accreditation Schemes

According to Schwarz and Westerheijden, who analysed the emergence of accreditation schemes in 20 countries participating in the Bologna Process, the "accreditation schemes with evaluation activities" existed in 1998 only in four Central and Eastern European countries as well as in the U.K. and in Ireland. Five years later, in 2003, such accreditation systems existed in 18 of the 20 countries analysed. The process of establishing accreditation schemes was undoubtedly very fast.

In comparing the 18 accreditation systems in Europe presented in the study, Schwarz and Westerheijden pointed out that seven characteristics were widely spread.

1. As a rule, study programmes were the *unit of analysis*.
2. As regards *coverage*, they noted that accreditation schemes addressed all degree programmes except for doctoral programmes in the majority of countries. Tere are notable exceptions, however. In Austria, an

accreditation system was established only for *Fachhochschulen*, and the accreditation scheme in Germany is only in charge of Bachelors and Masters programmes gradually established since 1998.

3. The *modes of inquiry and assessment* are similar with respect to some core elements. Site visits of external experts are customary. Altogether, there is a high degree of similarity between the new accreditation schemes and previously established 'elder brother' evaluation schemes.
4. Government, HEIs and academics, as a rule, are among the *reviewing and decision making actors*. Only in a few countries is a visible role allotted to students and to external stakeholders.
5. In the majority of countries, a *national accredi tation agency* was established with a *close link to government.*
6. In most cases where accreditation schemes were established in Europe, the statements made at the end of the review process are seen *ofcially as advice to government.*
7. In all European countries analysed, a *single scheme of government approval* exists.

Schwarz and Westerheijden noted substantial diferences between accreditation schemes as well.

- In some countries, *additional accreditation schemes* play a role, for example those run by professional accreditation and foreign accreditation schemes.
- Accreditation of *doctoral programmes* varies substantially by country. In some cases, accreditation of doctoral programmes is more or less identical with that of the regular degree programmes, in some cases it difers substantially and, in others, doctoral training is not accredited.
- The European accreditation schemes difer substantially in the *weight put on input, process and output or outcome criteria.*
- The *period of validity* difers substantially. It ranges from 2 to 10 years.
- *Appeal procedures* are arranged diferently across European countries.
- *Funding of accreditation* varies as well. In some countries, government bears all the costs. In other countries, HEIs have to pay the costs for the accreditation process, while government pays the costs for the accreditation agency.

- The varying *links between accreditation and approval* might be viewed formally and *de facto*. In some countries, accreditation serves as instrument of approval, in others it has the formal character of recommendation to the government to improve. In other cases, accreditation has no clear link to any approval decisions, and, in some cases, no supra-institutional programme approval procedures exist. With regard to the informal link, i.e. the extent to which government approval follows the accreditation decisions, the authors of the comparative analysis suggest that ownership of the accreditation schemes plays a role: the closer the accreditation agency is linked to government, the more likely the accreditation decision will lead to the approval.

In addition to these formal similarities and diferences of the accreditation scheme, it would be interesting as well to note the extent to which the standards of accreditation are similar across Europe. Obviously, European accreditation agencies are encouraged in the Bologna Process to co-operate in order to establish similar procedures, if they can be considered 'good practice', and to communicate about standards. The call for the establishment of European 'qualifcation frameworks' might lead to an additional mechanism of discourse about standards. But altogether, accreditation schemes in Europe do not serve directly the establishment of joint standards of study programmes in Europe. They might help at most to increase mutual trust in the quality of various programmes without any measured evidence.

THE FUTURE OF ACCREDITATION SYSTEMS

Accreditation systems were established in a large number of European countries over a short period.

They were encouraged by ideas to establish a threshold for the right to exist through a relatively transparent mechanism of academic involvement in the assessment process which eventually leads to a 'yes' or 'no' decision. Motives to establish accreditation were manifold. Notably, accreditation was expected to make assessment of study programmes more powerful than in mere improvement-oriented evaluation schemes, to identify black sheep more clearly amid trends towards greater vertical diversi-fcation, to create assessment less closely linked to governmental power than traditional government approval schemes, but still linked to ofcial government approval, and, last but not least, to increase the comparability of study programmes across Europe.

Actually, the accreditation schemes established in Europe have some elements more or less in common, but the diferences of the formal procedures vary in many respects. They difer in the extent to which they fulfl the various expectations named above. And we do not know how similar or diferent they are to determine the bottom line of accreditation: nobody knows the extent to which quality standards vary in accreditation schemes across Europe. Yet, accreditation might be helpful in facilitating recognition or non-recognition of study for border-crossing students and graduates in Europe, because they might help to increase the "zones of mutual trust".

The evaluation schemes established in Europe since the mid-1980s were modifed regularly at a remarkably quick pace. Terefore it should not come as a surprise to note a process of substantial change in accreditation schemes over time as well. Schwarz and Westerheijden made a distinction between an "internal drive for dynamism" and "contextual dynamics". With regard to the former, one cannot only expect learning from experiences, but also: "routine, bureaucratization and window dressing are dangers lurking behind". With regard to the latter, we obviously note a process of constant realignment of power to the actors and 'stakeholders' of higher education as well as growing expectations that accreditation has to play a role in the conficting co-ordination process between national prerogatives and European convergence.

It is premature to establish clearly the role accreditation plays in the overall patterns of evaluation exercises within the various countries, the power of accreditation in the actual decision about the right to exist and not exist and the role accreditation plays with respect to harmonization or diversity of quality standards across Europe. But certainly it is possible to note one clear trend: concern seems to grow that higher education is increasingly sufering from an overcomplexity and overload of assessment schemes. Obviously, an 'evaluation fatigue' (or 'assessment fatigue') is spreading. It is premature to predict as well how the overall activities of assessments of institutions, departments, programmes or individual scholars will be trimmed to a feasible size. But the price for this persistence might be enormous: improvement-oriented evaluation schemes, which can be more benefcial for the quality of all higher education programmes, obviously have already sufered setbacks in various European countries as the consequence of the accreditation boom, and they might fade away in many European countries.

Accreditation in The Netherlands

Key dates of the accreditation system in The Netherlands are as follows:

- 1985 Agreement about external quality assessment
- 1988 First cycle of external programme reviews
- 2002 From improvement to accountability
- 2003 A system for accreditation in The Netherlands
- 2005 A Dutch–Flemish accreditation organization

In 1985 the Ministry of Higher Education and Science published a document entitled *Higher Education: Autonomy and Quality*. According to this document, quality was the responsibility of the HEIs (higher education institutions) and they were therefore accountable for their internal evaluation. The external quality assessment was seen as a task for a newly created inspectorate for the universities.

In the opinion of the universities, however, quality assurance is the responsibility of the institutions themselves, and in 1986 it was agreed that the institutions would take care of quality assessment through evaluation. They would do that by internal evaluation and by periodical external quality assessment. The institutions would develop a co-ordinated and public external quality assessment system. In 1988, the first experiences were gathered.

In 2002, a shif was made from the Scylla of improvement to the Charybdis of accountability. Some people judged the existing system to be too lenient and were in favour of more external pressure and a possibility of sanctions against weakly performing institutions. A function of improvement was not enough, they wanted to add a function of accountability.

In 2003, a system of accreditation was introduced in The Netherlands. Accreditation is described as "a formal judgment that the quality of a degree course or an institution meets certain standards. This judgment is based on quality assessment. And precisely this necessary quality assessment shows that accreditation and quality assurance are connected.".

In 2005, the Dutch–Flemish accreditation organization was formally founded. This organization decides whether the programmes of the HEIs meet the legal requirements. Programmes have to meet a basic quality in order to be allowed to deliver certifcates which are recognized by the government. A positive decision qualifes the degree course for funding by the government.

Description of The Chosen External Quality System

The chosen external quality system can be described in the following points:

- Internal quality care as a starting point
- Writing of a self-study report
- Visit of an external review committee
- Report of the external review committee
- Meta-evaluation by the inspectorate

At the beginning, the internal quality care was accentuated. Greater autonomy and more freedom were welcomed by the universities. Autonomy and quality assurance as two sides of the same coin were not disputed. But the HEIs could not agree to external quality assessment being the task of an authority outside the institutions themselves.

Writing a self-study report was the first step in the evaluation process. A format for this self-study report was given. The report had to cover topics such as objectives, structure and content of the programme, input–throughput–output of students, teaching and learning environment, feasibility, quality of the graduates, efectiveness of the organization, and quality of personnel, facilities, internationalization and internal quality care.

Next, a visit of an external review committee was organized. In this committee, peers, an educationalist and sometimes a student participated. On the basis of the self-study report, this committee discussed matters with the board, teachers, students and graduates. Clarifcation, verifcation and gathering of additional information were the aims of these discussions. Similar programmes of diferent institutions were visited by the same committee.

Strengths and points of attention were described in a report by the external review committee. The aforementioned self-study report topics directed this description. Since the committee visited all similar programmes, descriptions of some general aspects of the discipline were possible. The function of improvement was important in the reports of the external review committees.

A meta-evaluation was performed regularly by the inspectorate. In this way, some additional remarks could be made if external review committees were too positive or not positive enough. The inspectorate also had an opportunity to formulate warnings to the programmes. These warnings could lead to visiting activities by the inspectorate or to special attention of the review committee by the next round.

Important Characteristics

The following are important characteristics of the quality assurance system:

- Final responsibility by the institutions
- Peer assessment has an important role
- Formal sanctions as an exception
- Improvement as an important issue
- Trust as a leading principle

For the first 15 years, the quality assurance system was based mainly on internal quality assessments. The responsibility for the quality care was given to the HEIs. Although there was an external review committee and a meta-evaluation by the inspectorate, no important decisions were made by external agencies. The autonomy of the institutions was respected.

Another leading principle was that peers were viewed as being the most competent reviewers in a system of external quality assessment. Traditionally, there was no inspectorate for the universities in The Netherlands. It came by surprise in 1985. The universities tried to keep or even broaden their autonomy as fast as possible. They accepted the authority of peers, but there was a resistance to accept the authority of the inspectorate.

The external quality assessment was not threatening, because there were no formal sanctions. Nevertheless, the system had a positive infuence. The self-study reports were public, there was a growing openness about educational programmes, external review committees brought ideas from elsewhere and there was a positive drive for improvement at the HEIs.

The function of improvement turned out to be very important. Exchange of ideas, co-operation, common projects and action programmes followed the reports of the external review committees. The reports concentrated on strengths and points of attention and not on weaknesses. Tere was a growing interest of the institutions for education as distinguished from research.

This first period of external quality assessment was based on a positive attitude. The function of improvement had an important role, and there was less suspicion and fear. Tere was hardly any reason for distrust because the consequences of the external review were limited. The institutions learned a lot by writing a self-study report, and most external review committees were very helpful in fnding improvements.

Description of the Chosen Accreditation System

The accreditation system can be summarized by the following steps:

- Periodical accreditation as an obligation
- Writing a self-study report
- Visit by an external review committee
- Report by the external review committee
- Decision by the Dutch–Flemish accreditation organization

Since 2003, there has been an obligation of an accreditation system. All educational programmes of HEIs need an accreditation every 6 years. Accreditation qualifes the degree course for government funding, students of the course receive study grants and the institution that provides the course is entitled to issue degree certifcates that are recognized by the government.

Writing a self-study report is still the same. However, the requirements are more specifc. The format asks for six subjects, which together cover 21 facets, and are related to a number of explicitly formulated criteria. Instructions about measurable indicators are less ambivalent. The possibility of appendices is nearly endless, which leads to an immense amount of papers, reports, regulations, plans and so on.

A visit by an external review committee is still on the agenda. This visit is organized by an intermediate organization which is responsible for the resulting report. An important diference is that this committee has to judge the six subjects in terms of excellent, good, satisfactory and unsatisfactory. The available criteria, however, are not clear and are ambiguous. Terefore these decisions are not based on very strong foundations.

The accreditation decision is taken by the Dutch–Flemish Accreditation Organization. The self-study report is not available for this organization. They have to decide on the basis of the report of the external review committee, but they have an opportunity to gather additional information on their own. Tere is a fear that bureaucratic elements dominate the approach of the Dutch–Flemish Accreditation Organization.

Important characteristics

Tere are various important characteristics of the accreditation system:

- Final responsibility by an external organization
- Doubts about the value of peer review
- A possibility of rigorous formal sanctions
- Accountability as an important issue
- Distrust as a leading principle

The introduction of an accreditation system introduces at the same time a more important role for the external authorities. The authority of the peers is more or less replaced by the authority of the governors. Both peers and governors are necessary in the existing system. A danger, however, is that now governors use the weaknesses in the arguments of the peers in order to justify the decisions of the governors.

The new accreditation system seems to illustrate some doubts about the value of peer reviews. A bureaucratic view of the accreditation organization is superior to the report of an external review committee from peers. This can lead to a vague mixture of professional and governmental arguments. Both sets of arguments are valuable, but a vague mixture will lead to a lot of misunderstandings.

*Dittrich state*s: "A n advantage for the government is that these decisions on accreditation may subsequently also can be used for political decisions". This statement makes clear that it is acceptable to mix professional and political decisions. This seems to be an unacceptable solution. Professional and political arguments have their own value, but hiding political decisions in professional arguments is misleading and unwanted.

Preference for a function of improvement does not mean that accountability is not important. Accountability, however, has to specify its own criteria. Tere are several possibilities for this specifcation in terms of realized results, average costs, impact on national and international projects, and so on. Trying to transform professional criteria into political arguments is misleading and generates distrust and suspicion.

Distrust seems to be a factor in moving from improvement to accountability. It is understandable that peers try to defend their colleagues. It is hard to solve this problem. Replacing professionals with governors leads to a mixture of arguments and not to a clarifcation of the situation. Arguments based on the quality of peers have to be distinguished from arguments based on political arguments. A mixture of arguments leads to unclear situations.

Arguments for Accreditation

Arguments in favour of accreditation include the following:

- An impulse to improve quality
- International benchmarking
- Transparency of the quality of education
- Clear governmental consequences
- Keeping variety in quality assessment

An impulse to improve quality is expected from the introduction of accreditation. The existing quality assurance system was seen to be losing some of its efectiveness. Some routines were developed and the intended improvements were not always realized. It was expected that a more severe approach would lead to a new and more efective system for quality assurance. Accreditation was the result.

International benchmarking as stimulated by the declaration of Bologna was also seen as an argument for introducing a system of accreditation. Comparable information about educational programmes in education is needed in order to facilitate mobility of students within Europe. The Bologna process tries to stimulate mobility of students and therefore a comparison of relevant information is needed. Accreditation can enable comparisons between countries.

By developing a system with a limited number of subjects, specifed in a number of facets and related to clear formulated criteria, a greater transparency of the quality of education may be expected. To make subjects, facets and criteria explicit is undoubtedly an important contribution to the improvement of comparability and transparency of programmes of the HEIs.

Accreditation leads to clear governmental consequences. A positive decision on accreditation qualifes the degree course for government funding, students of the course receive study grants and the institution that provides the course is entitled to issue degree certifcates recognized by the government. A decision not to award accreditation has the opposite consequences.

The detailed format of accreditation in subjects, facets and criteria makes it possible to demonstrate the variation in programmes for higher education. Programmes are able to choose a specifc profle. Up to now, it is unclear whether institutions make use of this opportunity. Some people think that there is also a great risk of unwanted uniformity.

Subjects in the Accreditation System

The accreditation system looks at the following subjects:

- Objectives of the programmes
- Quality of the programmes
- Quality and quantity of personnel
- Available facilities
- Internal quality care
- Realized results

The judgment about the objectives of the programme has to be at least satisfactory. Facets which have to be included are the level and orientation of the programme, and domain-specifc requirements. For both facets, some criteria are formulated to be fulflled.

The quality of programmes is subdivided into the following facets: (i) relationship between objectives and content of the programme; (ii) requirements of professional and academic orientation of the programme; (iii) coherence of the programme; (vi) feasibility; (v) congruence of curriculum design and curriculum content; (vi) assessment and testing; (vii) 'master proof'; (viii) fnal professional proof; and (ix) admission requirements.

Personnel is a very important factor in education. This leads to the following facets: (i) quality of personnel; (ii) professional or academic orientation; and (iii) quantity of personnel.

With respect to the available facilities, there is a distinction between the following facets: (i) material facilities; and (ii) guidance of students.

The subject internal quality makes a distinction between the following facets: (i) evaluation of the results; (ii) measures for improvement; and (iii) involvement of co-workers, students, alumni and professionals.

Realized results distinguish two facets: (i) realized level of education; and (ii) output of the educational programme.

Institutional Expectations about Accreditation (Priorities)

Expectations of HEIs about accreditation include the following priorities:

- Improving the quality of education
- Keeping the function of improvement
- Acceptance of decisions about accreditation
- Growing mobility of students
- Growing diferentiation in education
- Rejecting many requests for accreditation

Recently, the Dutch–Flemish accreditation organization gathered information about the accreditation system. Teachers and students were asked to choose priorities out of six possible efects of accreditation.

Improving the quality of education was appointed as the most preferable outcome of accreditation. This probably refects the growing attention given to the improvement of the quality of education. The visiting review committees are partly responsible for this growing attention. These committees accentuated the improvement of quality.

Next was to keep the function of improvement. This is apparently important for teachers and students. Tere is probably a fear that accreditation, with its sanctions, hides improvement behind accountability. The respondents want to keep the function of improvement.

Acceptance of statements from the accreditation organization was number three. Acceptance of decisions was seen as a positive sign for accreditation. It is unclear whether the respondents had some doubts about the acceptance of accreditation. A great majority of decisions by the accreditation organization is clearly accepted.

A growing mobility of students was mentioned as the next priority for a successful accreditation system. To stimulate the mobility of students is an important element in the declaration of Bologna, but its weight in this inquiry was not that high. Quality improvement is rated higher by the responding teachers and students.

Increasing diferentiation came next on the scale of positive expectations. The system of accreditation makes it possible to formulate specifc objectives and to create a local concept of education. Increasing diferentiation, however, does not score very highly in this enquiry by teachers and students.

Rejecting many requests for accreditation is the least popular expectation in this inquiry. This topic is probably somewhat controversial. If higher education is seen as a possibility for the happy few, one can be in favour of rejecting requests for accreditation. But rejecting requests will not support the broadening and expanding of higher education.

Some Important Changes

Important changes in the accreditation system include those:

- From improvement to accountability
- From trust to distrust
- From peers to bureaucrats
- From institutions to government
- From decentralization to centralization

A comparison of the first quality assurance system with the new accreditation system points at some important changes.

The function of improvement is more and more replaced by the accountability function. By keeping the self-study report and the visit of the external review committee, one tries to keep the function of improvement. The severe sanctions, however, are not an invitation to a great openness by the HEIs. These sanctions are probably an invitation for hiding the problems and window dressing.

Some distrust seems to be introduced by the system of accreditation. In 1985, the responsibility of HEIs for quality assurance was accepted by the government. Some 15 years later, it was decided to introduce an accreditation system with a substantial responsibility for an accreditation organization which was labelled as independent from the HEIs. Did something go wrong and where is this documented?

A quality assurance system with a central role for peers is replaced by a system that makes non-professionals responsible for the fnal decisions. Accountability decisions can be made by non-professionals, but they have to be made on the basis of their own criteria. The professional information from the external review committee is not a sound basis for accountability decisions. They are better as a starting point for improvements.

The main responsibility for quality assurance is taken away from the HEIs. An independent newly created organization is responsible for the accreditation decisions. This implies that political and non-professional arguments can play a more important role in the development of the system of higher education. Because the criteria are explicit, but still allow for diferent interpretations, some uncertainties (sometimes with bad consequences) are introduced.

Unwanted Effects of the Accreditation System

Unfortunately, there are unwanted efects of the system, such as:

- Accreditation is very expensive
- Accreditation stimulates bureaucracy
- Accreditation leads to uniformity
- Accreditation stimulates window dressing
- Accreditation hinders real innovation

The accreditation system is not accepted without critical remarks.

The accreditation system is seen as expensive. Compared with the existing assurance care system, the costs are doubled. The extra accountability results in additional procedures and more paperwork and costs. These costs are allocated to the Dutch– Flemish accreditation organization, by the visiting and assessing institutes and by the HEIs.

Increasing bureaucracy is seen as a second disadvantage of the accreditation system. The information which has to be given by the institutions grows and grows. The regulations for institutions, external review committees, visiting and assessing institutes, and the accreditation organization grow and expand. Even the communication between these actors becomes more and more complicated.

Tere is a fear that accreditation leads to uniformity. It is easy and safe to conform to traditional patterns because these traditional patterns are generally accepted. In this view, accreditation is an obstacle for innovation. New ideas and new views are risky because they can be rejected by the accreditation organization. In order to avoid risks, institutions can prefer traditional and generally accepted approaches.

A negative accreditation decision has important consequences for an HEI. This can be seen as an invitation for window dressing. Positive points are described as extensively as possible, and negative points are hardly described in the self-study report. The overall efect is that an artifcial situation is created and that the external review committees have to act as detectives.

Innovation is not stimulated by accreditation. Traditional criteria seem to be leading in the process of accreditation and institutions do not want to take risks. Nevertheless, innovation is a must in a world of increasing technological possibilities. Critical remarks related to the existing educational programmes have to be taken seriously and this means that it is unacceptable if accreditation hinders innovation.

The importance of accreditation decisions can be seen as an invitation to concentrate on fgures and measures instead of on ideas and innovations. More and more fgures and measures are asked for, and there is a risk that innovations are not recognized as innovations. Accreditation tends to be conservative, which is why traditional and well-known solutions will be preferred over innovative and unknown solutions.

In an accreditation system, external requirements tend to dominate internal requirements. Comparability, international benchmarking and political decisions can play an important role.Developments within a discipline, educational concepts of an HEI and try-outs of innovations will fnd it hard to be acknowledged in an accreditation system.

The quality assurance system which was introduced in 1988 was accepted well by the HEIs. The accreditation system is still criticized on several grounds: it is expensive, it is conservative, it is bureaucratic, it is complex and it is punitive. Of course, all of these characteristics can be changed, but there are no important initiatives to do so.

In 1995, Vroeijenstijn wrote a book entitled *Improvement and Accountability: Navigating between Scylla and Charybdis*. It is clear that it is very difcult to combine improvement and accountability in only one system. Changing the quality assurance system from 1988 into an accreditation system seems to illustrate that improvement and accountability require a diferent approach.

The desirability of a function of accountability is not criticized here. Criticism is related to the combination of improvement and accountability in one and the same system. The introduction of an accreditation system seems to be an obstacle for the function of improvement.

References

Maassen, P. (2000) Editorial. *European Journal of Education* 35(4), 377–383.

Ranson, S. (2003) Public accountability in the age of neo-liberal governance. *Journal of Education Polic y* 18(5), 459–480.

Corbett, D. (1992) *Australian Public Sector Management*, 2nd edn, Allen and Unwin, Sydney.

Orsingher, C. (ed.) (2006) *Assessing Quality in European Higher Education Institutions*, Physica-Verlag, Heidelberg.

Welsh, J.F., Alexander, S. and Dey, S. (2001) Continuous quality measurement: restructuring assessment for a new technological and organisational environment. *Assessment and Evaluation in Higher Education* 26(5), 391–401.

Drennan, L. (2001) Quality assessment and the tension between teaching and research. *Quality in Higher Education* 7(3), 167–178.

Saroyan, A. and Amundsen, C. (2001) Evaluating university teaching: time to take stock. *Assessment and Evaluation in Higher Education* 26(4), 341–353.

Worthington, A.C. (2002) The impact of student perceptions and characteristics on teaching evaluations: a case study in finance education. *Assessment and Evaluation in Higher Education* 27(1), 49–64.

8

Peer Evaluation

Science rests on peer review. Peer review is the method by which grants are allocated, manuscripts published and study programmes improved. As 'gatekeepers' of science, the task of peers or colleagues asked to evaluate applications, manuscripts or study programmes is to ensure high standards in higher education and research. Peer review is regarded as the embodiment of the principle of mutual control. Proponents of the system hold that peer review is more efective than any other known instrument for self-regulation in higher education and research. As stated by Eisenhart, "equals active in the same field are said to be in the best position to know whether quality standards have been met and a contribution to knowledge made". Thus the producers of science, the specialists, become the gatekeepers of science.

Peer evaluation in research means a process by which a selective jury of experts in a given scientifc field is asked to evaluate the undertaking of scientifc activity or its outcomes. Such a group of experts may be consulted as a group or individually, without the need for personal contacts among the evaluators. Although there is evidence that peer review improves the quality of the reporting of research results, critics of peer review argue that: (i) reviewers rarely agree on whether or not to recommend that a manuscript be published or a grant be awarded, thus making for poor reliability of the peer-review process; (ii) recommendations and decisions in peer review are frequently biased, that is judgements are not based solely on scientifc merit, but are also infuenced by personal attributes of the authors, applicants or the reviewers themselves; (iii) the process lacks predictive validity, since there is little or no relationship between the judgements on applications or manuscripts and the subsequent usefulness of the proposed or published research to the scientifc community, as indicated by the frequency of citations to the research in later scientifc papers.

Usually, peer-review-based study programme evaluation begins with internal self-assessment, whereby an academic programme or institute conducts its own analysis of strengths and weaknesses for a self-evaluation report. The next stage is external evaluation. Here, peer reviewers conduct a site visit of the programmes or units under evaluation and prepare an external evaluation report. The follow-up stage entails implementation of the reviewers' recommendations. Despite agreement on the general course of proceeding, national quality assurance systems difer greatly in the details. The peer-review-based evaluation of study programmes has long come under critical fre. Tere are complaints, for instance in Germany (as well as in other countries), about the supposed high costs and burdens of evaluation, including both fnancial and personnel costs, and about the lack of consequences following evaluation. In the face of scarce public funding, it is said that study programme evaluation serves merely to supply political decision-makers with information that is used for cost-cutting purposes and for changing the self-determination by professors into external control.

In recent years, a number of published studies have addressed these and other criticisms that have been raised against peer evaluation in higher education and research. Studies that involved meta-evaluations of journal and grant peer-review procedures are presented below.

Grant Peer Review

As an assessment tool, peer review is asked to be reliable, fair and valid. Should a stock-taking of research on peer review fnd no evidence for the reliability, fairness and predictive validity of recommendations and decisions in peer review, one would have to question peer-reviewed contributions (publications and approved grant applications) as a measure of scientifc advancement and of scientists' productivity.

Agreement among Reviewers

If a scientifc contribution meets scientifc standards and is a contribution to the advancement of science, it is reasonable to expect that two reviewers would agree on its value. Manuscripts and applications are rated reliably when there is a high level of agreement between independent reviewers. However, high agreement alone cannot result in high reliability, because a certain level of agreement can be expected to occur on the basis of chance alone.

Not all editors see reviewer disagreement as a negative factor; many see it as a positive method of evaluating a manuscript from a number of diferent perspectives. If reviewers are selected for their opposing viewpoints or expertise, a high degree of reviewer agreement should not be expected. It can even be argued that too much agreement is in fact a sign that the review process is not working well, that reviewers are not properly selected for diversity and that some are redundant. Whether the comments of reviewers are in fact based on diferent perspectives is a question that has been examined by only a few empirical studies. One study, for example, showed that reviewers of the same manuscript simply commented on diferent aspects of the manuscript: "In the typical case, two reviews of the same paper had no critical point in common… [T]hey wrote about diferent topics, each making points that were appropriate and accurate. As a consequence, their recommendations about editorial decisions showed hardly any agreement".

It has also been pointed out that the low degree of reviewer agreement refects the low levels of cognitive consensus that exist at the research frontiers of all scientifc disciplines. At the frontiers of research, it is usually impossible to make an 'objective' evaluation of new work.

Fairness of the Peer Review Process

Journal submissions or grant applications are supposed to be judged solely on the basis of their scientifc merit. The ideal Mertonian norm of universalism prescribes that the evaluation of new contributions should be based upon objective scientifc criteria and not on the characteristics of the author, applicant or assessor. Surveys of grant applicants and authors show, however, that they still have fears about a lack of objectivity in peer review. As many as 41% of the applicants of the NIHR (National Institute of Handicapped Research), now NIDRR (National Institute on Disability and Rehabilitation Research) (Washington, DC, U.S.A.), disagreed with the statement "the peer reviewer comments were fair".

Reviews of peer review research name up to 25 diferent potential sources of bias in peer review. In these studies, it is usual to call any feature of an assessor's cognitive or attitudinal mindset that could interfere with an objective judgment a bias. Other studies show that replication studies and research that leads to statistically insignifcant fndings stand a rather low chance of being judged favourably by peer reviewers. Research on bias in peer review faces two serious problems. First, the research fndings on bias are inconsistent. For example, some studies investigating gender bias in journal review processes point out that women scientists are at a disadvantage. However, a similar number of studies report no gender efects or mixed results.

Secondly, it is almost impossible to establish unambiguously whether work from a particular group of scientists (e.g. junior or senior scientists) receives better reviews and thus a higher acceptance rate due to preferential biases afecting the review and decision-making process, or if favourable review and favourable judgements in peer review are a simple consequence of the high scientifc quality of the corresponding manuscripts or applications.

Presumably, it will never be possible to eliminate all doubts regarding the fairness of the reviewing process. Because reviewers are humans, their behaviour, whether performing their salaried duties, enjoying their leisure time or writing reviews, is infuenced by factors that cannot be predicted, controlled or standardized. Terefore it is important that the process of peer reviewing should be studied continuously. Any evidence of bias in judgements should be uncovered for purposes of correction and modifcation of the process.

Predictive Validity of the Peer Review Process

What is peer review for? One answer to this question is that it is a method for selecting the best grant applications for funding and the best manuscripts for journal publication. It is difcult to test this aim, because there is no agreed upon definition of what constitutes a good manuscript or a good application. A conventional approach is to use citation counts as a proxy for research contributions, since they measure the international impact of the research by individuals or groups of scientists. Critics of peer review claimed that manuscript refereeing is without validity in forecasting the subsequent usefulness of a work to scientists as refected in citations of the work in other scientifc papers. On the contrary, based on citation rates for accepted manuscripts and previously rejected manuscripts published elsewhere, editorial decisions in all of the four existing studies showed a high degree of predictive validity. Similar results were reported for grant peer review.

The most serious limitation of research on the predictive validity of recommendations and decisions in peer-review processes is the very small number of studies.

In a study on the peer-review process of *Angewandte Chemie,* one of the most important chemistry journals worldwide, we traced the fate of rejected manuscripts. Of the manuscripts rejected by *Angewandte Chemie,* 71% were later published in other journals. These 'rejects' were published in a total of 39 journals. However, none of the rejected manuscripts appeared in a journal that had a greater impact factor than *Angewandte Chemie.* In addition, papers accepted by *Angewandte Chemie* were on average cited twice as frequently as manuscripts that had been rejected on the basis of reviewers' recommendations, but were later published elsewhere. The editor of the *Journal of Clinical Investigation,* Jean Wilson, the editor of the *British Medical Journal,* Stephen Lock, and the editor of *Cardiovascular Research,* Tobias Opthof, established very similar results

A review of the study on the peer-review process of *Angewandte Chemie* described above raised an argument against this form of validity test, stating that papers accepted by *Angewandte Chemie* may have been cited on average more frequently than those published elsewhere simply because they appeared in a journal with a high JCR (Journal Citation Report) Impact Factor (provided by Tomson Scientifc, Philadelphia, PA, U.S.A.), i.e. in a journal with high visibility. However, the citation rates of journal articles do not seem to be detectably infuenced by the status of the journals in which they are published.

In a study on committee peer review for the selection of doctoral and postdoctoral research fellowship recipients, we analysed the predictive validity of the peer-review process followed by the B.I.F. (Boehringer Ingelheim Fonds, Heidesheim, Germany), a foundation for the promotion of basic research in biomedicine, in two steps. In a first step, we examined 2039 articles by 120 former fellowship recipients that had been published between the date of approval of the fellowship and December 2000. The results showed that the research articles by B.I.F. fellows were cited considerably more ofen than the 'average' paper (average citation rate) published in the journal sets corresponding to the fields 'Multidisciplinary', 'Molecular Biology and Genetics' and 'Biology and Biochemistry' in ESI (Essential Science Indicators) from Tomson Scientifc (most of the fellows publish within these fields).

In the second step, we conducted a citation analysis for articles published *previous* to the applicants' approval or rejection for a B.I.F. fellowship. On the basis of the model estimation (negative binomial regression model), journal articles that had been published by applicants approved for a fellowship award (64 applicants) prior to applying for the B.I.F. fellowship award can be expected to have 37% (straight counts of citations) and 49% (complete counts of citations) more citations than articles that had been published by rejected applicants (333 applicants). Furthermore, comparison with international scientifc reference values revealed that (i) articles published by successful and non-successful applicants were cited considerably more ofen than the 'average' publication, and (ii) excellent research performance can be expected more from successful than non-successful applicants. All in all, the fndings of the two steps of the comprehensive analyses confrmed that the foundation is not only achieving its goal of selecting the best junior scientists for fellowship awards, but also successfully attracting highly talented young scientists to apply for B.I.F. fellowships.

Meta Evaluation of Peer Review based Study Programme Evaluation

The International Centre for Higher Education Resrmany) initiated an analysis of procedures and the efectiveness of the evaluation processes of the Central Evaluation and Accreditation Agency Hanover (ZEvA, Zentrale Evaluations- und Akkreditierungsagentur Hannover) and the Consortium of Universities in Northern Germany (VNU, Verbund Norddeutscher Universitäten) in the evaluation of study programmes. The study is the first comprehensive and representative investigation of peer-review-based study programme evaluations in Germany, and it assesses the two most tried-and-tested and best-known evaluation procedures in Germany [in all, there are eight evaluation agencies in Germany for systematic study programme evaluation at HEIs (higher education institutions)] from multiple perspectives and using multiple methods. VNU is a consortium of six German universities, and ZEvA is a common agency for Lower Saxony HEIs; both have conducted peer-review-based study programme evaluations since the mid-1990s. They completed the first evaluation cycle in 2001.

The study data were collected in a questionnaire survey by mail of all former external reviewers and members of institutes ('members of institutes' refers to all members of an evaluation working group formed within an institute under evaluation, including students) who participated in evaluations conducted by ZEvA and VNU. A total of 648 returned questionnaires could be included in the analysis, with a response rate of 41%. In addition to the questionnaire survey, 33 interviews were conducted and examined using content analysis. The interview participants were university heads and the authorized agents or contact partners at the diferent HEIs, the spokesperson of VNU, the scientifc director at ZEvA and the managing directors and staf members of VNU and ZEvA.

Overall Assessment of The Evaluation Procedures

To tap overall assessments, the members of institutes and reviewers were asked whether the peer-review-based study programme evaluation (internal evaluation, external evaluation and implementation of recommendations) proved to be useful and efective, whether the evaluation process achieved the goals of quality assurance and improvement, whether the results of the evaluation were commensurate to the efort required, whether they were satisfed overall with the process and whether participation in the evaluation process proved worthwhile for them personally.

The majority of the respondents were satisfed overall with the evaluations conducted at the individual universities (68% of institute members and 95% of reviewers). The majority of the respondents also found that the evaluation process achieved the goals of quality assurance and improvement (65% of institute members and 93% of reviewers) and that participation in the evaluation proved personally rewarding (61% of institute members and 93% of reviewers). Whereas 82% of the reviewers saw the efort entailed as commensurate to the results of the evaluation, the majority of the institute members (55%) found the efort required to be disproportionate to the results. All in all, however, as the results show, peer-review-based study programme evaluation proved to be useful and efective in the opinion of the reviewers and the members of the institutes.

As an alternative to the multi-stage procedure, some German universities conduct evaluations of study programmes in only one stage. The one-stage procedure can be either an external evaluation or an internal evaluation only. In the case of an internal evaluation only, a university consultant may be asked to provide professional support. Exclusively external evaluations include, among others, structural evaluations by management consultants.The reviewers and members of institutes were asked to indicate possible preferences for certain types of one-stage procedures over the multi-stage procedure. As an alternative to a purely internal evaluation, 22% preferred to see study programme evaluation conducted in the form of an external evaluation exclusively, by review committee, and 5% in the form of an external evaluation exclusively, by one reviewer.

The interview participants also rated the evaluation procedure overall as positive. The majority of the interviewees believed that the evaluations were necessary and that they proved to be useful and efective. They emphasized as particular strengths of the evaluations that in their design the evaluations were university-independent, self-critical and well-structured and organized. On the other hand, some interview participants ofered the criticism that the purpose of the evaluation was clarifed insufciently, that the personnel situation in the institute was not taken into account sufciently and that the evaluation did not take a sufciently international orientation.

Linkng Study Programme Evaluations with Rankings, University Funding, Evaluation of Research and Accreditation

In our meta-evaluation of peer-review-based study programme evaluation, the written questionnaire respondents were also asked (i) whether there should be a ranking of the universities participating in the evaluation, (ii) whether they would like to see evaluation results linked to funding decisions, and whether the study programme evaluation should be linked to (iii) the evaluation of research or (iv) accreditation.

Evaluation of Study Programmes

In line with common practice in European higher education, the evaluation procedures of ZEvA and VNU do not aim to produce a ranking of the participating institutions. An item on the questionnaire asked whether they had nonetheless feared during the diferent phases of the evaluation that their institute would be ranked. The fndings show that 62% of institute members and 80% of reviewers had not gained the impression that the evaluation was aiming towards ranking.

Both the questionnaire respondents and interview participants were asked whether they would have found a ranking of the participating HEIs desirable. The clear majority of interview participants spoke against ranking.

Nearly three-quarters (72%) of the survey respondents rejected ranking. Among the 28% that found ranking desirable, members of institutes (31%) were somewhat more strongly represented than reviewers (19%). Overall, the fndings as to ranking of HEIs participating in evaluation make it clear that the majority of people involved in evaluations neither fear nor are in favour of ranking.

Evaluation of Study Programmes and The Issue of Linkage to Funding

In the discussion on higher education policies in Germany, some voices have considered linking the amount of funding allocated to an institute to the results of evaluations. This linkage could result in funding increases or cuts. On the survey questionnaire, the respondents were asked to assess these proposals. They were asked whether evaluation results should be linked to funding increases only, to cuts in funding only, to both increases and reductions in funding, or not linked to funding at all. Regarding the linkage issue, members of institutes (42%) voted somewhat more frequently than reviewers (33%) for the alternative, namely no linkage to funding, while reviewers (46%) voted somewhat more frequently than the institute members (37%) in favour of linking evaluation results to funding increases or reductions.

Approximately 20% of both groups favoured linkage of evaluation results to funding increases only, and only 1% (institute members) and 2% (reviewers) approved of linkage to cuts in funding. The majority of the interview participants saw evaluation results becoming linked to funding decisions in future. Most of these interview participants viewed both positive and negative sanctions as appropriate. Still, a considerable number of the interview participants thought that linkage of evaluation to funding decisions would not be appropriate.

Evaluation of Study Programmes and the Issue of Linkage to Evaluation of Research

ZEvA and VNU evaluate study programmes. More than half of the questionnaire respondents (55%) indicated a preference for joint evaluation of teaching and research, while 39% voted for separate evaluations of these areas (6% of the respondents had no opinion). On this issue, the institute members and the reviewers are in agreement. The majority of the interview participants, in contrast, rejected the idea of a joint evaluation procedure for the two areas. The main reasons given by the interview participants were the following: (i) teaching would decrease in importance in comparison with research; (ii) research has a stronger interdisciplinary orientation; (iii) evaluations of research focus more strongly on the performance of individuals and less on the department as a whole; (iv) the objectives of the two evaluation procedures are too diferent; and (v) a joint evaluation procedure would require too much efort.

The interview participants found, however, that dovetailing study programme evaluation with research evaluation made sense. They stated that the time points of conducting the two evaluations should be co-ordinated and that a common statistical database should be used. For future decision-making afecting an entire department, co-ordination would make it easier for the results of both evaluations to be considered.

Issue of Linkage to Accreditation

The interview participants were rather reserved in their judgements on linking study programme evaluations to accreditation. The majority of the interview participants stated that the two procedures target diferent objectives and that the relationship between study programme evaluation and accreditation would first have to be clarifed. But considering the efort associated with both accreditation procedures and study programme evaluation, the interview participants were in favour of at least some kind of connection. A proportion of the interview participants stated the opinion that, in future, study programme evaluation, accreditation and evaluation of research should be conducted jointly or in co-ordination in order to minimize the efort and expense required for diferent procedures conducted in parallel. not justify the heavy work burden that the process entailed. In other words, a substantial proportion of institute members had concerns about the cost-beneft value of the evaluation process.To sum up, contrary to the diverse criticisms that are still being raised against peer evaluations in higher education and research, the fndings of the meta-evaluation studies confrm that peer review enjoys wide acceptance and can be seen as useful.

References

Laughton, D. (2003) Why was the QAA approach to teaching quality assessment rejected by academics in UK HE? *Assessment and Evaluation in Higher Education* 28(3), 309–321.

MacAlpine, M. (2001) An attempt to evaluate teaching quality: one department's story. *Assessment and Evaluation in Higher Education* 26(6), 563–578.

Neumann, R. (2000) Communicating student evaluation of teaching results: Rating Interpretation Guides (RIGs). *Assessment and Evaluation in Higher Education* 25(2), 121–134.

Smith, C., Herbert, D., Robinson, W. and Watt, K. (2001) Quality assurance through a continuous curriculum review (CCR) strategy: refections on a pilot project. *Assessment and Evaluation in Higher Education* 26(5), 489–502.

Spencer-Matthews, S. (2001) Enforced cultural change in academe: a practical case study: implementing quality management systems in higher education. *Assessment and Evaluation in Higher Education* 26(1), 51–59.

9

Improving Evaluation Methods

In 2005–2006, all universities were entered in the Reform Act of April 2002 (reform of higher education degrees) and the first balance sheets became possible. In March 2006, a new Evaluation Agency for Research and Higher Education (AERES) was set up by the law entitled 'Programme Planning Law of Research'. AERES is an independent administrative authority in charge of evaluating higher education and research institutions with regard to their missions and activities, research activities of research centres and higher education degrees.

How can we be sure of the quality of higher education degrees, especially of Higher Vocational Education (HVE) degrees? Particularly, how do we develop and improve the education– employment relationship? Are employers satisfed with higher education graduates' skills? Are the new graduates satisfed with their first jobs? Do they fnd a job related to their skills? Our analyses show that external evaluations are not enough; they fail to measure and to prove the actual quality of HVE degrees. Self-evaluations are needed and they can be used to build precise quality charts; when the majority of quality indicators are good, it becomes possible to look for an external accreditation by independent evaluation bodies, if possible at the European level. However, external accreditations are not enough. The conclusion examines the problem of governance at the university level: why governing bodies are not able to abolish degrees that are not relevant for the labour market, i.e. those which give poor job opportunities to their graduates? The conclusion deals with that question.

New Educational and Economic Contexts

Educational Context

In 2005–2006, all French universities were entered in the reform Act of April 2002, called 3, 5, 8, then LMD. The reform Act sets up a first cycle of 3 years (called '*licence*'), a second cycle of 2 years (called '*master*') and a third cycle ('*doctorate*'). However, all previous vocational degrees have not been suppressed. At the first level of higher education, the DUT (*Diplôme Universitaire de Technologie*, University Technological Degree), the BTS (*Brevetde Technicien Supérieur*, Upper Technician Degree) and the professional licence (*Licence Professionnelle*) are maintained as such. At the second level, the IUP (*Instituts Universitaires Professionalisés*) have been integrated into masters degrees, but the engineering degrees (*Titre d'Ingénieur*), the titles delivered by the Commercial schools (*Écoles de commerce*) and the MSG (*Maîtrise de Sciences de Gestion*, Masters in Management Sciences) still exist. The panorama of HVE degrees has been made more complex by the 2002 reform. The complexity has been criticized severely by employers and managers, interviewed in previous research. It is uncertain whether the National Repertory of Certifcations set up by a law (law of '*Modernisation Sociale*', January 2002) will make the panorama clearer: it has to include the list of all the vocational degrees (more than 15 000), but it is still in progress at the time of writing (June 2007).

First-level professional degrees The BTS, set up in 1959, is a professional two-year HVE degree (about 230 000 students and 110 000 graduates a year). The DUT, set up in 1966, is a professional two-year HVE degree (about 100 000 students and 50 000 graduates a year). The *Licence Professionnelle* is a new degree (1999) and corresponds to a third year of HVE (about 25 000 students in 2005–2006 and 17 000 graduates in 2005); year afer year, new *Licences Professionnelles* welcome a greater number of students (about 5000 a year). The three degrees have the same features, apart from one. The 23 industrial or service specialities of the DUT are regulated by law: the law prescribes the teaching and learning subjects, the number of teaching hours and the modalities of the exams; and it is the same for the BTS. On the other hand, the subjects of the *Licence Professionnelle* are decided at the local level in the context of the university autonomy; however, the yearly number of hours and the length of stages are prescribed; moreover, every *Licence Professionnelle* has to be ranked in a list of 46 national denominations, broken down into nine professional sectors.

Second-level Professional Degrees

The Reform Act of 2002 has set up two possible orientations in the masters degree: professional and research; the law says that selection is carried out at the beginning of the second year of the masters. Which are the changes? The curricula of the masters are proposed by the universities: there are no more national curricula (*maquettes nationales*). It is a big change and the result is that courses sharing the same name have developed with considerably diferent curricula, teaching and assessment methods and aims; so it is not easy for students to choose a masters and to compare the quality of the contents and of the degrees. If, for the second year of the masters, nothing has changed (the professional masters replaces the DESS, *Diplôme d'Études Supérieures Spécialisées*, and the research masters replaces the DEA, *Diplôme d'Études Approfondies*), an important change is located in the first year of the masters. Several solutions are possible with regard to the proposals of universities: common or separated curricula for the two orientations (professional and/or research); within each of the orientations, specialities are introduced from the first year or only in the second year; some universities have introduced the selection at the entrance of the first year of the master. Simultaneously, we have to remember that degrees in engineering, commerce and management are maintained. Universities have used the reform to create new professional degrees: an explosion in the number of curricula has been seen, as observed in Italy.

From the mid-1990s to the 2002 reform, the number of students in higher education was globally stable and the length of higher education studies was also stable. Nevertheless, among all higher education students, the number of HVE students and of HVE graduates or postgraduates was increasing every year. And the full impact of the reform is not yet known: statistical data are only available for 2003 and before. With the explosion in the number of curricula, the number of students and of graduates (particularly at the fve-year level) will probably be increasing.

So, more and more young people will have a degree in higher education. In 2004 (before the full impact of the reform), the proportion of young people with such a degree was more than 43%: 16% of the pupils who entered secondary education in 1989 have got a first-cycle higher education degree, and 27% have a second-cycle higher education degree; evidently, the proportion is very diferent with regard to the social origin. Probably, as an impact of the 2002 reform, the rate of 25% of young people getting a fve-year degree will be reached quickly. The problem is that the labour market does not need such a number of postgraduates!

Access to The Labour Market

The second context is the economic one. From 2001, the economic situation in France has been rather bad: economic growth is weak, and the rate of unemployment is at a high level (about 10%). All national and local surveys about students' placements reveal a constant degradation from 2001 For instance, APEC (*Association Pour l'Emploi des Cadres*) surveys reveal that, 6–9 months afer graduation from a four- or fve-year course of higher education, 49% of the graduates of 2003 and 2004 are unemployed and are looking for a job. From 2004 to 2005, the situation has deteriorated: only 49% of graduates have a stable job (60% of the 2003 graduates in 2004); 49% are managers (56% of the 2003 graduates); the average wages are about •1500 gross per month. In 2005, 18 months afer graduation, 11% of 2003 graduates are still looking for a first job and the global level of unemployment for the cohort is 20%.

In the 1960s, in the context of economic planning, a link was made between education levels and levels of job position, setting up an objective and subjective link between the degree and the job position; that link is a specifc French feature: a clear education–employment relationship. So, a postgraduate student waits for a stable job contract, a management position and high wages. That favourable situation is still known by the majority of postgraduates. However, if the deterioration observed in the last years goes on in the coming years, more than 50% of postgraduates would not have the awaited situation. Why the degradation?

Evolution of the labour market is structurally favourable to graduates and postgraduates. The number of upper job positions (*cadres* and *professions intellectuelles supérieures*) has increased more than 60% during the last 20 years; today it is more than 4.5 million. The proportion of graduates and postgraduates in upper job positions grows regularly: in 2002, 55% of *cadres* had a graduate or a postgraduate degree against 44% in 1990 (non-graduated managers have retired and have been replaced by young graduates or postgraduates). About 70% of managers less than 30 years old have a graduate or postgraduate degree (45% in 1990). Between 1982 and 2002, the growth in the number of *cadres* has been the highest for some jobs: teachers and recruiters (+341%), researchers and developers (+153%), data-processing experts (+147%), administrative, fnancial and accounting managers (+109%), communication and documentation professionals (+108%) and lawyers (+96%). The growth will go on between 2000 and 2010: it will be the highest for the same management positions; it will be relatively weak for teachers and civil servant managers.

How many graduates and postgraduates, with a higher education degree of three years or more, are recruited every year in France? On average, between 1998 and 2002, 112 500 beginners (i.e. young people present on the labour market for 5 years or less; most of them are less than 30 years old) have been hired in a managerial position (1 125 000=19% of managers' recruitments during a year). With regard to the proportion of graduates and postgraduates among the less than 30-year-old managers, the number of new higher education graduates or postgraduates who are recruited into a managerial job position can be estimated at about 80 000 per year. Is that number enough to face the number of graduates and postgraduates who yearly look for a job afer their graduation? The answer is no.

The growth in the number of higher education degrees which are awarded yearly is not linked to a demographical efect. Since 1995, it has not been linked to growth in the access rate to higher education. It is produced by the lengthening of higher education studies. That lengthening is not only produced by the difcult situation of the labour market, but also by the higher education reform: the students with a two-year higher education degree go on to get a three-year degree (a *Licence Professionnelle* for instance); the students with a four-year degree (the old *maîtrise*) go on to get a fve-year degree. With the implementation of the reform in all the universities in 2005–2006, it is clear that more and more students will get a licence or a masters.

Before the Reform Act of 2002 and especially with the implementation of the reform in all the universities, what happened and what will happen for the students with a graduate or a postgraduate degree? We have to remember the data: about 80 000 yearly recruitments of young *cadres* and, in 2003, more than 125 000 students with a fve-year degree who were looking for a job. The imbalance between the demand for managerial jobs and the number of managerial jobs ofered to beginners is clear and will increase in the coming years.

A bad education–employment relationship certainly explains the relative degradation observed on the labour market. The deterioration makes a vicious circle: deterioration of the labour market, downgrading at the entrance to the labour market for a signifcant proportion of graduates, lengthening of studies, increase in the number of students who get a degree at the highest level, reinforcing the degradation, and increasing the waiting list to have a job or a better job.

The imbalance between ofers and job demands, the source of unemployment, is particularly high in some professions, even in professions which know an increasing number of managerial positions, in professions which recruit young beginners with a higher education degree. Labour markets are segmented: they are diferentiated in terms of rates of higher education graduates' recruitments. Professional markets with regulated access and with student selection (*numerus clausus*) at the start of degrees (teachers and doctors, for instance) are open to beginners. Internal markets (internal promotions and beginners' selective exclusion) make compulsory a first entrance in non-managerial jobs. External markets put young beginners in general competition against experienced employees. French markets are more and more dominated by internal markets, and so beginners with a higher education degree have difculties in making a good entry into the labour market.

So, in spite of a high increase in the number of management jobs and a high rate of recruitment of young people, the unemployment rate is high for computer-science experts. Another profession (professionals in communication and documentation) which employs more and more young managers with a higher education degree, recruits about 5000 beginners a year, but about 25 000 young graduates and postgraduates were looking for a job in 2002. The explosion in the number of courses in computer sciences and in communication, and in the number of new graduates has caused a lot of damage. Moreover, there is a risk of a stronger deterioration if the economic situation does not improve and if the governmental policies to reduce the public defcits lead to a signifcant decrease in the number of civil servants, by not replacing departures caused by retirement.

Improving the Evaluation Processes

The conditions of access in the labour market are more and more difcult for the young higher education graduates and postgraduates. One of the main reasons is too many young people arriving yearly on the labour market with a higher education degree. It is partly because more and more vocational courses are available in universities. Why are there more and more degrees? It is linked to the 2002 reform and to the insufciencies of the national evaluation system. So, because it is difcult to change the national evaluation system, some universities and some courses develop self-evaluations and set up quality charts to prove the quality of their degrees, particularly the quality of job placements.

Insufficiencies of the National Evaluation System

The national evaluation system was set up in the mid-1980s. In the context of mass expansion of higher education and the increased expenditure, HEIs (higher education institutions) needed to be held accountable for the quality of their provision. Reinforcing the evaluation is prescribed by the 2002 reform and is pushed by the building of the European Space of Higher Education (development of quality assurance). The new law reminds us that evaluation of the degrees by students has been compulsory since the 1997 regulation; it also reminds us that the results of the quadrennial contracts (launched at the end of the 1980s) between the State and each university have to be evaluated more seriously. Nevertheless, the evaluation system has several shortcomings. The defaults are due to the absence of an actual lead by the Ministry of Higher Education. We observe a loss of control by public powers, showed by the fragmentation, the heterogeneity and the absence of co-ordination of the *habilitation* (authorization) processes. In that context, of a relative *laxisme* (laxity) from the State, universities do not have a direct interest in regulating or limiting the number of their courses. The logic of corporate professions (academic staf) is to increase the number of degrees in order to increase the number of students; more students mean a chance to get more academic staf.

Which bodies regulate the number of degrees (*ofre de formation*)? National commissions of experts give advice for the degrees proposed by universities. If the Ministry agrees the experts' positive advice, the degree is accredited (*habilité*) as a national degree and, because of that, it is fnanced by the State budget essentially with regard to the number of registered students. The first problem is the number of national committees: a committee for the DUT, one for the *Licences Professionnelles*, one for other licences and masters, not forgetting a committee for engineering degrees and another one for management degrees. More and more, the criteria which allowed professional and general degrees to be distinguished are less and less diferent: for the professional degrees, we observe a lower control of the number of courses, a lower selection at the entrance, fnancing problems and risks of deterioration of the access to the labour market. The Programme Planning Law of March 2006 set up a new national Agency for Evaluation with a mission of evaluating higher education degrees: its role in regard to the role of the existing committees is not yet clear; usually in France, new evaluation bodies do not suppress the existing ones.

The second weakness is the process of evaluation itself. Experts have to judge the quality of the new course before it exists. Committee members have to examine the content of proposals. When the proposal is to set up a new degree, their first job is to make a conformity control. Are the proposals in accordance with the Law? So, the committee members have to check the precise curricula, the distribution of the diferent disciplines, the numbers of training hours, the duration of internship, the career prospects, the selection procedures, the number of academic and professional staf, the state of economic partnerships, the resources brought by the institution, the advice given by the University Councils etc. Conformity control is not enough. Committee members also have to appreciate the coherency of the degree with the other degrees in the institution and to take into account the priorities elaborated by the HEI ('that degree is the most important for us'). They may check whether the economic partnership described in the proposal is real. In principle, they do not have to accept political or lobbying pressures. The process of *habilitation* is a long one: it takes more than 1 year. It is a process carried out from a distance and is generally seen as being time-consuming and bureaucratic.

In the process of assessment, the national experts judge the quality of the proposals and give their opinion (positive or negative advice) according to a written dossier, flled by the head of the project and certifed by the HEI; the content of the dossier is prescribed. Labour market relevance is a crucial point and it is measured by several criteria: list of jobs possible for the graduates, precise definition of the awaited skills, stability of the economic partnerships, professional teachers' involvement, place of traineeship and apprenticeship in the degree and attention paid to continuous vocational training. The labour market relevance is assessed at the national level. Teoretically, it is above all taken into account by the economic world representatives, members of the national commissions. Teoretically, their advice is based upon their knowledge of the labour market opportunities.

However, at the national level, do those representatives have a precise knowledge of the regional labour market opportunities? Do they actually participate in the national commissions? It is not always the case.

In an evaluation *ex an te,* the general problem for the national experts deals with the reliability of the written information given by the head of the project. Experts are able to check the conformity of the dossier to the national regulations. But how can experts check the degree of involvement of the economic partners, the actuality of the career prospects? They can check the partnership by reading the letters of frms included in the dossier (but is a letter of support a guarantee of involvement?). More surely, experts can be confdent if an ofcial agreement between the HEI and an economic partner is included in the dossier, i.e. agreement about stages, apprenticeship, recruitment, fnancial support etc.

All the forms used in France for the *habili tation* of a new degree have a part devoted to the career prospects of the future graduates. The HEI has to 'fll the cases'. Is it a reliable exercise or a formal one? Each HEI plays the game; it is theoretically compulsory to play the game, otherwise the national experts will formulate negative advice on the project. In fact, nobody is completely naïve: it is impossible to be sure of the actual career prospects for graduates who will reach the labour market in 1, 2 or 3 years. So, the remark could be: why is the information asked for? The best way to demonstrate that the preoccupations about the career prospects are actual ones would be promises ("we promise that we will hire the graduates in the future"), but such a promise is impossible: no frm is able to make such an engagement.

When the proposal is to renew an existing degree (process of *ré habilitation,* of revalidation), the committee members have to check the actual activities, resources and results of the degree during the 4 previous years. Activities: how many applicants for the degree? How many registered students? Resources: how many academic and professional staf? How many fnancial resources? Results: how many students have been awarded the degree? How many have dropped out? Which are the actual career prospects? So, it would be wrong to assert that the process did not address the relevance and responsiveness of vocational courses to the labour market. Because vocational degree programmes had been designed as vocational degrees, relevant to the needs of employers, they were judged against this aim. Moreover, the national committees are helped in their judgements by surveys, analysis and visits in the field carried out by national committees of follow-up; so the experts are able to identify globally the strong and the weak points of the courses. But here is the third weakness of the national process of evaluation. Most ofen, the statistical data included in the proposal of renewal are written by the people in charge of the degree. More rarely, the data are certifed by a local observer. It is clear that, in this second case, committee members may be more confdent in the data; it is better if the data are comparative (evolution of the fgures for several years, comparison of the local data with the data about similar degrees organized in other institutions). Until now, most degrees are *re habilités:* their good or bad job placements are not taken into account; nevertheless, things could be changed: in February 2006, the national committee of *Licences Professionnelles* had not delivered the *ré habilitation* for a signifcant proportion of the professional licences.

If a degree is *ré habilité* afer a period of 4 years, its human and fnancial resources stay the same as before: resources depend on the number of registered students, they do not depend on the efciency and efectiveness of the degree. The fourth weakness of the evaluation procedures is the absence of a link between the actual results and the amount of resources given by the State. Tere is no challenge for the courses which have strong partnerships with economic employers, good internships or apprenticeships and good job placements.

Quality Charts

In those contexts of the deterioration of the access conditions to the labour market, of an explosion in the number of vocational courses and of an absence of control and evaluation by the national evaluation bodies, how do we improve the evaluation of the education-employment relationship? How do we involve the economic world in the evaluation, in the quality assurance processes?

Several revolutions could be imagined. Each new project of course would be *habilité* only afer 2 years of experimentation, fnanced by the university resources; so, the results afer 2 years could be judged by the experts; in the case of *habilitation*, the university would receive the fnancial resources, including for the 2 years of experimentation. Probably, in that new context, universities would become more cautious to propose new projects! For the *ré habilitation*, a new procedure could be imagined. Every degree should have to produce a report including results obtained during the period, particularly in the field of the education–employment relationship, and including a plan to improve its weak points. The indicators should be notifed, certifed by an internal evaluation unit in the university (the internal evaluation units should be developed and may be compulsory) and by the economic partners.

From our case studies, we have observed that most of our interlocutors fnd that the graduates have a good theoretical knowledge and a good ability to learn; but they fnd their practical abilities and their problem-solving capacities insufcient. How do we improve graduates' weak points? The idea is to develop subject benchmark statements allowing a large degree of fexibility in provision (diversity was not viewed negatively). France is in a paradoxical situation: for the DUTs, 90% of the subject contents and the pedagogical methods are strictly regulated by law (it is not the case for the *Licences Professionnelles*). In spite of this, the local adaptations to improve the quality of subjects and of graduates are largely possible, partly because there no external inspections. However, the local adaptations, the good practices, are not always easy to implement: the evolutions can be limited by a lack of fnancial resources (difculty to buy new costly equipment) or by a reluctance from some academics (every evolution increases their workload and they are not paid for that increase).

The economic world wants graduates with capacities of autonomy, of problem solving. The 2002 reform insists on the pedagogy of project. For the HVE degrees, it exists by law, but it has to be implemented seriously. The reform also insists on the students' responsibility during their studies: they have to build their project of studies and their professional project; a greater possibility to choose the subjects is given to them. If the target is met, HVE graduates will have a greater capacity to organize projects.

Tanks to a quantitative survey, we have observed that there is a relatively weak involvement of companies not only in the daily functioning of the course, but sometimes also in the design of new degrees. A lot of companies are concerned, but the intensity of contact is weak. Nevertheless, the respondents say that the relationship between their company and the degrees are not developed enough. But they say that a higher involvement is difcult for their company, essentially because of a lack of time.

How do we involve economic partners more? It is certain that the initiatives to improve the partnerships have to be initiated by the HVE institutions. They have to make their continuous vocational training service more professional, their employment and internship service more professional, and the people working in those services more professional; in another part, the Centres for Training by Apprenticeship have to develop and to make their activities more professional. A solution to develop the participation of economic partners could be imagined, but would suppose a change in the regulation of continuous vocational learning. Currently, the participation of managers in HVE is not considered, for them and for their company, as an activity of continuous training; so their company may not include their external teaching in the so-called "fnancial participation to the continuous vocational training". If it was possible, maybe more companies would send their managers to teach and to manage the HVE degrees.

The ultimate step could be the implementation of quality charts. The first step of the chart should be the delivery of internal quality labels afer a rigorous internal evaluation: quality of information and communication for student and partners, quality of studentsw selection, quality of teaching and learning, quality of economic partnerships, quality of graduate job placements and quality in fnancial matters (diversifcation of resources and rationality of expenses).

Offensive Strategy of Evaluation

The development of quality charts and the difusion of their indicators would clearly show that there are, within universities, degrees of good quality and degrees of poor quality. In principle, poor quality courses should be abolished. It is not evident: quality charts are needed to improve the courses, but they are not sufcient. I have, as the former director of an observatory, the experience in university of 'bad' degrees which still exist. To understand that, we have to analyse the behaviour of university presidents with regard to evaluation results, to understand the university governance. Our survey on university presidents in France and in Italy reveals that only a few presidents develop an ofensive strategy of evaluation. Such a strategy consists of systematically difusing the evaluation results, in using the results in the decision-making process, in explicitly basing decisions on the results produced by evaluation (creating or abolishing a degree, increasing or decreasing the allowed resources). The ofensive strategy also shows that such decisions are needed to improve the implementation of the university missions, to have additional advantages in the competition between universities.

Why is the ofensive strategy difcult to set up? It is not easy because university presidents do not assume some political risks, do not have political courage. The first risk deals with the power of internal evaluation units. These units have a power from their rigorous analysis, from the independence of their judgements. If a president systematically takes into account the motivated advice given by evaluation units, he loses part of his power. The second political risk deals with the growth of conficts within the university. If a president decides, for instance, to close degrees with bad results revealed by evaluations he will have to face faculty directors and dissatisfaction will be growing in the university. If the dissatisfaction results in a coalition of faculty directors against the president, the president's power is threatened. The third political risk deals with the nature of the political power: exercising a political power is not only making decisions based on evaluation results, but also taking risks, experimenting, innovating, mobilizing people and giving dreams to them; presidents do not want to be accused of being only 'rational'. The evaluation dies if it is only a management control, the respect of constraint of decreasing the costs, the sanction of bad results. A 'political president' has to be able to loosen external constraints, to get new human and fnancial resources for his university.

How can a university that wants to excel in its teaching and learning missions prove that, in an ocean of thousands of licences and masters, its courses are particularly efective for graduates' job placements? That university has to develop a comprehensive strategy: only setting up degrees based on an important potential of academic staf, communicating about its degrees (precisely describing graduates' and postgraduates' skills), practising an equitable selection at the entry of vocational degrees, reinforcing the evaluation processes and taking into account the results, further professionalizing the degrees by the systematization of apprenticeship job contracts, and developing the partnerships with local and regional frms, getting quality certifcations. That university, with such an ofensive strategy and with regard to other universities, would increase its chances of guaranteeing good job placements to its graduates and postgraduates.

Stability Amidst a Storm of Evaluation

Japanese universities are amidst a storm of various types of evaluation and quality assessment. As is the case throughout Europe, the Japanese higher education system is faced with continuous pressure to reform in order to meet increasing societal expectations for universities and colleges to contribute directly to society.

Japan has developed a large and diversifed higher education system alongside a large private sector. In 2006, Japan had 744 four-year universities, most ofering postgraduate programmes, and 468 junior colleges, 64 colleges of technology and 2996 specialized training colleges issuing associate degrees or diplomas. The selectivity of the students among HEIs (higher education institutions) is highly diverse. Some of the research-intensive prestigious universities are attracting highly talented students, while around 40% of the less-prestigious private universities are facing difculty in attracting sufcient numbers of students to ensure their continued survival.

This oversupply of higher education is still a relatively recent phenomenon, having started around 2000. A rapid decrease in the youth population afer the second baby boomer generation fnished their higher education in the first half of the 1990s, and a continuous increase in higher education supply based on deregulation policies for the establishment of new programmes are the main factors of this new transition from historical overdemand in the higher education market to the current oversupply condition. In recent years, more than ten new four-year universities have been opening their doors each year, while some universities are facing bankruptcy. It is now clear that the government has abandoned any idea as to how to control student numbers in the Japanese higher education system. On the other hand, the government has also begun to rely heavily on a new indirect control mechanism, namely 'quality assurance' or 'evaluation'.

The introduction of corporate-style management to the national university system in 2004 includes the assessment of six-year cycle medium-term goals and plans, the achievement of which is closely linked with fnancial allocation. Assessment is not only implemented as an audit of institutional management, but also considers performance in education and research. National universities now submit annual reports to the Ministry of Education, Culture, Sports, Science and Technology (MEXT) evaluation committee, the assessments of which are made publicly accessible. Adding to this national university evaluation scheme, all national, local, public and private universities and colleges have to go through a seven-year cycle of 'certifed evaluation', which could be regarded as accreditation. Many project-based funding schemes for excellence in research and teaching have also been introduced, with universities competing for the number of incentive fund projects they can attract.

Quality assurance and evaluation in Japanese higher education is becoming increasingly complicated. The increase in the number and type of assessment and evaluation programmes incurs considerable costs for the preparation and submission of documents. The question is raised: do these quality assessment and evaluation tools lead to any real change in Japanese higher education?

Development of Evaluation in Japanese Higher Education

The practice of accreditation in Japanese higher education is not altogether new. Under the U.S. occupation, Japan established a new university system by creating four-year undergraduate and American-compatible two-year masters and three-year doctorate programmes. Changes at this time also included the integration of rather European-compatible 'imperial' and other universities and polytechnics in 1949. The Ministry of Education (then *Monbusho*) had already maintained an authorized process of establishing pre-war universities, especially with regard to private ones. Under the idea of 'university autonomy', the U.S. occupation government supported the practice of voluntary assessment by the Japan University Accreditation Association (JUAA), and University Standards were utilized for authorizing new universities. Afer Japan regained her independence in 1950, the Ministry of Education set-up its own Standards for University Establishment, upon which JUAA's accreditation process became a completely non-governmental voluntary activity.

In the late 1980s, a new type of debate concerning university evaluation started. The model generally referred to at that time was that of the American system rather than the newly starting European quality assessment systems. At the time, the existing governmental authorization system was regarded as a type of British 'chartering', with the American-type regular-based accreditation system referred to as a preferable future model for the Japanese university evaluation system. Up to then, the JUAA had not implemented any cyclical accreditation process; once a university became an accredited member, it was able to hold member status without time limitations. Only around one-third of Japanese universities had been accredited, mainly because there was no efective sanction for non-accredited universities.

In 1991, the University Council, an advisory council of the Ministry of Education recommended that universities "make eforts towards self-evaluation and monitoring" The model of this self-monitoring and evaluation process would be the self-study of the American accreditation process. The University Council also argued that Japan should develop an American-style accreditation system in the future, with JUAA regarded as the organization best suited to take the lead role.

The University Council also recommended the drastic deregulation of the Standards for University Establishment to allow university education programmes to adapt to changing social needs in a more fexible and meaningful way. At the same time, the government loosened national controls of student numbers which had been implemented under various higher education plans since the mid 1970s.

In the 1990s, university evaluation initiatives became active. By 2000, 92% of universities had implemented some type of self-monitoring and evaluation, and 83% of national universities and 24% of private universities had also implemented 'external evaluation' by organizing 'external review committees' under their own initiative. JUAA also became more active, issuing manuals for self-monitoring and evaluation, implementing 'mutual evaluation' as a kind of external evaluation and also acting as a body to re-accredit existing member institutions.

'Third Party' Evaluation and Establishment of A National Evaluation Organization

The direction of the evaluation debate in Japan changed drastically in the late 1990s. As part of the administrative reforms in general, arguments for the privatization or incorporation of national universities became stronger from the Ministry of Finance and other supporters of the privatization of public services. Initially, the Ministry of Education, Science, Sports and Culture (the newly restructured *Monbukagakusho*)[2], as well as JANU (Japan Association for National Universities) was opposed to the idea of the privatization and incorporation of national universities. Arguing that incorporation was not necessary for national university reform, the Ministry of Education started to examine the possibility of strengthening the external assessment system of higher education in order to demonstrate accountability and performance. At the same time, some leading academics supported the idea of concentrating public research funds among top universities so that they can survive global academic competition.

In 1996, JANU sent a delegation to the U.K. to study ongoing external quality assessment in that country. Following this visit, British and Continental European trends in quality assessment of education and research became frequently referred to in discussions of higher education policy. In 1998, the University Council issued a report recommending the introduction of 'third-party' evaluation for quality improvement and accountability of universities and colleges. The Council report mentioned neither the incorporation nor the privatization of national universities, but did recommend the establishment of a national university evaluation organization, arguing that the results of third-party evaluation should be used as a determining factor in fnancial allocation. The 'third-party' evaluation debate was not limited

to within the higher education system, but was also ongoing in public services in general at that time.

Acceleration of 'Higher Education' Reform 2000–2004

In 2000, the newly created NIAD-UE (National Institution for Academic Degrees and University Evaluation), comprising approximately 100 academic and non-academic staf recruited mainly from national university stafs and faculties, commenced university evaluation activities. NIAD-UE implemented three types of pilot evaluation programmes as follows:

1. Evaluation of research activities. The Ministry of Education nominated a limited number of collaborative faculties from national and local public universities in ten broad academic fields. Evaluation results were published, with ratings and recommendations for the improvement of research activities and management as informed by respective institutional missions, including the examination of academic standards as refected in individual academic staf profles (stated in terms of rankings ranging from excellent through good and ordinary to unsatisfactory).
2. Evaluation of educational activities. The Ministry of Education nominated a limited number of collaborative samples from national and local public universities in ten broad academic fields. Evaluation results were published, with ratings and recommendations for improvement of education activities and management as informed by respective institutional missions.

3. Tematic evaluation. Implemented for all national and selected local public universities on selected topics such as social contribution, international linkage and general education.

Under accelerated administrative reforms of the Koizumi Cabinet, the then Minister of Education Atsuko Toyama proposed further university reforms which included a plan to foster the development of 30 'top' or 'world-class' research universities. This proposed ofcial selection of 30 universities and the associated concentration of financial resources sparked heated debate over the future direction of Japanese higher education. Smaller-sized and rurally located national universities were especially opposed to this idea on the grounds that they support the basic infrastructure of Japanese research activities. A compromise was eventually reached in the 21st Century Centre of Excellence (COE) Program, which re-conceptualized reforms as aiming to foster the development of top 'research units', as opposed to top institutions.

The 21st Century COE Program was utilized as a funding scheme to ofer an incentive for excellent research units, and top national, local, public and private universities to compete for 'COE21 units', which are recognized as good indicators of domestic academic status. Funding comes from MEXT, with selection carried out by the JSPS (Japan Society for the Promotion of Science). Each COE21 research unit represents 5 years of funding and can lead to the employment of full-time researchers for projects. The results of selections to date have been surprisingly consistent with the traditional public image ranking of top universities. Namely, the University of Tokyo and other former imperial universities, the Tokyo Institute of Technology (the top national engineering university), and Keio and Waseda (top private universities) consistently appear among the top ten rankings.

The COE21 scheme, however, was positively received, at least by the leading universities which benefted from this incentive fund. Following the COE21 scheme, MEXT started similar funding incentive schemes for educational activities, such as the 'Support Program for Distinctive University Education (Good Practice in Education)'. This incentive fund is provided by MEXT, with selection and monitoring implemented by the JUAA. Funding for this initiative is considerably less than that provided under the COE21 scheme, and each institution can submit only one project for consideration. However, this incentive fund ofers opportunities to more teaching-oriented universities and colleges, which can use the award to fund advertising and student marketing. In 1999, the Cabinet had decided to incorporate all national universities within five years, to provide them with greater autonomy. MEXT organized a special taskforce with JANU to be responsible for the system design to guide incorporation plans. Here, the performance assessment scheme for national universities became a core issue, leading to the establishment of the National University Corporation Evaluation Committee (NUCEC) within MEXT.

Around this time, discussions on quality assurance in transnational higher education also came to the fore, infuenced by the rapid development of the international student market in East Asia. Japan became actively involved in international quality assurance debates in the WTO (World Trade Organization), OECD (Organisation for Economic Co-operation and Development) and UNESCO (United Nations Educational, Scientifc and Cultural Organization), as a country with a higher education system capable of both sending and receiving large numbers of students. Furthermore, this debate served to stimulate policy discussion on the national quality assurance system of university education, and, in 2004, the Japanese government introduced the 'certifed evaluation' system, which can be understood as an accreditation system legally required by School Education Law amendment.

The Koizumi Cabinet's administrative reforms afect higher education policy in additional ways. Decentralization policies led to the establishment of the Special District for Administrative Reform as a pilot project of deregulation under which municipal governments can apply to earmark special districts for specifc deregulation. For examples, Osaka city and the Chiyoda district of Tokyo applied for and received approval to deregulate for-proft universities operated by stock companies. This process also included the drastic deregulation of campus property; whereas in the past universities basically had to own their campus facilities, legal amendments now allow the borrowing of campus facilities for both non-proft, private universities and colleges.

The quality assurance debate for cross-border education services also led to the establishment of an ofcial designation system for Japanese branches of foreign universities. Although, in practice, some American university branches in Japan had already started operation by the end of the 1980s, their existence was not yet ofcially recognized by MEXT. The aim of this designation is to protect students by providing a system of ofcial recognition of quality providers of education.

Further Change in Evaluation since 2004

In 2004, all national universities, junior colleges and colleges of technology in Japan were incorporated. National universities are now operated as newly established NUCs (national university corporations). The Ministry of Education sets medium-term goals for each NUC, upon which each institution bases medium-term plans. NUCEC assesses the achievement of those medium-term goals and plans every 6 years; similarly, NIAD-UE evaluates education and research activities and reports to NUCEC every 6 years. National universities and colleges are requested to publish annual reports, which are evaluated by NUCEC annually.

The Certifed Evaluation (accreditation) scheme, as discussed above, has also recently come into being, under which MEXT, in consultation with the Central Council for Education, certifes evaluation organizations which implement certifed evaluation programmes.

Tere are two types of certifed evaluation, as follows.

1. Institutional level certifed evaluation. Compulsory for all national, local, public and private universities, junior colleges and colleges of technology, which must undergo these programmes every 7 years. MEXT, in consultation with the Central Council for Education, certifes 'certifed evaluation organizations' according to guidelines requiring the publication of evaluation standards, processes and results. As for authority to designate 'certifed evaluation organizations', JUAA, NIAD-UE and the newly established Japan Institution for Higher Education Evaluation (JIHEE) applied for and received this power from the Ministry. Universities, junior colleges and colleges of technology are free to choose the certifed evaluation authority to which they apply. In theory, while HEIs are required to apply for certifed evaluation, MEXT does not have direct legal authority to close institutions that do not receive favourable results.
2. Certifed evaluation for professional graduate schools (programme level). The professional graduate school system (such as law schools and business schools) started in 2004, as separate from existing, rather academic-oriented postgraduate programmes. For these professional graduate schools, certifed evaluation is required within every 5 years. MEXT, in consultation with the Central Council for Education, designates 'certifed evaluation organizations' according to published

guidelines. Professional schools may select the certifying evaluation authority to which they apply. In theory, while professional schools are required to apply for certifed evaluation, MEXT does not have direct legal authority to close those institutions that do not receive favourable results.

In addition to these certifed evaluation schemes, universities and colleges are faced with several other types of evaluation. Only 1 year afer the deregulation of authorization procedures for new university programmes in 2004, MEXT started to re-examine the idea of shifing from *ex ante* (before establishment) to *ex post* (afer establishment) evaluation, which had been decided upon 1 year earlier. The 2005 Central Council for Education report stressed the importance of both *ex ante* Governmental Authorization and *ex post* certifed evaluation. Although the authorization process itself was deregulated, MEXT started an ‘afer care’ scheme of governmental authorization; afer starting the programmes, site visits by the University Establishment Assessment Committee were implemented, and the results posted on the governmental website.

From 2004, MEXT also strengthened its ability to infuence poorly performing universities and colleges; it can now issue recommendations and advice to national, local, public and private universities and colleges in addition to using the existing ‘order for closure’ power, which has not been used thus far. In addition to this, COE21 projects have to go through the interim and *ex post* evaluation, with results published to reveal achievement ratings. The number of ‘good practice’ projects is also increasing, and, together with the existing ‘Support Program for Distinctive University Education’, the government has also started the ‘Support Program for Contemporary Educational Needs’, the ‘University Education Internationalization Promotion Program’, the ‘Support Program for Professional Graduate School Formation’ and the ‘Program to Support Medical Education Corresponding to Community Health Care and Other Social Needs’, as shown below. These rapidly increasing incentive budgeting programmes are basically welcomed by the institutions, while the cost to submit proposals is obviously increasing.

1. Support Program for Distinctive University Education (2003–present). This programme supports the eforts of universities to achieve distinctive and outstanding education, and provides information to greater society by holding forums, publishing collections of case studies, etc. (Projects: FY2003: 80; FY2004: 58)

2. Initiatives for Attractive Post-Graduate Education (from 2006). This programme intensively supports highly motivated and distinctive postgraduate education in order to strengthen the fostering of creative young researchers who can meet contemporary social needs (Project: FY2006: 46).
3. Support Program for Contemporary Education Needs (2004–present). This programme supports the outstanding eforts of universities and other institutions to respond to recommendations of various councils and policies refecting strong social demands (Project: FY2004: 86).
4. University Education Internationalization Promotion Program (2005–present). This programme supports eforts to further internationalize university education through overseas student and staf dispatches, active co-operation with overseas universities, etc.
5. Support Program for Professional Graduate School Formation (2004–present). This programme supports eforts to develop and enhance educational content and methods in graduate law schools and other professional graduate schools (Project: FY2004: 63).
6. Support Program for High Quality Teacher Training (2006–present). This programme supports eforts to strengthen university teacher-training programmes and ongoing education of school teachers, in order to improve the quality of teacher-training programmes in universities.
7. Program to Support Medical Education Corresponding to Community Health Care and Other Social Needs (2005–present). This programme supports eforts by university hospitals to cultivate medical professionals who will be responsible for holistic medical care, by developing medical education based on community health care and other social needs.
8. The 21st Century COE Program (2002– present). This programme supports the formation of global research and education centres by introducing the principle of competition through third-party evaluation.

Adding to these incentive programmes, in 2005 the Central Council for Education issued a report focusing on improving the international attractiveness of postgraduate education in Japan. The report recommends subject-level-certifed evaluation of postgraduate programmes, along with existing institutional-certifed evaluation and professional school evaluation.

Discussions on the precise implementation of medium-term goal evaluation and plans for national university corporations are ongoing. How, and to what extent, NIAD-UE implements the evaluation of education and research activities of national universities will be particularly key factors in determining the future of university evaluation in Japanese higher education.

Increasing Evaluation Costs with Dubious Results

Considering the rapid increase of evaluation-related programmes, it is clear that documentation work, monitoring and related evaluation tasks by both the evaluation organizations and HEIs has drastically increased, and will continue to increase for the foreseeable future. Although it may be too early to assess the impact of this ongoing rapid development of university evaluation, concrete gains to justify the increasing costs of evaluation work are not readily apparent from the viewpoint of universities and colleges.

First of all, medium-term plans and goals do not sufce as institutional 'strategic plans' for HEIs. Considering the very complex nature of university management, medium-term goals and plans as applied to the 'Independent Administrative Corporation' scheme for public service agencies in general do not suit the inherently entrepreneurial nature of corporate-oriented strategic planning within HEIs. Some university managers point out the need to develop strategic plans and plans for efective university management separate from medium-term goals. Secondly, linkage of performance with fnancial allocation puts pressure on universities to avoid stating clear numerical goals for implementation. Thirdly, universities and colleges may have to make eforts for quality improvement, although actual implementation plans for the evaluation of research and education have not yet been fully decided. Annual budgeting still continues, even afer incorporation, even though the linkage between evaluation results and budgeting remains unclear.

Although still in the early stages, problems regarding the implementation of various types of evaluation scheme are becoming apparent. First, it is very difcult to identify the victims of certifed evaluation. All of the certifed evaluation programmes of various certifed evaluation organizations issue evaluation results with threshold decisions, namely 'pass', 'withhold' or 'fail'. In practice, however, it is very difcult to draw such clear-cut borderlines between qualifed institutions or programmes and those which are unqualifed. In the first annual results published by JUAA in March 2005, only 2 out of 34 universities were 'withheld', with the remaining 32 universities passing the certifed evaluation. In the second year, NIAD-UE published their first results in March 2006, with all 23 national and local public universities and colleges which applied for evaluation meeting the required standards. All universities and colleges which applied to the JUAA and JIHEE also passed.

Secondly, the impact of evaluation practices on existing images of university rankings, based mainly on student selectivity, has been relatively small. As for research activities, the top ten universities which gained the largest number of COE21 research units were dominated by the seven former 'imperial' universities, including the Tokyo Institute of Technology, and Keio and Waseda Universities. This result is exactly the same as the existing image of hierarchy among Japanese universities. Incentive fund schemes for educational activities may have some impact by highlighting particularly efective practices, some of which were not well known. The fact that these institutions received incentive funds was and is nevertheless utilized for promotional purposes.

Stability Amidst a Storm of Evaluation and Power Plays

One of the reasons for the stability of ranking order despite the introduction and implementation of a variety of new assessment and evaluation systems could be the highly domestic nature of any evaluation process. While some non-Japanese committee members are frequently involved, all of those involved speak the Japanese language and are highly committed to Japanese higher education. Furthermore, evaluators and committee members tend to come from current and retired senior managers and academic leaders. These otherwise successful reviewers tend to have high confdence in the 'past successes' of Japanese society, and therefore have a tendency to defend the status quo, albeit perhaps unwittingly. Even experts in the international higher education arena seem to experience great difculty in comprehending precisely what is going on in the Asia Pacifc academic order. For example, there is a considerable gap in the rank positions of Chinese universities between the *Times Higher Education Supplement* World University Rankings and Shanghai Jiao Tong University Ranking. As a country located in the Asia Pacifc region, Japanese higher education stakeholders have to seek their positions in comparison with Western and Asian Pacifc universities. However, the internationalization process of Japanese university evaluation practices is far behind its counterparts in Europe, the Asia Pacifc and North America.

In terms of research performance assessment, the usage of performance indicators such as number of publications and citations may help to maintain a meaningful international comparison in some academic fields. MEXT initially made great eforts to collect such 'objective' performance data during the COE21 selection process, but these indicators were utilized only as factors for reference, with the peer-review process (among those who speak the Japanese language) ultimately utilized as the decisive method of selection.

The tools for grasping the international position of Japanese higher education are still very undecided, and the language barrier of academic activities also tends to limit the discussion of 'global standards' to a mere slogan. At the same time, however, some HEIs are beginning to gain 'international' accreditation from American accreditation bodies. Considering the relatively small size and rather hierarchical structure of the predominantly Japanese-speaking academic community, it is difcult to reject criticism that selections were infuenced by traditional domestic power plays.

Old Boys' Club to Meritocracy?

The evaluation storm is brewing not only at the system level, but also at the institutional level; it is certainly changing the academic culture in Japan, especially among the younger generation. In particular, the diference in the academic lives of the first baby boomer generation (around 60 years old) and that of the second baby boomer generation (around 30 years old) is signifcant.

First, the globalization of the academic market is having a great impact on academic culture. Traditionally, a limited number of leading postgraduate schools dominated the production of new academics, and inbreeding and nepotism were frequently seen in the Japanese academic labour market. Systematized doctoral programmes and the rapid increase of self-fnanced overseas postgraduate students, however, are leading to the establishment of more equal relationships between established and newly entering academics.

Secondly, mobility and competition among researchers is increasing rapidly. While Japanese universities have a long tradition of tenured faculty, even among junior positions, these junior positions have been gradually replaced by short-term contract positions since the end of the 1990s.

Thirdly, increasing transparency in assessment, recruiting and application for competitive funding is improving opportunities for those institutions that demonstrate efort and improvement, and therefore merit. As information regarding academic performance and student satisfaction becomes more transparent, nepotism will become more difcult to cloak.

Lastly, the increasing power of university president ofces coincides with the decreasing power of 'chair' professors; the organizational structure of most faculties and departments has thus become more fat. Academic performance and performance assessment in teaching, such as are refected in student satisfaction surveys, enables able young researchers to escape from seniority customs to some extent.

The Danger of Perfectionism in Evaluation Practice

The present public management and 'evaluation storm' has undeniably changed the style of 'collegial' dialogue in Japanese higher education. Dialogue within academia is becoming more transparent, clear and assertive. Japanese society in general, including its universities, has long been sufering from a tradition of *honenuki* culture. *Honenuki*, meaning the 'boning of fsh' in Japanese, can be equated to the 'removal of teeth' in English; both expressions basically connote the weakening of power or infuence; in this case, *honenuki* explains that the real impact of any reform may be subject to the desire of existing powers to protect their positions by taking out the core part of the reform to prolong the current regime. However, this *honenuki* custom is now faced with strong criticism under the rather fundamentalist ideology of new public management. The evaluation process is apparently evolving as a thorough system. For example, under the certifed evaluation scheme, university self-evaluation reports are posted on institution websites, with the evaluation process highly transparent, including both the objections of institutions and responses from evaluation committees.

Efforts to eliminate *honenuki*, if not carefully managed, may result in a kind of perfectionism, whether it is real or only perceived, which is equally undesirable. An overly detailed and mercilessly critical approach to evaluation would only represent an afront to sensitive academic activities. Perfectionism could therefore be regarded as a potentially dangerous attitude in evaluation arguments. Recognizing the risk of confusion, most evaluation organizations are now starting to stress that evaluation is a means and not an end. The 'improvement' function of university evaluation is now being stressed, probably because the goals of the entire exercise are at risk of being misunderstood, and hence resented. The end of *honenuki*, and the beginning of more rigorous transparency and assertiveness in the context of the university evaluation storm, is exactly what the provocateurs of university evaluation and new public management intended. At the same time, if not properly managed, the end of *honenuki* may leave the Japanese academic community lost in a storm of excessive evaluation, with little to show for their eforts.

References

Yonezawa, A. (2002) The quality assurance system and market forces in Japanese higher.

Kimura, T., Yonezawa, A. and Ohmori, F. (2004) Quality assurance and recognition of qualifcations in higher education: Japan, In *Quality and Recognition in Higher Education: The Cross Border Challenge* (Larsen, K. and Momii, K., eds), pp. 119–130, OECD, Paris.

Central Council for Education (2005) *A Vision for the Future of Higher Education in Japan (28 January 2005).*

Scott, G. and Hawke, I. (2003) Using an external quality audit as a lever for institutional change. *Assessment and Evaluation in Higher Education* 28(3), 323–332.

Welsh, J.F., Alexander, S. and Dey, S. (2001) Continuous quality measurement: restructuring assessment for a new technological and organisational environment. *Assessment and Evaluation in Higher Education* 26(5), 391–401.

Yamanoi, A. and Kuzuki, K. (2005) A study on the fxed-term system for faculty members: focusing on the analyses of types, length of term and renewal. *Higher Education Research in Japan* 2, 1–20.

10

Assessment and Grading in Open and Distance Learning

Computer based assessment is becoming a major part of the experience of university students. This movement reflects developments in wider education and training. For example, within the United Kingdom, the Qualifications and Curriculum Authority QCA, the regulatory body for public examinations and publicly funded qualifications for the years of compulsory education, has adopted the universal availability of an e-assessment option in high stakes exams as one of its strategic goals. An example from training is the UK Driver and Vehicle Licensing Agency's use of a computer based test administered in testing centres as a 'theory' pre-test for those seeking a driving licence.

These examples involve high-stakes summative assessment. Alongside such developments, there has been a trend towards the embedding of computer based tests within blended learning processes. For example, it is now commonplace for major textbooks to be accompanied by online 'homework' packages that include computer based tests. Here the computer based assessment is formative.

The drivers for uptake of computer based assessment are economic, entrepreneurial and pedagogic. The growth of accountability and increasing employment mobility has fed a demand for portable qualifications and for cost effective means of testing. With such a market emerging, it is not surprising that there is increasing commercial involvement, particularly though not exclusively in the USA, and a growing experience in the design of computer based tasks. Rapid technological progress is facilitating the design of computer based tasks that, with ingenuity, reflect authentically the intended learning outcomes of course and programmes.

The strength of the pedagogic driver is contested, with anxieties such as the loss of direct human contact and judgement balanced against operational advantages such as immediacy, flexibility of use and scalability. One means of analysing the pedagogic potential of computer based assessment is to use one of the frameworks designed so as to assist audit of assessment practice. Both Nicol and Macfarlane-Dick and Gibbs and Simpson have provided such frameworks. The list below indicates the scope of the conditions that Gibbs and Simpson suggested were required for assessment to support learning effectively. For simplicity, their eleven conditions have been collapsed into five.

1. Assessment should encourage a strong and consistent level of engagement in learning activities
2. Assessment should encourage student effort that is at an appropriate level and intensity.
3. Feedback should be provided in time and in sufficient detail to affect learning.
4. Feedback should be insightful and appropriate in its focus.
5. Feedback should prompt an active response from the student

Can computer based assessment provide an effective means of satisfying these conditions? In principle, yes. For example, engagement, the factor, underlying the first two conditions, has been encouraged by the use of frequent computer based progress checks, sometimes performed anonymously and sometimes with active monitoring. Progress checks and their results can be available at any time via the internet, a major advantage for students who have constrained timetables and other responsibilities. Perhaps the strongest area of potential pedagogic advantage is in the provision of rapid feedback, in the form of both marks and comments, with the potential for the immediate shaping of future learning (Condition 3). Conversely, there is a potential weakness in the composition of the feedback. To date, very few implemented systems provide rich individually-tailored feedback and, therefore, there may be a failure to meet Condition 4.

There have been a number of analyses of the adoption of e-assessment. Whitelock and Brasher's analysis for the UK's Joint Information System

Committee, which sets out a roadmap and vision for e-assessment, identifies the drivers for adoption as; perceived increases in student retention, enhanced quality of feedback, flexibility for distance learning, strategies to cope with large student/candidate numbers, objectivity in marking and more effective use of virtual learning environments. They assert that the principal barriers to uptake are the need for academic staff development and resistant autonomous departments. The longer-term vision they offer is one in which e-assessment is supporting personalised learning. The analysis of Warburton is framed in terms of a dual path model of uptake of innovatory practice with one path involving high-impact high-risk approaches and the other involving lower-risk incremental tactics. Within this analysis, coordinated central action and support is required for high risk reform, for example of exam processes, whilst bottom-up reform is more likely to prosper in lower stakes formative activities. An additional insight is provided in a report commissioned from PriceWaterhouseCoopers by the Qualification and Curriculum Authority. The authors analysed the e-assessment process models of four UK Awarding bodies. The report provides a valuable insight into crucial process issues, e.g. the provision of effective appeal procedures, that may be of significance in adoption decisions.

Assessment Systems

Institutions and teachers who wish to make use of computer based assessment can now choose from a large number of systems and services.

A large proportion of university level computer based assessment is constructed using the functionality embedded within virtual learning environments VLEs such as are provided by Blackboard Inc. and the open-source Moodle community. The available functionality has been limited and the large majority of assessments produced in this way are simple in design and aim. However, market pressure is requiring VLE providers to augment their internal functionality so that customers can present their programs within a monolithic VLE context. As a result, the capabilities of such systems are increasing rapidly,

The most advanced computer based assessment systems have been constructed use specialist packages, e.g. Questionmark Perception. In addition, several systems have been developed within individual universities or university consortia or for specialist purposes e.g. Tripartite Interactive Assessment Delivery System TRIADS, OpenMark at the Open University

UK and Maple TA, Questionmark Perception is a richly configured system that has been adopted widely. According to the company, the software supports 21 question types, though many of these can be regarded as technical variants on the same fundamental task, e.g. there is no fundamental difference between a multiple choice question and one that is based on a drag and drop operation. A useful facility provide by the package is an interface that allows incorporation of Java or Flash elements. Adams et al have provided a relevant and powerful illustration of the use of this platform. Of particular interest are their laboratory preparation questions that allow the student to construct a virtual experiment, thereby involving themselves in a learning task that transcends the superficial requirement for recall. The Questionmark Assessment Management System provides a flexible means of reporting results, as well as workflow management and integration tools.

Maple Testing and Assessment is an example of a product that is oriented towards a narrower market – students studying mathematics. It is based around the Maple mathematics engine, which provides symbolic manipulation, and supports 'complex, free-form entry and intelligent evaluation of responses'. The system has been exploited elegantly by Greenhow and colleagues to provide mathematics questions that, through the use of variables in the authorship, can be instantiated with random values (within physical limits) to yield endlessly repeated variants and appropriate feedback.

These and similar systems incorporate a range of item and assessment management functions, including authoring tools. Recently, there has been an increasing emphasis on assessment for learning and the provision of differentiated feedback. OpenMark is a system developed by the Open University that is used for both formative and summative online assessment. It supports the full range of question types available on other systems. In addition it has a strong focus on interactivity, e.g. drawing lines, placing items, controlling simulations, building molecules, and the provision of multiple layers of feedback. These emphases reflect the use of OpenMark within open learning where the student may lack some mechanisms for encouraging engagement or providing feedback support.

The interactive functionality of OpenMark is being further developed in response to specific academic need. For example, by embedding sequential video elements, it becomes possible for students to pursue a decision making sequence within a practice environment. Furnished with appropriate feedback, such a package constitutes a learning experience. Another example is the use of controllable virtual experiences, e.g. a virtual microscope or journey, with the student's control choices providing the assessed output and feedback providing information on future choices.

Design of Assessment Tasks

All of the systems described have rich potential for grading and learning. However, even within the community who are engaging with such powerful tools, there is limited realisation of more complex assessment tasks. This is the conclusion of an unpublished study by Ross and Swithenby at the Open University UK who examined sample CBA tasks and resources from eight expert academics at different UK universities, in each case considering the tasks alongside the guidance offered to students on the relevant learning outcomes. The analysis used a framework of generic learning outcomes and level descriptors. Overall, the majority of the questions were found to test recall or knowledge and understanding, rather than higher order cognitive or subject skills (Table 1).

Table 1 Percentages of sample computer based questions at different levels from 3 universities. The data is illustrative rather than representative.

	Knowledge	*Understanding*	*Cognitive and subject skills*
Example 1	27%	43%	30%
Example 2	46%	42%	12%
Example 3	21%	62%	17%

There are two hypotheses that might explain these observations. The first is that these examples are drawn from the broader sciences and that the focus on content and the assimilation of knowledge reflects the curriculum as understood by the science community. Alternatively, or additionally, there is a sound pedagogic rationale for the observed focus if it is being used to motivate engagement with another learning activity, e.g. a lecture. Engagement and effective feedback are, after all, the overriding requirements if assessment is to drive learning.

However, within the assessment tasks that were examined in Ross and Swithenby's study, a significant minority tested higher order cognitive skills, and some tasks included, within the response process, a requirement to organise knowledge in a way that would facilitate understanding and rehearse higher order subject skills. The conclusion drawn is that it is possible to devise CBA tasks that are relevant to the large majority of learning outcomes at all levels of achievement though, in some cases, the task may not have the authenticity required for appropriate grading. Most such difficulties are concentrated on the demonstration of practical or communication skills.

This brief review of existing systems would not be complete without noting the incompatibility of most computer based assessment systems. Their analysis is centred on the well developed interoperability Question and Test Interoperability QTI specification. Although several systems claim QTI compliance, the capability is fragile in most cases and import of questions from a different package may not be a practical option for the non-technical user. It is not clear whether QTI compliance will increase as the advantage of compliance is of limited value to vendors.

Role of Publishers

Perhaps the most important trend in e-assessment is the involvement of publishers. To an increasing extent, large publishers have become aware of an assessment market that is complementary to their conventional textbook offerings. It has become commonplace to receive e-resources with the purchased book or for a publisher to offer a set of integrated Web resources that include texts, activities and diagnostic 'tests' with teacher reports. For example, in 2006 John Wiley and Sons are offering ~20 'Wiley PLUS' packages that are based on prominent standard texts and are compatible with the Blackboard environment. Usage data suggests that university teachers are finding it attractive to adopt the embedded computer aided assessment, at least for non-summative purposes.

Summative Assessment

The summative role of computer based assessment has been limited by many factors. There is the perception that machine generated tasks are too closed to represent authentically the full range of learning outcomes of a given programme. Other anxieties are; collusion, plagiarism, the logistical problems of engaging simultaneously an entire cohort, recognition of partial achievement, and, by no means least, institutional policies. The culture of regarding an unseen pen and paper and exam as the 'gold standard' is still strong, in spite of the rapid advance of screen-based high-stakes assessment at secondary levels and in skills-testing by, for example, the UK Driving Standards Agency with its national network of testing venues.

Conservatism in the use of summative computer based assessment is not universal. From 2007, the Medical College Admission Test, which is a required part of any application to a medical school in the USA, will only be available online and will be administered via nationally distributed testing sites. The total test takes 5½ hours. The advent of large commercial concerns offering 'total assessment solutions on a global scale' to professional bodies, Government agencies, universities and companies is an indicator of a trend which will undoubtedly affect universities.

In summary, present practice in computer based assessment in tertiary education is characterised by the following.

1. Uptake that is focused in the broader sciences.
2. Assessment tasks that involve recall rather than higher order skills.
3. A multiplicity of providers, both commercial and institution specific.
4. Assessment system capabilities that are greater than authors use.
5. A growing publisher involvement with tasks devised centrally.
6. The growth of Web Services that include assessment.
7. Limited university use for summative purposes.

Drivers and Barriers for E-assessment in Open Learning

Analyses of the uptake of computer based assessment highlight a number of factors, particularly;

> Limited academic skills in devising more complex CBA tasks.
> Social and regulatory conservatism. High entry costs

The first and third of these may be illustrated by OpenMark production processes. The code on which OpenMark is based is most practically generated by collaboration between an academic who has the subject expertise and a learning technologist/software engineer. Given the need for the production of code and pedagogically valuable feedback, a single item may require 1-4 days of professional level staff input. Scaling this input to create the volume of items required for a module or programme is prohibitively expensive.

Although the position portrayed here may be extreme - OpenMark is a rich system – the problem of time investment exists for all systems. Warburton highlights this issue and notes the tension between the need for technical and pedagogical design skills in the design of advanced computer aided assessment and the traditional academic ownership of teaching in parts of tertiary education.

Authoring tools and item banks provide two potential ways of overcoming the expertise problem.

Authoring tools are generally available in commercial systems and there have been attempts to provide generic open-access solutions. The Technologies for Online Interoperable Assessment TOIA initiative aimed to 'remove many of the barriers for teachers who wish to move into computer-assisted assessment - and avoid lock-in to a particular proprietary system.' Although not widely used, its use of Web based templates that are structured so as to provide the information necessary to work within the interoperability framework provided by the Question and Test Interoperability QTI specification may provide a route that wins eventual acceptance.

Although there are now several item banks available, the largest and most accessible resources are provided by commercial text book publishers. Sclater et al and Sclater have analysed in some detail the technical, legal and process issues involved in the running of a national item bank service. Greenberg and Swithenby have suggested that 'a demonstration of an implemented interoperable assessment system drawing on diverse sources of content and with tangible benefit would be of immense value' and have highlighted the need to reconcile high production costs with the need for local ownership, a prerequisite to overcoming social barriers to adoption.

Specific Issues for Distance Teaching Universities

Many of the factors discussed above are relevant to both residential and distance teaching universities. However, there are a number of factors that should promote enhanced interest in open and distance learning.

- Potential for enhanced engagement in part-time students. One of the Gibbs and Simpson conditions for assessment that supports learning is 'strong and consistent engagement', a condition that is hard to meet by students who have other major responsibilities and an interrupted study schedule. Frequent low-stakes assessment based around rich interactive Web-accessed tasks is a teaching tactic available to distance teaching universities.
- Potential for enhanced feedback to dispersed students. The tasks identified above will have greatest value if feedback is provided 'in

time and in sufficient detail to affect learning'. Although support of remote students can be optimised so that, in quality of interaction, it meets or surpasses the standards in residential settings, it is likely that there will be delays in students receiving academic support and advice. The feedback from computer based assessment can be immediate and tailored to the student. The value of providing such feedback has been noted in several studies, for example Rayne and Baggott and Jordan and Swithenby.

- Access to large markets that justify investment. Even with expected increases in efficiency in item generation, the costs of learning experiences based around computer based assessment are front-end loaded. The scale of operation of large distance teaching universities allows such costs to be distributed within a single institutional 'market'.
- Collaborative opportunities in item bank generation. The successful creation and adoption of item banks depends crucially on local acceptability and each negotiation required to achieve such acceptability carries complexity and costs. Collaborations between a few large partners are potentially more viable than the marshalling of a larger and more fragmented community.

Future Capabilities

There is a stark contrast between such activities and the writing of an extended essay or report with a free format. Given that there is a strong belief that such open-response formats are needed to assess higher order learning outcomes, it is reasonable to ask whether computers can grade and provide feedback on essays. Some progress has been made. These studies are limited to short free text answers but have achieved impressive results. Marking of longer texts is less developed though there are well established tools for automatic feedback on writing style: content, grammar, usage, style, organisation etc. Educational Testing Services provide a range of relevant products. Work in this area and in the complementary problem of marking free diagrams is continuing and progress may be expected.

In the above discussion, the assessment function is at the core of the design of the experience. However, there is an increasing interest in computer based activities that are designed as constructivist learning experiences. Examples are; simulations and virtual practice environments, e-conferences, Wiki construction, e-portfolio generation, etc. In each case, integrated assessment could generate input to an automatic grading and feedback tool. Such approaches are only now emerging with an accent on monitoring the quantity and timing of activity rather than the quality of the contribution. Distance teaching universities may benefit from these developments, as it will become easier to monitor and therefore assess group activities that are difficult to construct for a dispersed student body.

A pedagogic strategy that has attracted significant interest recently is peer assessment. This has the merit of engaging the student with the criteria for success and can engender a feeling of community responsibility. Such strategies might be facilitated by the user of computers. The extension of such work to non residential students is an important and interesting aspiration.

Grading in Distance Education

Both the traditional practices of 'marking' and the relatively recent innovation of 'grading' are concerned with reporting and interpreting examination/test results. While marking of learning outcomes is measured and expressed with the help of numerical or quantitative indices (say 40, 60, 65, etc.), grading is related to the quality of performance or expression of learning outcomes in qualitative terms (say, first/second, higher/lower, etc.). Let us discuss both the practices, marking and grading, and examine to what extent the latter is an improvement over the former.

Marking vs. Grading

In our examination system, marking has been followed for a long time and most of the educational institutions/systems depend on the same practice. In the practice of marking, the examination results of individual papers are expressed on a scale ranging from 0-100. It is assumed that whatever the student has learnt over a year can be expressed in terms of his/her performance on a three hour test and the performance is measured in numerical scores. But in grading the 0-100 scale is reduced to a five point scale. Grading provides an overall estimate of human ability which is more reliable. Unlike marks, grades are not influenced by the variations in subjects/disciplines.

The advantage of marking is that it is convenient to express the measurement of learning outcomes/performance in numerical indices scores. Another advantage is that the easy comparison of the scores of a number of students helps the educational authorities to select and admit them into various courses. Though this process is easy, it may not be valid and in fact it is not. And by tradition/convention we didn't/don't question this practice. Though it has many disadvantages, we will concentrate on three issues.

- The foremost disadvantage of marking is its unattainability of the assumption on which it is based. There are varied and at times different, learner tasks and it will be wrong to analyse these tasks into exactly hundred constituent 'bits'. Moreover, in a 101-point scale, the difference of 1, for example, between 1 and 2, between 40 and 41, and between 76 and 77 may not have the same connotation.
- The second disadvantage is that the hundred constituent 'bits' (in the scale of 0-100) are spread differently (i.e., in different proportions) in the three domains of learning, viz., cognitive, psychomotor and affective. For example, a score range of 30-45 measuring learning outcomes in the cognitive domain is different from the same score range measuring learning outcomes in the psychomotor domain. Moreover, it is difficult to express human abilities, especially at affective domain, in numerical indices or scores.
- The third, but very important, disadvantage is the 'error' that is involved in the practice of marking. This error creeps in due to 'marker variability' and 'subject variability' in marking the answer scripts. Let us briefly discuss errors in marking due to these two types of variations.

Marker Variability

Reliability of scoring objective type/fixed answer items/questions is guaranteed even if the same answer script is checked and marked/scored by a group of examiners. But scoring of essay type/free response items by more than one examiner does not provide objectivity. In fact, it can't be possible because of the fact that it is impossible to predetermine rigid 'bits' constituting a response or an answer, and it is difficult on the part of one individual marker/examiner to consistently distinguish the variations in one response/answer given/attempted by a group of learners/students.

There is no justification for awarding a particular score (neither more or less) to an answer. The correctness of the decision of an examiner to award 55 and not 56 out of 100, and vice versa can always be questioned.

Moreover, the probable 'error' in awarding one score, say 55 in this case, to one answer script by the same examiner varies from 5 to 7%, and in 50% of the cases of answer scripts checked, this error is more than 5%. So the true mark of a student who has been awarded 55 may well fall between 55±5, i.e., 50 to 60. To put it precisely, besides inter marker variability (variation between examiners) in scoring the same answer script, there is intra marker variability (variation in one examiner at different occasions) in scoring many answer scripts at the same period of time. So, the decision of labelling 39% marks as "fail", 40% marks as "Pass", and 60% marks as "First Division", and so on has no sound theoretical basis. Also, it is wrong to declare a student scoring 55% as "Second Division", for if we allow an error (of scoring) of 7% the same student would have secured either 48% ("Third Division" or "Pass") or 62% ("First Division").

Subject Variability

In the traditional practice of marking, most of us are used to the 0-100 scale. If you look at the 'range' of marking or the 'spread' of marking in various 'disciplines' including yours, you may find that the lower and the upper limits of this spread/range vary from discipline to discipline. In Mathematical Sciences the whole range from 0-100 is utilized in marking/scoring, while in Literature the range may fall approximately between 15-60. Obviously, then, a score of 60 in both Mathematics and English Literature may not have similar connotations. Likewise, a student of Science securing 60% marks in aggregate may not be equaled with a student of English Literature securing the same percentage of marks in aggregate.

So, because of these variations in the range of scores across subjects/ disciplines, it becomes difficult to compare the scores of students from different subjects/disciplines. Moreover, equalisation of aggregate marks across disciplines, without taking into consideration the respective spread or ranges of scores, at the time of admission to courses and recruitment to jobs may be fallacious. For example, a student securing 65% marks in Statistics may not necessarily be considered superior to a student securing 55% marks in Sociology because, for instance, the score-range of students of Statistics may vary from 45% to 85% while that of Sociology from 30% to 65%. In that case both the Statistics and the Sociology students may be considered nearly equal in their respective abilities/knowledge in their respective disciplines.

Advantages of Grading

As against marking, the acceptance of the principle of grading is an honest confession of our inability to be so precise in assessing human qualities. Unlike marks, grades are not influenced by the variations in disciplines/ subjects. If almost all human qualities and achievements can be measured quantitatively, only then scoring/marking is justified. But this is not always the case.

Given below are a few advantages of grading.

- Grading is more 'precise' and 'reliable' than marking. It is 'precise' because the 0-100 scale is reduced to a five point, or seven or even nine point scale. As we have seen earlier, marking (with its numerical scale of 0-100) ensures a false precision in the measurement of human abilities. Grading, on the other hand, provides an overall estimate of human ability which is more realistic and so 'reliable'.
- The accuracy in assessment cannot be fully ensured, whether it is marking or grading. But the chances of error of judging the ability of one individual to be better or worse than that of the other are much less in grading. At the same time, because of a very precise scale with a short range, error due to marker variability in grading the same assignment response is minimised.
- In all subjects whether Literature or Mathematics there is a greater possibility of utilising the whole grade range in the system of grading. Therefore, the error due to subject variability is lower because grading minimises the disparity in the value of scores/grades in different subjects.
- Another reason why grading is more realistic and reliable is that it is based on two standards.

Let us briefly discuss these two basic standards of grading before examining the techniques of grading assignment responses.

Bases of Grading

Grading is based on two standards — relative and absolute. A standard is an external criterion or a set of external criteria. While grading, the standard or the model is kept in view against which a grade to a particular assignment response is awarded. For example:

- When the relative grading standard is followed in grading the assignment responses of a group of learners on a given question or task, the criterion is the performance of the whole group of learners on that task.

- In case of absolute grading standard the criterion may be the ideal performance on the given task, irrespective of anybody's performance.

Both relative and absolute grading standards are elaborated in the following pages.

Relative Grading Standard

As said earlier, in relative grading standard the performance of the whole group of learners is kept in view as the standard against which grades are to be awarded. Before assessing the assignment response, a decision is made regarding the number of learners to be allocated/put under various categories within the range of the scale, say five point, seven point, nine-point, etc. The preferred mode of distribution determines the number of learners to be put in various grade categories. For example, if 500 learners take one assignment question and prepare assignment responses, the distribution in a five point scale would be even and balanced on either side of the central figure, i.e., 38% in C grade, and 24% and 7% in B/D and A/E grades respectively. This can be practically presented in a tabular form (both in case of 5 point and 7 point scales) when the assignment responses of 500 learners on a given assignment question are to be evaluated.

Table 2: Distribution of "population" (N = 500) on 5-point and 7-point scales

	5 Point Scale			*7 Point Scale*	
Grade	*% of Students*	*No. of Students out of 500*	*Grade*	*% of Students*	*No. of Students out of 500*
A	7	35	O	3	15
B	24	120	A	7	35
C	38	190	B	22	110
D	24	120	C	36	180
E	7	35	D	22	110
			E	7	35
			F	3	15

Table 2 suggests that if a 5 point grading scale is to be followed, the number of learners out of 500 to be awarded grades A, B, C, D and E would be 35, 120, 190, 120 and 35 respectively. The middle portion (i.e., grade C) has 190 learners and the rest 310 learners are equally distributed on both the sides of the scale. Similar principle is followed in case of 7 point scale.

Though very easy to use and handle, the limitations of relative grading standard are many.

- First, the grades do not tell the teacher exactly "how much" of "what" the learners have mastered in a subject. This standard may be helpful to, for example, Recruitment Boards of Universities which make select/reject or pass/fail decisions respectively for their purposes.
- Second, grading a learner's ability in relation to the overall performance level of the class/group does not convey much meaning to him/her unless accompanied by a clarification on group performance. A learner who has secured 'B' grade in one class/group may secure 'D' grade in another class/group. This inconsistency challenges the reliability of grading learners' performance.
- Third, in a 5 point scale for example, at least 7 % of learners are to be given 'E' grade (which means "poor' or "unsatisfactory") even if they have written good assignment responses. If these 7 % learners do better next time, they may come up to 'D' grade, which further means that 7 % of learners from D grade have to come down to 'E' grade. This not only causes injustice to learners but also creates misunderstanding among them.

Now let us see in what way "absolute grading standard" overcomes these drawbacks in grading learners' performance.

Absolute Grading Standard

Unlike relative grading where a fixed number of learners are put in each category of grades, in absolute grading a range of scores is put against each grade.

Table 3: Absolute grading: distribution of range of scores across grades

Grade	*Range of scores*
O	90-100%
A	80-89%
B	70-79%
C	60-69%
D	50-59%
E	40-49%
F	Less than 40%

So, unlike relative grading, there is no prefixed hard and fast rule to put a fixed percentage of learners under each grade. In absolute grading, for example, a situation may arise when no learner gets F grade, and the average learners may fall within 50-59 score range (which is not the mid portion). Though ideal in evaluation and grading learners' performance, it is not easy to follow this standard of grading. Much depends upon the type of item/question/assignment response, which is being used to evaluate learners' ability.

Grading Mechanisms

For essay type items/questions, the range of scores can be a 7 point scale putting the evaluation of responses into a wide range of qualitative judgments. The interpretation of the scale consisting of seven grade points can be done as given in table.

Table 4. Interpretation of 7 point scale

Grade points	*Interpretation*
6	Outstanding
5	Excellent
4	Very Good
3	Good
2	Satisfactory
1	Pass
0	Failure

When grading is done, especially of essay type items/questions, certain criteria regarding

- content (viz., relevance, adequacy, appropriacy, etc.);
- form (viz., clarity, coherence, etc.); and
- presentation (viz., imagination, intelligence, resourcefulness, etc.)

of the answers/responses are taken into consideration. The objective items may be "Yes/No" type or "multiple choice" type having only one correct answer, and so they cannot be spread over a 7-point scoring scale. Similarly, essay type items cannot be put within two point scale of right/wrong answer.

Grading Different Item Types and Combining Grades

Let us consider the grading of answer scripts of learners appearing at the term end/final examination.

- Suppose the final examination "Paper 1" consists of:
  i) four essay type questions,
  ii) eight short answer questions, and
  iii) sixteen objective type questions.
- Suppose again that the instructions say that the essay type questions are to be graded on a 7-point scale (from O to F or 0 to 6), the short answer questions are to be graded on a 3-point scale (from A to C or 0 to 2), and the objective type questions have two alternatives (Yes/No) and so have 2-point scale (0-1).
- In the examination, for example, Mr. Y, has secured grades C,B,D,E in the four essay type questions (on the 7-point grading scales), grades A, A, B, C, C, A, A, C in the eight short answer questions (on the 3-point grading scale) and has given 11 correct answers to objective questions (on the 2-point grading scale).

Now let us calculate grades for each of the three items (question types) and find out the final grade.

Step 1

Sum of grade points on essay type items (on 7-point scale)

$$= \frac{\text{Combined grade for essay type items} \times 6}{\text{No. of essay type items} \times 6}$$

$$= \frac{[C + B + D + E] \times 6}{4 \times 6}$$

$$= \frac{[3 + 4 + 2 + 1] \times 6}{4 \times 6}$$

$$= \frac{60}{24} = 2.50 \text{ or Grade 'C'}$$

(Where 6 is the maximum grade point on a 7-point scale)

Step 2

Combined grade for short answer items (Converted into 7-point scale)

$$= \frac{[A + A + B + C + C + A + A + C] \times 6}{8 \times 2}$$

$$= \frac{[2 + 2 + 1 + 0 + 0 + 2 + 2 + 0] \times 6}{8 \times 2}$$

$$= \frac{54}{16} = 3.38 \text{ or Grade 'C'}$$

(where 6 is the maximum grade point on a 7 point scale, and 2 is the maximum on a 3-point scale)

Step 3

Combined grade for objective types items $= \frac{11\times1}{16\times1}$

(converted into 7-point scale) = 4.13 or Grade 'B'

(wher 6 is the maximum grade point in a 7 point scale, and 1 is the maximum on a 2-point scale)

We can find out the overall grade for this question paper consisting of three item types (essay, short answer, and objective type) by calculating the average of the grade points of the three item types.

Step 4

$$\text{The overall grade for Mr. Y is} = \frac{\text{Sum of Grade - points on different subsets}}{\text{Total number of subsets}}$$

$$= \frac{C+C+B}{3} = \frac{3+3+4}{3} = \frac{10}{3}$$

= 3.33 or Grade 'C'

In certain cases, the subsets (essay type, objective type, etc.) in a question paper may carry different weights for which weighted grades are to be calculated.

For example, in the present case if subset I (essay type) has a relative weight of 2, subset II (short answer type) a relative weight of 3, and subset III (objective type) a relative weight of 1, then the weighted grade and the overall grade will be as given in table.

Table 5. Tabulation of scores on subsets of different weights

Subsets	*Relatice Weight*	*Grade-point obtained*	*Weighted Grade*
I	2	2.50	5.00
II	3	3.38	10.14
III	1	4.13	4.13
Total	6		19.27

Overall grade $= \frac{19.27}{6}$ = 3.21 or Grade 'C' (Good)

For converting GPA or grade point average to corresponding grades and verbal description of those grades, a conversion table may be prepared that might help in easy calculation of the overall grade for individual learner. Following is an example of such a conversion table for a 7-point scale of grading.

Table 6. Conversion table of GPA into letter grade

Grade range	*Grade point*	*Letter Grade*	*Verbal Description*
5.50 and above	6	O	Outstanding
4.50 to 5.49	5	A	Excellent
3.50 to 4.49	4	B	Very Good
2.50 to 3.49	3	C	Good
1.50 to 2.49	2	D	Satisfactory
0.50 to 1.49	1	E	Pass
Less than 0.50	0	F	Failure

It notice that each grade point has a corresponding grade range. The grade range for a particular grade point is ±.50 to that grade point. For example, the grade point of 3 has the lower limit of 2.50 and the upper limit of 3.49. Any calculated GPA falling in between the range of 2.50 to 3.49 is converted into the letter grade of C, which means "Good" (GPA of 2.49 is Grade D whereas 2.50 is Grade C). In the foregoing example, we find that the GPA of Mr. Y is 3.33 which falls in the grade range of 2.50 to 3.49 and is represented by a letter grade of 'C', meaning that the performance is "Good". Similarly GPA falling in between the range of 3.50 to 4.49 indicates "Very Good", 5.50 and above indicates "Outstanding" and 0.50 and below indicates "Failure".

The evaluator as per his/her judicious estimation awards grades to the questions in accordance with their national values while assessing the assignments relating to Diploma and Certificate Courses.

References

Allan, J.. *Learning Outcomes in Higher Education*, Studies in Higher Education, 21, 1, 93-108.

Gibbs, G. and Simpson, C. (2004-5). Does your assessment support your students' learning? Learning and Teaching in Higher Education (on-line), 1(1), 3-31.

Jordan, S. and Swithenby, S.J. On-line summative assessment with feedback as an aid to effective learning at a distance. Proc of 2004 ISL Symposium Diversity and Inclusivity (Ed C. Rust) Alden Press, pp 480-485.

Ross, S.M. and Swithenby, S.J.. Probing the limits of applicability of computer aided assessment: a learning-outcomes led analysis. EARLI Assessment Conference 2006 Roundtable workshop.

Whitelock, D. and Brasher, A.. Roadmap for e-assessment. Joint Information Systems Committee Report June 2006.

11

Assessment Versus Accountability

There is confusion about what kind of assessment is appropriate in higher education. There is also misunderstanding over the relationship between assessment and accountability. Even when institutions and state policymakers use similar assessment information they do so for different purposes. Faculty are focused on improving educational programs while state leaders are interested in holding their public higher education institutions accountable for their performance.

Our goal is to improve our understanding of assessment and accountability and the relationship between them. We do so through the following steps: First, we present a rationale for a set of assessment principles to implement in higher education. Second, we argue that states have an important role in assuring accountability of their institutions of higher learning but that they must avoid a number of land mines if they wish to engage their institutions successfully. Moreover, to do so, basic rules in comparative methodology must be adhered to in the use of institutional level data for any aggregated comparisons. Third, we present an example of the application of these assessment principles in a set of testing activities we find useful elements for any strategy of rapprochement between higher education institutions and state-based authorities. We argue that assessment measures based on the principles stand the best chance to fill the gap between the two groups. These measures should be organized with other measures to form an assessment indicator system. Fourth, the terms of engagement between institutions and state-level policymakers must be carefully worked out.

The Focus

The need to improve our understanding of assessment and accountability cuts across public and private colleges and universities. Regional accreditation groups now require evidence of student learning success for the public and private institutions they accredit. Private and public colleges are frequent targets of Congressional concerns about the cost of undergraduate education. Such concerns occasionally translate into proposed legislation to deal with the problem. Most recently, the Commission on the Future of Higher Education, established by Secretary of Education Spellings, has brought accountability issues to public attention. Because of concerns about costs and quality, private as well as public institutions need to demonstrate that they add value, that they produce successful educational outcomes. Boards of trustees of private and public institutions now increasingly call for evidence of success. Finally, both public and private institutions are interested in using assessment to improve teaching and learning. Many of the points raised here are therefore relevent to both public and private institutions. However, we feature public institutions in this study because they are under the direct authority of governors, state legislatures, and state-based commissions of higher education directly charged to hold public institutions accountable.

The Argument

The "public" (taxpayers, legislators, governors) wants to be assured that their college students are receiving a quality education. This interest in accountability is fueled by the same factors that have led to higher tuitions, namely shrinking state budgets and the increasing cost of higher education. In the past, institutions relied on accreditation reviews and various types of actuarial data, such as graduation and minority access rates, to demonstrate quality. That approach is no longer adequate for colleges just as it no longer sufficient for K-12 education (as evidenced by No Child Left Behind legislation and the emphasis on statewide testing of students).

The public wants to know whether its education institutions are helping students acquire the knowledge, skills, and abilities they will need when they graduate. In addition, policy makers increasingly want to know how much students actually have learned, not how much they believe that they have learned. Forty-four states have established accountability systems for higher education. Within this group 27 states feature "report cards" that attempt to benchmark student learning outcomes. Thus, the measure of quality has been expanded beyond accreditation and actuarial data to include evidence that learning goals have been met. Seat time, course grades, and graduation rates are no longer sufficient. In short, the public is increasingly asking its colleges and universities to show that acceptable progress has been made in student learning.

To satisfy this demand for accountability, higher education institutions need to demonstrate that their students have acquired important skills and knowledge in addition to achieving other goals such as graduating, achieving necessary prerequisites for professional schools, and gaining employment. Institutional ratings, student and faculty surveys, and other indirect proxies are just not sufficient. The only credible way to show such learning is to test them over what they are supposed to know and be able to do. Instead, direct measures of outcomes are needed. Colleges and universities already assess students, but hardly ever for the purpose of demonstrating the value the institution adds to a student's knowledge and skills. At least until recently, their reasons for testing have had nothing to do with accountability. Instead, they test incoming students to make sure they have the skills that are needed to do their course work. Those who do not have sufficient skills are generally placed in remedial programs. In addition, some colleges administer tests at the end of the sophomore year to make sure students are ready for their upper division studies. These so-called "rising junior" exams, like the initial placement tests, focus on basic reading, writing, and math skills. These tests are focused on the individual student without attempting to measure the contribution of the institution to student learning.

Some colleges are now expanding their testing programs to include assessing other abilities, such as critical thinking skills, that are central to the college's mission but cut across academic majors. College administrators see this as a way to demonstrate the beneficial effects of the educational experiences at their institutions to prospective students and their parents. Nevertheless, most institutions continue to rely on their faculty to assess their students' content knowledge and skills. This is fine with the faculty who generally believe they already provide sufficient and appropriate assessments of student learning. They use midterm and final exams, term papers, classroom participation, and other evidence to assign grades. And, they feel these grades reflect how much students learn in their courses. Unfortunately, grades of professors are idiosyncratic. Two courses with the same title may cover different content areas, even at the same college. There also are large differences in grading standards among professors across colleges. B-work at one school may correspond to A- or C-work at another institution. The same is true across professors within an institution. There also has been substantial grade inflation over time. Hence, professor assigned grades cannot be relied on to provide a valid measure of whether the students in one graduating class are more or less proficient than those in another class or at another college. Nor are value added comparisons of the contributions of institutions to growth in student learning made. Some other metric is needed.

The search for another index has led some colleges to experiment with portfolios, grades in capstone courses, or other institution-specific indicators of learning. However, all of these measures have the same fundamental limitation as regular course grades, namely, the absence of a way to reliably and validly interpret scores outside of the context of a particular course or school at a given point in time. To correct that problem, the measures have to be administered under the same standardized conditions to everyone and the scores obtained have to be adjusted for possible variation in average question difficulty, reader leniency, and other factors. Locally constructed measures, like professor course grades or portfolios, do not have these essential features and therefore cannot be used for making valid comparisons within institutions over time or for comparisons among institutions at a single point in time.

Those limitations are not present with the measures that are used for statewide K-12 testing (such as the Stanford-9, Iowa Tests of Basic Skills, and the National Assessment of Educational Progress (NAEP)), college and graduate school admission decisions (such as the SATs, ACTs, GREs, and LSATs), or licensing exams in the professions (such as accountancy, law, medicine, and teaching). Thus, when results really matter, such as for high-stakes decisions about individuals, procedures are used that help to eliminate the effects of extraneous factors, such as who drafted the questions or scored the answers.

The Role of the State

States have a legitimate and critical role in assuring accountability in their higher education institutions.

Many states set objectives for:

- educational proficiency levels to be achieved by entering students
- participation rates by ethnic/racial groups
- minimum passing scores for law, medicine and other professional schools
- numbers of graduates in particular fields to be achieved such as teaching, nursing, and technology fields.

The states also provide the instructional budgets for public undergraduate education and infrastructure support, including buildings, library, and scientific equipment. States clearly have a right and a responsibility to require accountability from the institutions they support. Why, then, are we not further ahead in developing assessment systems of student learning that work from the point of view of the institutions and the states?

The problem is that the assessment measures used at the institutional level differ from most of the accountability measures states focus on. First, the concept of accountability must be specified. Most broadly, in the context of higher education, accountability can be defined as the extent to which public higher education institutions meet the goals set for them by the state. (In the best case these goals are mutually agreed to by both parties.) Just as faculty and institutions set assessment goals for a variety of purposes, states set accountability goals for different purposes. Most states desire accountability for prudent use of resources, or at the very least, absence of fraud. Some state leaders demand evidence of increased participation, retention and graduation rates for underrepresented groups. Still others, an increasing number, want to be assured that students have gained knowledge and skills from their educational experiences. Approaches and measures of student learning favored by faculty differ from those used by state leaders. Because of the growing interest in student outcomes, we are focused on this last goal of state-based accountability, evidence of student learning outcomes.

Approaches to student learning outcomes by faculty have the following characteristics: Their goals are to improve curriculum and pedagogy as well as set targets for students:

- They focus on individual students, departments, or institutions but are not focused on inter-institutional comparisons;
- Are content rich, tailored to the context of the institution and generated by faculty themselves and are often time intensive and costly;

- Because the emphasis is on content, they tend not to be replicable from one institution to the next.

In comparison, state-based approaches are:

- focused on accountability objectives;
- aggregated at the regional or state level and ideally replicable and comparable across institutions;
- focused on indirect proxies of student learning outcomes such as the percentage of passing rates for teaching examinations,
- nurses, and other professional school examinations; number and percentage of students that take the graduate record examination (GRE); retention and graduation rates;
- not rich in content or tailored to the context of the individual institutions and not developed by faculty;
- cost effective, making use of existing data.

The result is a disconnect between the faculty/institutions on the one hand and the state on the other.

Comparative Methodology

This disconnect is made worse because a number of state-based comparisons violate comparative methodological principles. The attempt at comparing states at the K-12 level is now being extended to the higher education level. It is not easy to make direct comparisons among states on student learning outcomes. Such comparisons are fraught with methodological hurdles, some of the more important of which are listed below:

- States differ dramatically in demographic and social-economic characteristics so that direct comparisons, say, between California and Rhode Island about the mean proficiency levels attained in math or reading make little sense.
- Comparing aggregated scores at the state level, rather than higher education institutions, makes little sense because such comparisons assume there are no differences in effects across individual higher education institutions within a state. If a state's scores go up (or down), is it due to one or all institutions? If a state's scores stay the same, is it because all the institutions functioned the same way or did the effects at one institution offset those at another? This is the fundamental flaw

that statisticians call "aggregation bias" or the ecological fallacy problem.

- The use of a variety of indirect, proxy measures is problematic for several reasons. Comparing GRE scores across states makes no sense because of concerns about selection bias, e.g., a state may have a large or small number of students who take the GRE exam; the context that drives the number differs substantially from state to state. Use of passage rates on licensing exams, such as for teachers, is similarly problematic because states differ dramatically in pass/fail standards (NAS study report). For example, a score that is far below the score required for passing in one state may be far above the score required in another state. Finally, graduation and retention rates are also not credible measures to compare across states on their own, because, again, they must be interpreted in context. A low retention rate may be purposeful at an institution dedicated to serving at risk populations. Does this mean that no state-based comparisons are possible? In fact states may conduct comparisons over time within their states to provide valuable benchmarking data about the quality of performance of graduates from their public institutions. Comparisons between states are also possible, States may also desire to establish minimum levels of performance outcomes for undergraduate graduates and benchmark them against the same measures in sets of states judged to be most similar to them.

Assessment Principles

Using measures whose scores are interpretable across professors, colleges, and time allows for making relevant comparisons within and between institutions. For example, the scores on such measures can be used along with grades on other tests (such as the SAT or ACT) as controls to assess whether the students at a school are doing better or worse on an outcome measure than would be expected given their entry-level skills. Measures that are applicable across institutions also may serve as benchmarks for interpreting the results with similar but locally constructed instruments or course grades. Measures that are designed to permit comparisons across institutions thus provide a signal of academic performance (and therefore motivator for change). Such signaling can indicate whether faculty and administrators need to take a closer look at the resources, curriculum, pedagogy, and programmatic structure underlying undergraduate teaching and learning. In short, such measures may help colleges document the progress they are making in fostering student learning. The measures also may contribute to improving academic programs by providing institutions with baseline and outcome scores to help identify the effects on learning of programmatic and curricular changes.

To accomplish these ends, cross-institutional measures must have certain essential characteristics. The scores must be reliable in the sense that they are not overly affected by chance factors. If the results are aggregated to the college level (such as to providing information about programs), then the degree of reliability required to identify effects is much less than would be needed for making decisions about individual students. The scores must be valid in the sense of providing information about student characteristics that are important to the institution's goals, such as improving their students' ability to communicate in writing and to think critically about issues.

The process of implementing such measures at the college level is fraught with land mines. For instance, any top-down effort to impose them on faculty and students is likely to run into trouble. Instead, it will be essential for the academic community to see them as a valuable adjunct to their own measures or even embed them into their own capstone courses. Similarly, attempts to use the results to punish institutions for having less than stellar or even average improvement scores would stop the assessment effort in its tracks. Instead, the results need to be used to identify best practices that other institutions could try as well as spot potential problem areas where additional support is needed

It is not feasible to measure all or even most of the knowledge, skills, and abilities that are central to a college's learning goals. Much of what is learned takes place outside the classroom. This situation leads to the concern that what is tested will be overly emphasized in the institution's instructional programs. In short, some will say that the only abilities that count are the ones that are measured. This position is akin to saying "you shouldn't measure anything unless you can measure everything." This concern can be addressed by varying the types of measures used over time and by augmenting the measures that are used across institutions with local program specific instruments. To make this discussion more concrete we next present the assumptions, goals, methods and results for the Collegiate Learning Assessment (CLA), a new initiative we have been developing.

Collegiate Learning Assessment

We have been working with diverse colleges around the country to explore the feasibility of implementing the foregoing principles on a large scale. This research has involved the following testing activities:

- Tests are used to assess student skills.
- All the measures are open-ended; i.e., students write essays or short answers to the questions in each task. These measures fit within Shavelson and Huang's framework for conceptualizing, developing, and interpreting direct measures of student learning.
- The measures are delivered to students over the Internet. The students take the tests under standardized exam conditions in their college's computer labs. This test administration procedure greatly reduces the costs of the assessment process and helps to insure data quality.
- The students enter their answers online, and the responses are processed and scored by computer. Computer software programs "learn" how to score the open-ended responses based on the task's scoring rubric and a sample of 400 answers that were graded by human scorers.
- A given student takes only a small portion of the entire set of tests administered at each college. This "matrix sampling" approach uses measures from several clusters of disciplines (e.g., natural sciences, social sciences, and arts and humanities) but only requires two to three hours of testing time per student.
- The students' SAT or ACT scores (which are obtained from their campus' registrar's office) are used to put the scores from the admissions tests on a common scale and to adjust for differences in admissions and grading standards across colleges.
- The "unit of analysis" is the college. Although data are collected on individual students, these data are aggregated to the institution, because that is the locus for program improvement. However, this focus does not preclude examining separate colleges or programs within a large institution.
- Colleges are informed about the average of their students' scores (individual scores are only reported to the students). They also are advised about whether their average is above or below what would be expected given their students' mean SAT or ACT scores. Although

anonymous institutional averages are presented (such that a college can compare itself to others in the sample), no college's identity is disclosed to any other institution.

- Research is conducted to assess the reliability and validity of the scores assigned, the relationship between these scores and other measures, the interaction between task type and student characteristics (including demographics and academic major), student motivation, the characteristics of the schools that have average scores that are above or below the expected level, and other factors.

Conducting the above-listed activities, a proof of concept study was conducted with 14 colleges and universities testing 1365 students in the 2002-2003 academic year. The tests were administered in computer labs where most students typed their answers on computer discs provided for the purpose based on instructions and questions provided on paper. Five findings emerged from our feasibility study (Klein, et al., 2004): the measures satisfy psychometric standards for reliability and validity; the graders agree highly with each other in the scores they assign to an answer; students exhibit consistent performance across tasks; and after controlling on their college admissions scores, seniors and juniors earn significantly higher scores on our tests than do freshmen and sophomores. This latter finding indicates the measures are sensitive to the amount of education a student receives (recognizing that learning occurs both in and out of the classroom). In addition, the substantial correlation between these scores and the students' college GPAs suggests that the types of tests we are using measure abilities that are relevant to the educational process. Finally, we replicated the findings of others who have reported a high correlation between human and computer scoring of open-ended responses by comparing hand scoring of writing prompts with computer scoring done by the Educational Testing Service (ETS). For example, we obtained a 0.95 correlation between these two scoring methods when the school is the unit of analysis. The major advantages of computer scoring and Internet testing are the substantial savings in test administration, scoring and reporting costs, and elimination of the numerous problems associated with reading hand writing and handling hard copy, and much faster turnaround time in reporting results.

The feasibility study further found that some colleges had average scores that were significantly higher or lower than would be expected on the basis of their mean SAT scores. Subsequent results, based on testing 45 institutions in the academic year 2004-2005 refine and extend the findings of value added within and between institutions.

Notes for Reconciliation

States are increasingly developing assessment systems that emphasize accountability. Resistance by faculty to accountability oriented systems of assessment (that are focused on indirect, proxy measures of student learning) also continues and is unlikely to change. This is an unfortunate, even problematic situation if, as we believe, the state level demand for accountability is only going to grow. We should reject the argument that the unit of analysis for accountability must be only the state or the argument that the unit must only be the institution. How might we reconcile the implications of the two units of analysis? We argue that the prime focus of accountability should be on student learning. And we will also argue below the focus on the institution as the unit of analysis does not foreclose the possibility of doing comparisons across states. However, such comparisons need to be based on carefully developed ways to compare institutions in a state with institutions in other states.

Representatives of the state and institutions, including both their administration and faculties, will need to work out the equivalent of a legal agreement that both parties will adhere to. In most cases the venue for this activity will be the state-based higher education coordinating commissions. These rules of engagement must give both parties incentives to cooperate. What should the rules of engagement be? First, there must be agreement on the measures to be used. The measures must meet faculty objectives but the ability for inter-institutional comparison should be built in to satisfy the needs of the state. Although the two parties need to agree on common measures to be used, their goals are different. Since faculty are primarily interested in assessment for educational improvement objectives while the state is primarily interested in assessment for accountability goals, the two parties will need to reach agreement on what information from the assessments may be aggregated at the regional or state level. Relations between the institutions and the state will be considerably improved if there is agreement that the focus should be on improvement in the value-added contribution of the institution to student learning over time rather than a focus on absolute levels achieved. Indeed, if there is agreement that the value-added approach is appropriate, there can be a time lag built in during which institutions identified as being below minimum levels of quality can be asked to show improvement over a several year period. Since institutions, as well as the state, are interested in demonstrating that they are improving, this strategy should provide common ground between the two groups. Eventually, parties using the CLA will also want to establish criterion referenced norms to define a reasonable minimum standard for CLA performance. Currently, for example, each state defines and, if it so desires, changes its own cutoff points for satisfactory performance in high stakes testing in K-12 education. The National Assessment of Educational Progress (NAEP), developed by education testing experts, at least offers an alternative way to think about these norms. Thus it may be more appropriate that higher education testing experts take the lead in establishing cut off levels for satisfactory to excellent performance on the CLA. Clearly having comparative data is a necessary condition for helping to decide what a fair standard should be.

Governance of this partnership will also need to be considered carefully. Ideally, an independent commission might be set up to govern the relationship between the state and the institutions. This is unlikely to occur. What is more likely is that existing higher education coordinating commissions will be given the responsibility to implement any agreement to assess higher education institutions within their states. What is most important under these circumstances is that the agreements be carried out faithfully and consistently, within the terms of the rules of engagement. Anything else will lead to breakdown between the institution and the state.

There is a disconnect in assessment and accountability goals focused on student learning between the institution and the state. Can it be overcome by the state exerting control through its levers of power, i.e., the power of the purse or regulation? Probably not or, to put it another way, the result would certainly be a pyrrhic victory with no winners on either side. Can the disconnect be bridged? The answer is yes. It appears that, increasingly, state leaders will be judged on how well they improve the skills of their workforce to make their states more competitive economically. If they do not succeed in doing so, they will not be successful in raising the nature of their state-based economy up the curve of valued added economic activity which, in turn, will mean the best educated members of their workforce will leave. Faculty and administrators should come to recognize the right of state political leaders to be concerned about the quality of undergraduate education and therefore have the right to set goals for improvement in student learning outcomes at higher education institutions in their state. Education is the main venue to accomplish this goal. Therefore we can expect heightened attention by state leaders on the performance of their higher education institutions as well as their K-12 system. Eventually, along with the growing recognition that the role of the state in setting goals is reasonable, should also flow state-based incentives, accepted by higher education leaders as appropriate, to encourage their public higher education institutions to meet those goals. This is so because of the growing recognition, by all parties, that human capital is the most important asset a region, state, or nation has. However, in the case of higher education, reliance on the experts (the faculty) to define the most appropriate methods of assessment is, necessarily, a prerequisite to success. This recognition of the need to work together by faculty and administrators at colleges, on the one hand, and state leaders, on the other, may well take some time and the road getting there will likely be bumpy. However, if human capital is as important as we believe, state and national leaders will ultimately be entrusted with the task of setting standards for improvement in student learning. If they do not, the consequences in a globally competitive economic environment will be severe. However, if we reach a wider consensus on how to implement this principle, we will be able to develop policies and practices in assessment that benefit the institution and the state and, most importantly, the citizens both serve.

A Strategy for State-Based Comparisons

We suggest the following strategy for within and across state comparisons. Instead of making direct comparisons among states on such measures as graduation and retention rates, passage rates on licensing exams for teachers or nurses, the logic of the CLA approach suggests that one make comparisons among institutions grouped by states. If one simply aggregates the scores of all institutions within a state to create a single state score, this eliminates the ability to understand the range of variation of the value added scores of specific institutions which, in turn, could seriously skew the results.. Second, instead of making comparisons in the level of student performance between states, the CLA method calls for comparing the value-added scores of colleges within and between states. Why look at value added compared to absolute level of student learning outcome levels? The answer is that while absolute levels achieved are interesting to note, the CLA approach places the focus of attention on improvement. We believe this is a more realistic and fruitful strategy to pursue. In addition, after a period of time in which the value added growth of a state's colleges are benchmarked, goals for value added improvement for the colleges may be established. And, eventually, state and college leaders across states and/or within a state may work to establish minimum levels of student performance on the CLA instruments.

To do what the CLA requires, we always need an input measure that is applicable across all the institutions in the study (mean SAT or ACT scores or a measure correlated with SAT or ACT scores for all students taking the CLA tests).

The CLA approach can be used to make comparisons between states by computing the proportion of a state's schools and/or students that are well above, above, on, below, or well below a plotted regression line. This comparison answers the question of how effective are a state's colleges in improving student performance on the outcome measures assessed relative to the effectiveness of the colleges in other states.

References

Association of American Colleges and Universities (AAC&U) (2002). *Greater Expectations: A New Vision for Learning As A Nation Goes to College.* Washington D. C.: AAC&U.

Banta, T. W., J. P. Lund and F. W. Oblander, (eds.) (1996). *Assessment in Practice: Putting Principles to Work on College Campuses.* San Francisco: Jossey-Bass.

Coady, T. (ed) (2000). *Why Universities Matter: A Conversation about Values, Means, and Directions.* St. Leonards, Australia: Allen & Unwin Pty.LTD.

Klein, S., Kuh, G., Chun, M., Hamilton, L., & Shavelson, R. (2005). An approach to measuring cognitive outcomes across higher-education institutions. *Journal of Higher Education*, 46, No. 3, 251-276.

Pascarella, E. and P. Terenzini. (2005*). How College Affects Students: A Third Decade of Research.* Jossey-Bass.

12

Management of Educational Assessment

A few decades ago, it was not taken for granted that university staf should be formally and regularly assessed, except when they were candidates for promotion. Most universities saw this as a task that had to be done by peers, with other stakeholders seldom being included in this process. Senior colleagues assessed whether a young colleague was ft to move up in the academic ranks. His or her teaching and research behaviour was certainly discussed, but very seldom, if ever (depending on the country or university), was there any formal assessment by other stakeholders. This has now changed completely. There are probably very few HEIs (higher education institutions) today where there is no formal assessment of teaching and research procedures of the staf by peers and/ or students, although this practice is not always accepted and is certainly regularly criticized.

Social Context of Assessment

The reasons for the emergence of the assessment procedures of teaching and research are many. We will consider here only a few of them: mass higher education, globalization, internationalization and neo-liberalism.

Mass Education and the Growing Awareness of Stakeholders

The second part of the last century in Europe was characterized by increasing democratic access to secondary and higher education. The position of universities changed with their insertion either into a unifed higher education system or into a binary system by the upgrading of forms of secondary education into professionally oriented education or by the establishment of higher professionally oriented education. This diminished the elite status of the universities, but it opened HEIs to a larger portion of secondary school graduates than had ever been. In most European countries, access to higher education is beyond 15% of the age grade. This process was certainly an important advance for democracy, but it also had a tremendous infuence on the HEIs and on the related policies. To mention only a few of the consequences: rising costs (it is ofen claimed that higher education is underfunded), growing numbers of students in lecture halls, declining teacher/student ratios, increased distance between the student and the teacher, problems of HEI governance, commercialization of research and teaching, and declining teacher morale. At the same time, HEIs could no longer live without heeding the expectations of the growing number of stakeholders, internal (academic and non-academic staf, and students) as well as external (parents, taxpayers, employers, the state and international organizations). Most stakeholders no longer took for granted that HEIs by definition ofered quality education. More than one of them wanted a quality assurance system that ft this mass higher education and wanted HEIs to be accountable for what they did.

Globalization

The first strand is the economic one: "visible in the global fow of trade and investment, the availability of particular goods worldwide, and the multinational location of manufacturing and marketing". Seen to be marketable are not goods, but also services and especially education. The General Agreement on Trade in Services (GATS) could be an important factor in this respect. Another dimension of globalization is the political one. This is "characterized by the growth of supranational organizations addressing policy and regulatory matters beyond the scope of individual nations". Important actors in Europe are the EU (European Union), UNESCO (United Nations Educational, Scientific and Cultural Organization), the OECD (Organisation for Economic Co-operation and Development), and other international organizations, such as professional organizations. Although the Bologna Process was not organized by such a supranational organization, the decisions taken within this framework have far-reaching consequences for the HEIs. Thirdly, there is the cultural dimension: "the fow of cultural images and information about cultural practices around the world", also called 'McDonaldization'. Although these mostly Western values are not equally accepted everywhere, they still strongly infuence local values. The last dimension of globalization discerned by McBurnie is the technological one, which is, at present, being strongly supported by the integration of information and communications technology. This is, and could be even more so in the future, a very important contributor to the spread of higher education among groups that have not yet been able to enjoy higher education. At the same time, it is creating new challenges for HEIs because the distribution of knowledge is no longer their privilege, but has to be shared with all kinds of providers, who do it for free or for money (private proft-oriented universities and corporate universities).

The infuence of globalization on higher education policy is taking on diferent forms. Besides the infuence of other nation states, Dale discerns five forms of infuence coming from the globalization process: harmonization (EU), dissemination (OECD), standardization (of curricula), installing interdependence (because people are concerned about peace and the environment), and imposition (by an organization in exchange for support).

Internationalization

Already before globalization became an issue, internationalization was a natural part of higher education. Relative to the situation a few decades ago, the internationalization of higher education is now proceeding more rapidly and is taking on diferent forms. 'Internationalization of higher education' can mean many things and has been the subject of much discussion. Hilary Callan refers to the typology devised by Jane Knight, who distinguishes four types, the first being the 'activity approach', which refers to phenomena such as student and faculty mobility, international student recruitment, technical assistance, knowledge transfer and research co-operation. The second type concerns the outcomes and goals of students and lecturers as a product of international contacts. This is called the 'competency' approach. The third is a 'cultural' one, which occurs when the presence of academics of diferent nationalities on a campus infuences the local culture and organization. The last is the 'process' or 'strategic' approach and refers to parts of the first three types when they are integrated in a plan to give an international dimension to an HEI or to the higher education policy of a country.

The first three types have been present in higher education as long as higher education has existed. Some HEIs have always attracted scholars from diferent regions or nations. The number of international students (students studying in a country other than their own) is expected to increase greatly, and Böhm et al. estimated that, throughout the world, about 1.8 million international students were studying in HEIs in 2000 (mainly in the U.S.A.). They estimate that this fgure will be 7.2 million (70% of them coming from Asia) by 2025. Internationalization is currently a process that is included in the plans of most nations and HEIs.

Scientific knowledge does not stop at the borders of a nation state, and HEIs are not interested in knowledge that is confned to the work of the local researcher. Quite the opposite. International recognition of the research of local HEIs is seen as the main criterion for assessing the results of research. Without international recognition, an HEI has no future in a globalized world. In this context, the contribution of the ERASMUS (European Community Action Scheme for the Mobility of University Students) and Leonardo da Vinci schemes is important.

Neo Liberalism

As higher education in Europe was beginning to feel the infuence of globalization and internationalization, neo-liberalism became prominent. Although neo-liberalism has its roots in the old liberal thinking, Olssen (reviewed in) contends that it has its own characteristics. Neo-liberalism takes for granted that the state has to create 'an appropriate market' by providing the conditions, laws and institutions needed for the proper functioning of the market. This includes making the individual an entrepreneur who is ready to compete with the others on the market, but he is no longer seen merely as a *Homo economicus* concerned only with self-interest and being averse to the state. The citizen in a neo-liberal society has to become a 'manipulatable man' who is responsive to what the state expects. Everybody is supposed to be accountable for what he or she does. A neo-liberal state wants responsible citizens and so creates instruments for surveillance and appraisal.

It is not surprising that processes of deregulation and privatization are the key policy instruments in the neo-liberal state. Anything that makes goods and services unapproachable for others because of restrictive rules has to be abolished. This can have far-reaching consequences for the development of higher education. In its extreme form, it could mean for Europe, where higher education is seen as a public good, that higher education has to be privatized. Although the EU is applying this principle of liberalization of education, Commissioner Viviane Reding of the European Commission stressed that commitments of the EU countries in the GATS refer only to privately funded education services. Not only is higher education in Europe not privatized, but also, in many respects, it is not deregulated. For instance, many European countries still have control over first-level degree fees, and they also demand a quality assurance system in HEIs.

Nevertheless, there is no doubt that higher education cannot be disassociated from the market thinking that is currently prevailing in Europe. Oficial governmental declarations notwithstanding, higher education is being treated as a product to be marketed, and a rating system for HEIs is seen as a helpful supporting instrument for this. Higher education is something that can be sold, even in a society where most of the cost of higher education is covered by the government. Tooley (reviewed in) distinguishes two concepts of the market in relation to higher education: 'education of the market', which is gaining space in higher education, and 'markets for education'. Education is becoming a commodity that can be commercialized and sold on a market where the demand in our knowledge society is growing. HEIs have seen this as an opportunity for expanding their ability to improve the education they provide. The sale of education to professionals may not be seen as the primary task of a college of higher education, which is providing academic education for beginning students. By delivering training to professionals, the college enters the market for education, which Tooley (reviewed in) has defined as "educational opportunities delivered by markets, i.e. not provided, largely funded or largely regulated by government, with supply-side liberated and the price mechanism in place". Even in the higher education systems of the EU, where the main part of the budget is provided by the state, HEIs are acting more and more as suppliers to the education market. This is done not only on the market of postgraduate higher education, but also at the undergraduate level. Students are approached as individuals whose right of free choice and self-interest on the education market have to be protected. Gibbs stresses that, on the HEI market, the rights of the individuals are protected by the government. Students are primarily consumers, and consumers of education must obtain an education that is 'consumable'. This means that education should be organized according to the capacities of these consumers, which is expressed in forms of modularization, semesterization and self-directed learning. Education here, Gibbs contends, is outcome-driven and is directed to make accredited people "able to use their educational outcomes (or competencies) to further their economic desires". This may place a burden not only on the relationship between the teacher and the student, but also on the relationship between the HEI and the teacher, who has to be prepared to carry higher academic loads in order to increase the proft of the HEI. Young people may become less interested in academic excellence than in employability. Consequently, HEIs may be more interested in ofering curricula that ft the demand for vocational training and skills. Professional profles that are successful on the labour market may guide the construction of curricula more than does the problem of how to make a young person an educated and moral person.

Management and Quality Assurance

As noted, globalization stimulates nation states to copy from each other policy principles, culture, the organization of economy and education, etc. Moreover, the supranational organizations contribute to harmonization, dissemination, standardization, etc. This is also visible in HEIs in Europe as far as institutional governance and management are concerned.

On the basis of a comparative study in several member states, the OECD concluded that "higher education is moving towards a new system of governance, where the power of markets and the power of the state combine in new ways. Government is generally withdrawing from direct management of institutions, yet at the same time introducing new forms of control and infuence, based largely on holding institutions accountable for performance via powerful enforcement mechanisms including funding and quality recognition". Similar observations have been made by Amaral et al.. State governments still have their say in HEIs, but, instead of direct control, they prefer to steer at a distance. Although most universities in the 11 countries of the OECD study are state universities, they are very autonomous as far as the spending of the budgets is concerned in order to achieve their objectives, and they are also very autonomous as regards the hiring and fring of academic staf. There is also much independence of HEIs in these countries in the setting of academic structures and course content. For all the domains of governance, however, there are many diferences between the countries.

Not only have the states changed their policy, but also institutional governance has changed. Without doubt, many HEIs are visibly developing from collegially managed institutions to institutions in which the institutional management is being granted to experts who did not formerly belong to the academic staf or to academics who change from being teachers and/or researchers to managers. The belief that HEIs could only be managed by experts of the scientific disciplines is no longer shared by policy-makers and HEI managers. Moreover, it is ofen held by policy-makers that collegial decision-making structures for HEIs are not efcient enough to make the rapid decisions needed in a time of rapid change and increasing challenges for HEIs. Indeed, HEIs have lost their monopoly on teaching and research (e.g. corporate universities). If they want to survive, they have to adapt to the new situation. At the same time, an adage of industry is being applied to HEIs, namely that it is not possible for insiders to see the problems of the institution. Only governors and managers coming from outside the HEIs are able to see the problems and make the hard decisions necessary for survival (see, e.g.,). Of the 15 countries covered by the OECD report, in nine of them, the board is composed of mainly external members, and the leaders of the HEIs are appointed by the board. Only in six of the 15 countries are the leaders of the HEIs elected from the staf. In some of the countries, the leaders are recruited internally, in others, recruitment is external.

Not only has institutional governance changed, but also the management style has changed. Very ofen the concept applied here is 'managerialism'. The least that can be said of this concept is that it pinpoints to a phenomenon that is not always understood in the same way by its users. This distinction also explains why institutional governance did not change in some universities, whereas, at the same time, principles or organizational modes were introduced to obtain more efcient management than could be provided by collegial management, which invests much time in meetings. However, it is clear that quality assurance is being organized according to widely accepted principles, even in collegially managed HEIs.

What are the characteristics of managerialism? It is not easy to fnd a definition of this phenomenon that is shared by all researchers. Reed speaks of a governmental and institutional order 'which has existed under the traditional compromise between corporate bureaucracy and professional association'. Amaral et al. did not stipulate in advance what the diferent contributors to the book had to understand under managerialism, but they did state that most of the contributors came to accept some common characteristics, although they did not agree on all. To name some of them:

accountability based on performance, target setting, funding based on results, collegial leadership and decision-making replaced by individual leadership and decision-making, marketization, commercialization, bureaucratization, appointment of leaders, more external members in the central governing body, a loss of professional autonomy of academics, and deprofessionalization of the academics. At the same time, however, they recognized characteristics linked to the old collegial type of governance. Some examples are democratic decision-making, the promotion of consensus within the community, consultation and persuasion of members of councils, and recognition of the university as a professional organization. In other words, HEIs may adopt managerialist principles, but still maintain some principles of the old collegial structure. Amaral et al. conclude: "whatever progress the onward march of managerialism may be making within specifc systems, and granting that there are important similarities between some of these, taken as a whole, these diferent case studies present a picture of our continuing diversity at the national level. It cannot (at least yet) be convincingly argued that there is a multinational convergence towards new methods and processes of management, paved by the brutal expansion of the new managerialist ideology".

All of the contributors to this project mention the resistance of the academics against these innovations. The academics accused the new system of having reduced their freedom in teaching and research and of creating corporate professionals who lose their independence and have to work for a company instead of the university. Academics sometimes blamed the administrators for spending money that could be more valuably used for research.

Administrators, for their part, got worked up by the inability of academics to perceive the necessity of having a structured policy for the total institution. Both parties ofen underwent a difcult process in the search for new principles for the management of HEIs. This was caused not only by the administrators coming from outside the institutions, but also by academics who had turned into administrators, but could not forget to apply the old collegial values. This new system will also change the hierarchy of loyalty of the academics. Traditionally, it was said that academics were in the first place loyal to the discipline, then to the department and then to the university. Because of the new positions in a manage-rially organized university, it is likely that academics have to be first loyal to the HEI, the institution that pays the salary.

Although none of these studies stressed that a managerial structure is widespread, it has become clear that many characteristics of managerialism have been incorporated into HEIs. One of these characteristics is accountability of the HEIs and the members of these HEIs. This fts perfectly in a society where neo-liberalism has become the mainstream political and economic philosophy. Citizens should be accountable for what they do, and this also applies to institutions that are supported by the state. The neo-liberal states have given more independence to educational institutions to attain their targets, but they have to be responsible not only to the state, but also to other stakeholders for the way they use the resources that the state provides. And there is more. Even when it is hard to say what the core of manage-rialism actually is, it is clear in many countries that accountability is one of the management principles, whether it is in a country or in an HEI where the leaders of the HEIs are elected by peers from among peers or where the leaders are appointed by boards mainly consisting of external members.

What is the meaning of accountability? Although the concept is in the current vocabulary of policymakers, one is not sure whether this concept has the same meaning for all of the participants in the conversation. Ranson gives the following general definition: "to be accountable, conventionally, is to be held to account, defining a relationship of formal control between parties, one of whom is mandatorily held to account to the other for the exercise of roles and stewardship of public resources. Such a report, moreover, is always an evaluation of performance according to established standards".

Vidovich and Slee actually rely on two typifcations, one by Corbett and the other by Ball et al.. Corbett distinguishes four reforms of accountability: *upward accountability* is the accountability of public servants in function of legal and constitutional prescriptions to their superiors and also to the courts and administrative tribunals; *outward accountability* is the accountability to the client groups and other stakeholders in the community; *downward accountability* is the accountability of a manager to his subordinates; and *inward accountability* is the accountability of an actor toward his personal conscience. Ball et al. mention market and political accountability. When actors justify what they do to consumers, we can speak of *market accountability* (and *managerial accountability*). *Politically accountable* is the person who acts on behalf of the electorate and has to answer for what he has done.

Ranson, referring to the British educational system, distinguishes between professional accountability and four other forms of accountability linked with the neo-liberal era (commencing in the early 1980s for the U.K.; it came later on the continent). *Professional accountability* is the accountability of the professional and is based on specialist knowledge and reported in internal reports. For the age of neo-liberalism, Ranson cites four forms of accountability: *consumer accountability*, whereby the responsible actors have to take into account market competition and to pay attention to the choice of the consumers; *contract accountability*, whereby schools have to be accountable for costs and efciency, and assessments are ruled by criteria of technical efciency and costs; *performative account ability*, whereby schools are accountable for the attainment of the national standards and targets, with test scores and league tables being used to assess it; and *corporate accountability*, whereby schools are accountable to a private person or corporation (e.g., public–private partnerships) and rely on criteria of proftability in order to assess policy success.

Vidovich and Slee, describing the higher education policy in Australia and England, come close to Ranson's characterization. They speak of a 'managed market', which means that they recognize managerial accountability (upwards-oriented) as well as market accountability (outwards-oriented). They stress that the managerial forms of accountability are stronger in both countries than the market forms. Governments are more interested "in providing information to students as paying customers, to inform their market choices". This 'managed market' form is easier to link to teaching than to research. There is no doubt that students and employers belong to the customers of teaching, while it is not always clear who the customers of research are. Although it is very important for researchers to fnd money on a competitive market, they are still more strongly oriented towards their peers than to customers. In systems where the resources depend on the level of performance of the HEIs, it is important for the institution to meet the governmental standards. When governmental resources are scarce, HEIs will look for resources in the private sector, which brings them into more of a market position. They will try to demonstrate that they do what they are expected to do by showing how good their position is in a ranking system for education and research. This system is perceived diferently by elite universities, which are less dependent on government resources. For them, market accountability will be more important than governmental accountability.

This diagnosis of the accountability of the educational system by Vidovich and Slee is certainly not directly transferable to other European countries, as has been shown above. Nevertheless, most of European countries have accepted that HEIs have to be accountable, at least to the national government, which provides the majority of the resources for most of the HEIs in most European countries. However, in most of them, accountability is not only upward, but can also be downward, inward and/ or outward. Whatever the position of a country in this respect, most European countries expect HEIs to establish a quality assurance system, and staf assessment is a very widespread method within this system, although a survey in France has shown that only 22.9% of the respondents had undergone 'formalized teaching evaluation' in their faculty.

Staff Assessment Instruments

Staf assessment instruments are probably not used in isolation from a global quality assurance system in HEIs. A reader edited by Orsingher presents the quality assurance systems of six universities. Among the many examples, I refer here to only one. Welsh et al. describe a quality measurement system developed by and in an American university together with a private company. They wanted to create a system that continuously measures all the quality indicators of the university with valid and reliable instruments. This instrument concerned the opinions not only of the teachers and the other staf but also of the students, alumni and the employers. Surveys are conducted continuously among students, alumni of diferent years, employers of graduates, library users, IT (information technology) users, parents, donors and many other groups. All of the data are collected on a monthly and/or a semester basis and are uploaded to a central server. The data collection, management and analysis are all automated. Within 7–10 days, the results of the surveys are available for the interested members of the university. All members are allowed access to parts of the data, depending on their position, since, for example, the head of a department has diferent interests to a faculty member. Therefore each of them has permission to check diferent parts of the database. If someone has to report on a particular quality issue, he has up-to-date information available in the database.

According to the authors, the advantages of this quality assurance 'machine' are many, one being the common platform for the whole university concerning assessment, and another being the philosophy supporting the assessment, so no discussion is needed when an evaluation has to be delivered. It also ofers the advantage of presenting the results of previous actions taken. It is seen as an instrument for decentralizing actions in a function of evaluation and/or accreditation. Departments can produce self-evaluation reports and instruments to benchmark programme performance. With this instrument, the university is able to integrate the quality assurance system and report to the state. The instrument is not only efcient for quality assurance, but also cheaper than a less-organized system.

Such a quality assurance machine seems to be the perfect answer to the problem of quality assurance for a managerial system. It is hard to resist the impression that we have here a perfect machine for detecting problems, seeing the roads to solutions and, ultimately, enabling stakeholders to measure improvement. Is this actually the case? Such an assessment would require more information than is given in the report by Welsh et al.. Nevertheless, research has been carried out on the strengths and the weaknesses of the current instruments for staf assessment.

Based on the information from some 20 research papers (published since 2000), I have come to the conclusion that there is a wide acceptance of the reliability and the validity of the instruments to measure SET (, for example). Moreover, this is supported by the numerous references afrming such a judgement in each paper. This information certainly contributes very much to the trust of managers in these instruments. The question is whether this trust is general among all stakeholders. Not at all. Many reasons have been put forward by observers of this phenomenon. Basic questions are what the evaluation of teachers by students means and why the evaluations are made.

SET is ofen seen as a rating activity by students of the overt teaching actions and the assessment by students of the perceived consequences of the teaching on their learning behaviour. Others use the concept of teaching efectiveness. Although the concepts are closely related, researchers do not agree about the dimensions that should be studied when we try to collect a picture of teacher efectiveness. Some mention two dimensions (e.g. clear instructional presentation and management of student behaviour), others give more (e.g. caring, systematic and stimulating, or respect for students, organization and presentation skills and ability to challenge students). Obviously, researchers and stakeholders can use the same concept, but it is not certain that the concept covers the same phenomenon.

On the basis of papers published in *The American Psychologist* in 1997, Saroyan and Amundsen conclude that there is little discussion about the level of construct validity of the rating instruments of teacher efectiveness. The instruments seem to enable students to provide an accurate measurement of efectiveness. The results seem to support a moderate correlation with efective teaching and with student achievement. Nevertheless, it is observed that they are more suspicious about the discriminatory validity of the ratings, i.e. indicators were found that did not support efective teaching, but rather correlated with the ratings.

Although some authors consider this to be a minor problem, a growing number of researchers are criticizing the lack of attention given to this problem. The reason for this may be linked with the criticism of lecturers of the validity of the instruments for measuring teaching efectiveness and the consequences of validity for the learning behaviour of students. Some of these remarks have been confrmed by research, but they have also been refuted. This has not stopped the use of SET, but it has contributed to discussions among stakeholders about the utility and the legitimacy of the use of SET for assessing lecturers. What are the most important conclusions?

First, data in more than one survey gives evidence that there is a strong relationship between grading leniency and ratings of teaching efectiveness. Strong evidence is also found in web-based voluntary student evaluations in the U.S.A. Felton et al. found a correlation of 0.61 between the teaching quality of the lecturers and level of difculty. Since teaching efectiveness has certainly nothing to do with lowering the standards, such a situation can hardly support the use of SET.

Secondly, class size may also infuence the results of SET. While the results are not so outspoken, the data show that the largest and the smallest classes give the highest ratings.

Thirdly, instructor enthusiasm can be another factor that reduces the real signifcance of SET. If the instructor is enthusiastic, it does not mean necessarily that he or she contributes much to the learning behaviour of students.

Fourthly, research has also found that students who have "a positive and/or social view of the lecturer" will rate a lecturer higher, even though it is not certain that this lecturer contributes more to a better understanding of the study material. Shevlin et al. took this statement as a starting point for their research. They concluded that the charisma factor can explain 69% of the variation in the lecturer's ability rating. In other words, a signifcant proportion of the SET's scale variation is a refection of the charisma of the lecturer and/or of the expectations of the students towards the lecturer. This positive attitude might also come from a judgement by the students about the 'sexy appearance' of the lecturer. Felton et al. concluded on the basis of data collected in a voluntary web-based assessment of teaching efectiveness in the U.S.A. that the results were determined by how sexy the instructor was, but this was countered by a study of students of a Spanish university.

Fifhly, when students have high expectations about their grades, they are prone to rate the lecturers higher, which is confrmed in the research by Worthington, but not by Greimel-Fuhrmann and Geyer. As for other variables, grading does not seem to have a consistent infuence on SET.

Sixthly, the ethnic background of the students could have an important infuence on the assessment of lecturers. Worthington found evidence in other surveys that the ethnic background of students did not show a 'systematic racial bias' in the assessment of lecturers.

Seventhly, gender is one of the signifcant divides in our society, and so researchers reasonably hypothesized that SET results could be diferent for male and female students and also diferent for male and female lecturers. Greimel-Fuhrmann and Geyer discerned a signifcantly more favourable rating for female lecturers, while Worthington states that female students assign a lower rating to their lecturers, but he admitted that he could not check whether these lower ratings were more determined by the teaching style of the lecturer than by the gender of the student.

Eighthly, age is another variable that shows important divides in our society. Worthington decided that students older than 30 were more inclined to give lower ratings to lecturers. This statement is not very convincing in view of the smallness of the sample in this study and the probability of a negative assessment by students older than 30. In any event, they do not constitute a major group of students.

The rating of teachers also depends on the subject taught by the lecturer. If a lecturer is teaching a course that is linked directly with the subject the student is interested in, the rating is more positive than if this is not the case. Greimel-Fuhrmann and Geyer make this statement on the basis of students in accounting. Looking at these research results, it is understandable that Felton et al. came to the conclusions that the instruments used by students to rate teaching efectiveness do not rate teaching efectiveness, but measure only a perception of teaching efectiveness. If this is true, it supports the lecturers who are reluctant to accept the application of SET either for assessment or for providing a basis to improve their teaching.

The critique of the researchers delivers more support for the opponents of SET than for the defenders. Criticism has also been delivered concerning the organization of the SET (does the lecturer's concept of teaching correspond with that of the students?) and the poverty of the instruments being used to measure teaching efectiveness. Therefore some researchers propose paying more attention to a new concept of teaching. Saroyan and Amundsen, for example, develop a complex teaching concept, although this cannot be measured by means of the usual simple SETs. They propose including in the teaching concept a knowledge and an action component, and also the instructional context. In the knowledge component, attention should be given to knowledge of subject matter, knowledge of the pedagogy and knowledge of the learners. The action component includes the preparation of the teaching task and the teaching itself.Not only do the instruments not ft a more up-to-date concept of teaching, it has been complained, but also there are parts of teaching that infuence its efectiveness that are hardly perceptible to the students and consequently hardly assessed by them. Ballantyne et al. mention that students do not have enough information on, for instance, "problems caused by class sizes, a lack of staf collaboration, inadequate university support and the lack of staf development opportunities". Therefore some observers plead for other approaches to assess teaching efectiveness, such as peer evaluations in class and teaching portfolios in addition to SET, and analysis of the thought processes underlying teaching actions, self-evaluation, student journals, free writing, teacher observation and inventories.

Stakeholders' Reaction to Instruments

Important in this discussion is not only the opinion of researchers, but also the opinion of the stakeholders. We will look at some of the reactions of lecturers, students and HEI policy-makers.

Resistance is also felt among lecturers depending on the alleged function of the SET. Nasser and Fresko discern four functions of SET: (i) ofering feedback to the lecturers in order to improve teaching; (ii) assigning the capacities of the staf for promotion; (iii) helping students to select a course; and (iv) providing information for educational research. Although these four functions are theoretically reasonable, they are all certainly not served in some (many?) HEIs. For instance, if the results of the SET are not made public, and this is not unusual, it will be hard for them to be used to help students choose their subjects. Moreover, summative evaluation by SET is ofen criticized by lecturers because research activity has much more infuence on promotion than does teaching.

This critical attitude of lecturers may be supported by the criticism by the students. Greimel-Fuhrmann and Geyer observed that one-third of the students of their sample had doubts about the usefulness of SET for the assessment of lecturers. They question the fairness of the measurements because they think that students with low grades or who do not like a teacher will express these feelings in the scores. The fgures confrmed this opinion, albeit very weakly. However, they also saw that two-thirds of the students thought that they could inform the teachers about their teaching in order to improve the quality of teaching. Nevertheless, other research is less optimistic about the contribution of students and shows that not all students are interested in flling in SET questionnaires. Smith et al. experienced that the response rate was highest when the survey was administered during lecture time (70–75%) and was much lower if special classes for the survey were organized (46%) or if the students were asked to send in the questionnaire later (26%). The reason for this non-participation is, among other reasons, that they are oversurveyed or do not believe that their opinion will contribute to the improvement of teaching. This is not totally wrong. Nasser and Fresko reported that only a small portion of the lecturers admitted having been stimulated to change something in their teaching under the infuence of SET and then it very ofen concerned only minor interventions.

There is some uncertainty among researchers about the positive contribution of SET to the improvement of teaching. Kember et al., for instance, mention diferent reasons for the weak infuence of the SET in the university of their research, but could not decide which one was the most infuential. They mention the following possible reasons: teaching quality has attained an acceptable level; SET was not used efectively; lack of incentives to use the results of SET; the instrument was more directed towards appraisal than towards teaching improvement; and SET was too teacher-centred. If improvement was observed in connection with SET, these researchers found that the collection of data with the help of a SET questionnaire went together with specialized counselling, an approach that has been confrmed by other researchers.

There is not just criticism of the instrument for measuring teaching efectiveness. Other resistance is reported by more than one researcher. Interesting in this respect are the observations made by Laughton in relation to the teaching quality review in the U.K. It should be stressed that these are opinions that are not necessarily confrmed by facts. First, some lecturers wonder whether the money spent on testing the quality is in proportion to the efects of the test. Secondly, others report that testing the quality of education contributed to grade infation. Thirdly, assessment of teaching revealed again the diferent position of the old universities in the ranking and the more recent established ones. Fourthly, assessment might contribute to compounding the dropout rates. Fifhly, mistakes are possible during the collection of the data, i.e. the system is not reliable enough. Sixthly, because some academics do not trust the instrument to be reliable and valid, they might react with non-compliance, lip service and sabotage of the system. Laughton describes these reactions as a part of the struggle of academics for power among themselves, with the management of the university, and with the government. The system is inspired much more by a desire for accountability than for teaching improvement. Teachers felt that they lost part of their autonomy and were convinced that these are some of the first steps taken by managers led by manage-rialism, a management principle imported from the business world. Using these new techniques for the assessment of teaching could push the lecturers on an educational track that was not their choice. The reactions, collected in 2001, contributed to a change in the system of quality assurance.

Laughton did not associate the diagnoses with direct experience of managerialism in the university of the respondent. Managerialism is indeed experienced diferently in the diferent universities in the U.K. On the basis of 135 interviews in 16 universities in the U.K., Fulton paints the following general picture. He fnds that only one of four manager-academics felt comfortable in the new procedures of managerialism. Even the culture of managerialism was not taken for granted by these decision-makers. Nevertheless, at the level of the departments, the pressure to inform the top and to work with targets is increasing, and assessment of teaching and research is part and parcel of the life of a department. These manager-academics, however, did not identify themselves with a top-down decision-making structure. Decentralization (devolved budgets, internal markets for space, responsibility for assessment of teaching and research, etc.), and markets for students, research and service were considered to be more important. This is not a portrait of an extreme form of managerialism, but some characteristics are certainly linked with it.

Similar reactions can be found in other countries. Hulpiau et al. reported on a Belgian university that clearly shows some characteristics of managerialism: accountability of the academics based on performance; target setting; internal allocation of the funding based on results of the departments or research units; a large part of the budget provided by other than state funds; the board being composed of the same number of external members as internal members; and so on. Nevertheless, the management of the university is still in the hands of a vice-chancellor, deans and heads of departments who are elected from and by the academics. Because of the management function, though, they do not teach anymore (or very little), hardly participate in department councils and have little frequent interaction with their former peers. At the top of the university, the decision was taken that each year all academics would be assessed for each course by all of the students. These assessments had been made previously, but not every year. Students could fll in forms on the Internet using an instrument composed of at least 11 multiple-choice questions, and lecturers could present more questions if they wanted. The results of these surveys were sent to the lecturer and the programme director. For many reasons, the staf reacted very critically once the system was applied. It was not only that the decision for this change of policy was taken at the top, but also at the same time new curricula had to be formulated as part of the Bologna Process, and many other decisions had come top-down. The presentation of an assessment system that did not ofer what it promised was not accepted by many of the academics, and the system was criticized at many meetings. This reaction was infuenced by the way it was imposed by the university managers, but also by concerns as noted above. Careful discussion with the staf made clear at the end that the academics of this university were not opposed to assessment as such, but that they expected that an instrument would be used that made a clear distinction between assessment for the evaluation of teaching and assessment of quality improvement of teaching.

Furthermore, the staf wanted an instrument that did not hinder education innovation.

The introduction to universities of quality assessment instruments that have traditionally been seen as instruments suitable for a factory was not readily accepted by the academics, who considered their independence to be a guarantee of quality work. Instead of collegial collaboration, they suddenly had to undergo the assessment by the youngsters that they themselves were assessing. Moreover, the general application of SET in Europe was not a decision taken by the academics, but emerged in the wake of neo-liberal education policy, where the state asked for accountability from the HEIs and where manager-academics were soon seen as those who could choke academic freedom. Staf had to be convinced that assessment would not touch their freedom of research and would not interfere with educational innovation. As seen in former examples, this takes time and planning.

A good example of the planning of this change has been reported by Dynan and Cliford in a small university in Australia. The action was taken because external quality audit agencies could come in and could make the functioning of the university difcult. The university also wanted a clear picture of its quality in order to inform the consumers (students) in the context of international competition.

Important in this process was that the change was prepared by a special committee in which all important groups of the university were represented. The change was not a free option, as the government wanted accountable universities. The committee did not take for granted that the staf would accept this enthusiastically. Therefore they drew up a fve-step plan based on a collaborative implementation model. The objective of the steps was to make the entire institution aware of the necessity of the quality assurance system as well as of the advantages that it could bring to the staf. Over a period of several years, they involved as many staf members as possible in the change process. According to the authors, the process was also quite successful because the main decision-makers (among others, the deans) were members of the Quality Management Committee. The staf realized that the main decision-makers considered this process important enough to invest in it. Moreover, staf members who took initiatives for the realization of the project received fnancial support for these initiatives. Another positive element was that the staf were familiarized with and trained in the new concepts of the plan, and an external professional quality manager was hired.

Staf and leaders were trained to see quality assurance as an integral part of faculty life not something additional to it. Quality assurance had to be part of the yearly planning of the faculties and was not to be seen as something coming from a foreign body.

In spite of the systematic programme for introducing quality assurance in this university, the authors noted that the implementation of formal quality management has not yet permeated in all areas of the university. Among the most receptive are the faculties and the research ofce. The implementation process could have been hindered by the sudden emergence of complex concepts (producing aversion to the process) and the creation of a bureaucratic system that is more keen to run the quality assurance process than to use the information for improvement. Once more, we see the same problems arising in this implementation process as in those described above. The authors cite the following problems: the external pressure was not liked by the staf, but accepted; it was hard to convince the staf that this SET could also be useful to themselves; the assessment instruments were weak; the time consumed by the evaluation process was felt by many to be a waste. To give the staf the feeling of ownership of the evaluation system was not easy, but a process of empowerment emerged for those who acquired it. This empowerment is still a problem afer 8 years, and there is a fear that the criteria of a coming benchmark approach will still be criticized by the staf.

HEIs in the EU operate in a globalized world, and most of them proclaim their intention to put their institution on the international track. There is no other way to survive in this world of international competition. At the same time, the neo-liberal ideology progressed in Europe and is now determining policy, including education policy. On the one hand, this policy has stimulated an open market and consequently deregulation and privatization, but, on the other hand, it has also made actors (individuals and institutions alike) responsible for what they receive from the state. HEIs, traditionally supported predominantly by the state, became more independent of the state, but also had to look for resources that were no longer being provided by the state. In some countries of the EU, a rather large group of independent HEIs was established. In the wake of this neo-liberal policy, the position of stakeholders of the HEIs changed. More of the stakeholders wanted to have a say in the policy of the HEIs and were interested in the development of the institute. HEI governance also changed in several countries: in some institutions, the main decision-makers no longer have to be elected from among the academics, but external specialists are hired as managers. This is also the case for the board:b external experts are ofen seen as those who will make the diference. In some institutions this new type of governance goes hand in hand with elements of a new type of management: managerialism. The collegial bureaucracy, however, has not totally disappeared. Research has shown that both systems live together. One characteristic of managerialism, however, is widely accepted by policy-makers and HEI managers, namely accountability. HEIs have to prove that they are providing quality education, and it is here, within a more general framework of quality assurance, that SET was established in most HEIs in Europe.

This establishment has not been without problems, some as yet unresolved. Research has given strong support for the application of the diferent measures of teaching efectiveness, but, at the same time, many researchers have criticized the weak spots, the primary one being the questionable validity of the instruments used for measuring teaching efectiveness. Because research has shown that the results of the instrument are infuenced by the appearance of teachers, the expected assessment results of students, and other factors that have nothing to do with teaching efectiveness, the application of the instruments for SET has regularly been challenged.

Moreover, in some institutions and countries, the introduction of the regular application of SET instruments has ofen been experienced as enforced by the top, without open consultation with the lecturers as has been the tradition. This change was not seen to be a collegial decision. Lecturers ofen felt that the traditional culture of the HEI in which the academic had great independence in the organization of the lectures was suddenly being determined by stakeholders who had never been involved in the assessment of their work. Control was accepted from peers, but not directly from other stakeholders, as is possible now with SET. The direct intervention by the government and the HEI managers was experienced as a devaluation of the position of the academic. As the cases presented above indicate, it has become clear that the introduction of SET was not always done with sufcient care. The HEI managers act from a more- or less-managerialist standpoint, while the staf are still thinking along the traditional collegial lines. Nevertheless, research has shown that the staf are not opposed to assessment, but that they are not happy with the method of implementation. Innovation takes time, which means that it takes many years before the innovation has been institutionalized. In order to attain this objective, many strategies are possible. When we take into account the widespread collegial culture of HEIs in Europe, a coercive strategy does not seem to be the most suitable. An old value system cannot easily be changed. More credit can probably be given to a collaborative model of implementation. This approach brings managers and staf together, opens discussions, and makes all participants aware of the difculties and the advantages of the system. It gives those who have to be assessed a better understanding of the functions of the assessment and their consequences. Moreover, it creates a basis for the inclusion of assessment in institutional and departmental policy. Research has shown that innovation is better accepted by teachers if they are involved in its planning and implementation. In this context, it will also be important to pay attention to the educational theory and the collegial values of the lecturers. A collaborative implementation approach fts better in the collegial culture, which still prevails in HEIs. Also important in this context is that lecturers and students are convinced that SET really contributes to improvement of teaching and that the SET instruments measure validly and reliably. As long as teachers and students do not believe in the value of the assessment practice, the assessment of teaching efectiveness will be a burden, not an instrument for improvement of teaching.

References

Amaral, A. and Magelhães, A. (2002) The emergent role of external stakeholders in European higher education governance. In *Governing Higher Education: National Perspectives on Institutional Governance* (Amaral, A., Jones, G.A. and Karseth, B., eds), pp. 1–21, Kluwer Academic Publishers, Dordrecht.

Breton, G. and Lambert, M. (eds) (2003) *Universities and Globalization: Private Linkages, Public Trust*, UNESCO Publishing/Université Laval/Economica, Paris/Quebec.

McBurnie, G. (2001) Leveraging globalization as a policy paradigm for higher education. *Higher Education in Europe* 26(1), 11–26.

Trow, M. (2000) From mass higher education to universal access: the American advantage. *Minerva* 37(4), 303–328.

Vidovich, L. and Slee, R. (2001) Bringing universities to account? Exploring some global and local policy tensions. *Journal of Education Policy* 16(5), 431–453.

Bibliography

Alkin, M. C. (2011). *Evaluation essentials*: From A to Z. The Guilford Press

Allan, J.. *Learning Outcomes in Higher Education*, Studies in Higher Education, 21, 1, 93-108.

Amaral, A. and Magelhães, A. (2002) The emergent role of external stakeholders in European higher education governance. In *Governing Higher Education: National Perspectives on Institutional Governance* (Amaral, A., Jones, G.A. and Karseth, B., eds), pp. 1–21, Kluwer Academic Publishers, Dordrecht.

Apple, M.W. (2001) Comparing neo-liberal projects and inequality in education. *Comparative Education* 37(4), 409–423

Association of American Colleges and Universities (AAC&U) (2002). *Greater Expectations: A New Vision for Learning As A Nation Goes to College.* Washington D. C.: AAC&U.

Banta, T. W., J. P. Lund and F. W. Oblander, (eds.) (1996). *Assessment in Practice: Putting Principles to Work on College Campuses.* San Francisco: Jossey-Bass.

Bickman, L. (Ed.). (1987). *Using program theory in evaluation.* San Francisco, CA: Jossey-Bass

Böhm, A., Davis, T., Meares, D. and Pearce, D. (2002) *Global Student Mobility 2025: Forecasts of the Global Demand for International Higher Education, Media Briefng*, IDP Education Australia, Sydney

Breton, G. and Lambert, M. (eds) (2003) *Universities and Globalization: Private Linkages, Public Trust*, UNESCO Publishing/Université Laval/Economica, Paris/ Quebec.

Callan, H. (2000) The international vision in practice: a decade of evolution. *Higher Education in Europe* 25(1), 15–23

Central Council for Education (2005) *A Vision for the Future of Higher Education in Japan (28 January 2005).*

Chen, Y. and Hoshower, L.B. (2003) Student evaluation of teaching efectiveness: an assessment of student perception and motivation. *Assessment and Evaluation in Higher Education* 28(1), 71–88.

Coady, T. (ed) (2000). *Why Universities Matter: A Conversation about Values, Means, and Directions*. St. Leonards, Australia: Allen & Unwin Pty.LTD.

Colton, D., & Covert, R. W. (2007). *Designing and constructing instruments for social research and evaluation*. Jossey-Bass

Corbett, D. (1992) *Australian Public Sector Management*, 2nd edn, Allen and Unwin, Sydney.

Dale, R. and Robertson, S.L. (2002) The varying aspects of regional organizations as subjects of globalization of education. *Comparative Education Review* 46(1), 10–36.

De Wit, K. and Verhoeven, J.C. (2001) The higher education policy of the European Union: with or against the member states. In *Higher Education and the Nation State: the International Dimension of Higher Education* (Huisman, J., Maassen, P. and Neave, G., eds), pp. 175– 231, Pergamon, Oxford.

Dill, D., Teixeira, P., Jongbloed, B. and Amaral, A. (2002) Conclusion. In *Markets in Higher Education: Rhetoric or Reality* (Teixeira, P., Jongbloed, B., Dill, D. and Amaral, A., eds), pp. 327–352, Kluwer Academic Publishers, Dordrecht

Drennan, L. (2001) Quality assessment and the tension between teaching and research. *Quality in Higher Education* 7(3), 167–178.

Dynan, M.B. and Cliford, R.J. (2001) Eight years on: implementation of quality management in an Australian university. *Assessment and Evaluation in Higher Education* 26(5), 503–515

El Khawas, E. (2006) Accountability and Quality Assurance: New Issues for Academic Inquiry. In *International Handbook of Higher Education*, vol. 1 (Forest, J.J.F. and Altbach, P.G. eds), pp. 23–37, Springer Verlag, Berlin.

Fulton, O. (2003) Managerialism in UK universities: unstable hybridity and the complications of implementation. In *The Higher Education Revolution?* (Amaral, A., Meek, V.L. and Larsen, I.M., eds), pp. 155–178, Kluwer Academic Publishers, Dordrecht

Gibbs, G. and Simpson, C. (2004-5). Does your assessment support your students' learning? Learning and Teaching in Higher Education (on-line), 1(1), 3-31. Available at http://www.glos.ac.uk/adu/clt/lathe/issue1/index.cfm (Accessed 9/11/06).

Gibbs, P. (2001) Higher education as a market: a problem or a solution? *Studies in Higher Education* 26(1), 85–94

Hinagi, T. (2004) Networking of quality assurance agencies in the Asia-Pacifc region and the role of Japan University Accreditation Association. *Quality in Higher Education* 10(1), 37–41.

Hulpiau, V., Masschelein, E., Van der Stockt, L., Verhesschen, P. and Waeytens, K. (2005) *A system of student feedback: considerations of academic staf taken into account*, 27th Annual EAIR Forum, Riga, Latvia, 28–31 August 2005

Joint Committee on Standards for Educational Evaluation, (2011). *The Program Evaluation Standards: A guide for evaluators and evaluation users* (3rd Ed), Sage Publications, Inc

Jordan, S. and Swithenby, S.J. On-line summative assessment with feedback as an aid to effective learning at a distance. Proc of 2004 ISL Symposium Diversity and Inclusivity (Ed C. Rust) Alden Press, pp 480-485.

Kimura, T., Yonezawa, A. and Ohmori, F. (2004) Quality assurance and recognition of qualifcations in higher education: Japan, In *Quality and Recognition in Higher Education: The Cross Border Challenge* (Larsen, K. and Momii, K., eds), pp. 119–130, OECD, Paris.

Klein, S., Kuh, G., Chun, M., Hamilton, L., & Shavelson, R. (2005). An approach to measuring cognitive outcomes across higher-education institutions. *Journal of Higher Education*, 46, No. 3, 251-276.

Laughton, D. (2003) Why was the QAA approach to teaching quality assessment rejected by academics in UK HE? *Assessment and Evaluation in Higher Education* 28(3), 309–321.

Maassen, P. (2000) Editorial. *European Journal of Education* 35(4), 377–383.

MacAlpine, M. (2001) An attempt to evaluate teaching quality: one department's story. *Assessment and Evaluation in Higher Education* 26(6), 563–578.

McBurnie, G. (2001) Leveraging globalization as a policy paradigm for higher education. *Higher Education in Europe* 26(1), 11–26.

Nasser, F. and Fresko, B. (2002) Faculty views of student evaluation of college teaching. *Assessment and Evaluation in Higher Education* 27(2), 187–198.

Neumann, R. (2000) Communicating student evaluation of teaching results: Rating Interpretation Guides (RIGs). *Assessment and Evaluation in Higher Education* 25(2), 121–134.

Orsingher, C. (ed.) (2006) *Assessing Quality in European Higher Education Institutions*, Physica-Verlag, Heidelberg.

Pascarella, E. and P. Terenzini. (2005*). How College Affects Students: A Third Decade of Research.* Jossey-Bass.

Patton, M. Q. (2011). *Developmental evaluation: Applying complexity concepts to enhance innovation and use.* Guilford Press

Ranson, S. (2003) Public accountability in the age of neo-liberal governance. *Journal of Education Polic y* 18(5), 459–480.

Ross, S.M. and Swithenby, S.J.. Probing the limits of applicability of computer aided assessment: a learning-outcomes led analysis. EARLI Assessment Conference 2006 Roundtable workshop. To be published.

Saroyan, A. and Amundsen, C. (2001) Evaluating university teaching: time to take stock. *Assessment and Evaluation in Higher Education* 26(4), 341–353.

Scott, G. and Hawke, I. (2003) Using an external quality audit as a lever for institutional change. *Assessment and Evaluation in Higher Education* 28(3), 323–332.

Scott, W.R. (1995) *Institutions and Organization*, Sage Publication, London.

Scott, W.R. and Meyer, J.W. (1991) The organization of societal sectors: propositions and early evidence. In *The New Institutionalism in Organizational Analysis* (Powell, W. W. and DiMaggio, P.J., eds), pp. 108–140, University of Chicago Press, Chicago.

Smith, C., Herbert, D., Robinson, W. and Watt, K. (2001) Quality assurance through a continuous curriculum review (CCR) strategy: refections on a pilot project. *Assessment and Evaluation in Higher Education* 26(5), 489–502.

Spencer-Matthews, S. (2001) Enforced cultural change in academe: a practical case study: implementing quality management systems in higher education. *Assessment and Evaluation in Higher Education* 26(1), 51–59.

Trow, M. (2000) From mass higher education to universal access: the American advantage. *Minerva* 37(4), 303–328.

Upcraft, M. L., & Schuh, J. H. (1996). *Assessment in student affairs: A guide for practitioners.* San Francisco, CA: Jossey-Bass

van den Berg, R., Vandenberghe, R. and Sleegers, P. (1999) Management of innovation from a cultural-individual perspective. *School Efectiveness and School Improvement* 10(3), 321–351.

van der Wende, M. (2002) *Hoger Onderwijs Globaliter: naar Nieuwe Kaders voor Onderzoek en Beleid,* Universiteit Twente, Enschede.

van der Wende, M. (2004) Globalisering, handelslib-eralisering en hoger onderwijs export. *Tijdschrif voor Onderwijsrecht en Onderwijsbeleid* 14(3), 234–241.

Verhoeven, J.C., Kelchtermans, G. and Michielsen, K. (2005) *McOnderwijs in Vlaanderen: Internationalisering en Commercialisering van het Hoger Onderwijs,* Wolters Plantyn, Mechelen.

Vidovich, L. and Slee, R. (2001) Bringing universities to account? Exploring some global and local policy tensions. *Journal of Education Policy* 16(5), 431–453.

Welsh, J.F., Alexander, S. and Dey, S. (2001) Continuous quality measurement: restructuring assessment for a new technological and organisational environment. *Assessment and Evaluation in Higher Education* 26(5), 391–401.

Welsh, J.F., Alexander, S. and Dey, S. (2001) Continuous quality measurement: restructuring assessment for a new technological and organisational environment. *Assessment and Evaluation in Higher Education* 26(5), 391–401.

Whitelock, D. and Brasher, A.. Roadmap for e-assessment. Joint Information Systems Committee Report June 2006 – Available from http://www.jisc.ac.uk/elp_assessment.html (Accessed 9/11/06).

Wholey, J. S., Hatry, H. P., and Newcomer, K. E., (2010). *Handbook of practical program evaluation,* (3rd Ed). Jossey-Bass.

Worthington, A.C. (2002) The impact of student perceptions and characteristics on teaching evaluations: a case study in fnance education. *Assessment and Evaluation in Higher Education* 27(1), 49–64.

Yamanoi, A. and Kuzuki, K. (2005) A study on the fxed-term system for faculty members: focusing on the analyses of types, length of term and renewal. *Higher Education Research in Japan* 2, 1–20.